Manual for Testing and
Teaching English Spelling

Manual for Testing and Teaching English Spelling

A comprehensive and structured system for the planning and delivery of spelling intervention

CLAIRE JAMIESON MSc, BA, PGCE
University College London

JULIET JAMIESON MRCSLT, TEFL
Child Development Centre
North Hertfordshire

Consultant Editor
MARGARET SNOWLING
University of York

W **WHURR PUBLISHERS**
LONDON AND PHILADELPHIA

First published 2003 by
Whurr Publishers Ltd
19b Compton Terrace, London N1 2UN, England and
325 Chestnut Street, Philadelphia PA 19106, USA

British Library Cataloguing in Publication Data

A catalogue record for this book is available from the
British Library.

ISBN 1 86156 372 8

Printed and bound in the UK by Athenaeum Press Limited,
Gateshead, Tyne & Wear.

Contents

Acknowledgements vii
Foreword ix
Preface xi

Guide to the Manual 1

Teaching Spelling 8
The Development of Spelling Skills 8
General Principles in Teaching Spelling 11
Teaching Letter Names, the Alphabet and Sound–Letter
    Correspondence 15
Teaching Spelling Patterns ("regular words") 18
Spelling 'key words' 19
Spelling and Syllables Stucture 22
Teaching Homophones 24
Teaching Silent Letters 25
Spelling Rules 26
Teaching Word Structure Related to Grammar 27

SECTION 1: *Testing Spelling* 31
Testing Alphabetic Knowledge 33
Screening Test 35
Test Words 1 36
Test Words 2 45

SECTION 2: *Spelling Vowel Sounds* 55
English Vowel Sounds 57
Index of Spelling Alternatives 58
Word Lists for Spelling Alternatives 65

SECTION 3: *Spelling Consonant Sounds*   **121**

English Consonant Sounds   123
Index of Spelling Alternatives   124
Word Lists for Spelling Alternatives
Consonant Clusters Index   181
Word Lists for Consonant Clusters (initial)   183
Word Lists for Consonant Clusters (final)   190

SECTION 4: *Homophones and Silent Letters*   **197**

Vowel Homophones   199
Consonant Homophones   206
Word Structure/Grammar Related Homophones   210
Silent Letters   211

SECTION 5: *Word Structure and Grammar*   **217**

Section Index   219
General Rules applying to Prefixes, Suffixes and Endings   224
Grammar Related Rules for Suffixes and Endings   234
Use of Apostrophe   292
Possessive Pronouns   297

References   **299**

Bibliography   **301**

Word Index   **303**

Acknowledgements

We would like to acknowledge the following people for their various contributions to the production of this manual. First we would like to thank the many teachers who, over the past ten years, have gained their RSA and OCR SpLD qualifications at the Department of Human Communication Science, University College London. Discussion with them about the problems that arise in the teaching of spelling, and their clearly expressed wish for a resource such as this have motivated us to complete this project. Our own students over the last twenty years, from young school children to university students, all of whom have found spelling a particular challenge, have also influenced the course our project has taken. In our own teaching we too have felt the need for this manual. Sarah Simpson has offered invaluable advice throughout the production of the manual, her involvement continuing until the very last minute. We are enormously grateful. Thanks too are due to Amanda Jamieson for her much appreciated contribution to the formatting and reformatting of the text. Our families have been supportive and patient, bearing with us, as we have become increasingly obsessive word nerds. Special thanks are due to them.

"When we use the word orthography, we do not mean a mode of spelling which is true to the pronunciation, but one which is conventionally correct." 1873 (OED)

Foreword

Understanding of spelling processes and their acquisition is much less well developed than is knowledge of reading and how to teach it. Indeed, spelling has sometimes been described as the "Cinderella" of reading research. Yet spelling poses a far greater challenge than reading to learners of all alphabetic languages and especially English. While contextual factors can facilitate word-level decoding during reading, spelling requires access to the full orthographic specifications of words. English is a particularly difficult spelling system to master because of its origins in many different languages and the many variations in spelling-sound consistency that it embodies. It is a fallacy that a child will learn to spell simply by reading words. While exposure to print via reading experience is a vital ingredient of successful spelling, research shows that a child's spelling proficiency depends upon phonological, morphological and syntactic awareness. Thus, at the basic level, spelling requires the ability to segment the speech stream into phonemic units and to transcribe these using knowledge of letter sounds. In English, this does not suffice and provides only a phonetic rendering of the to-be-spelled word. The child must also acquire implicit knowledge of the different orthographic forms that can be used to represent a phoneme [e.g., /s/ -> 's', 'ss', 'ce', 'ci', 'cy'] or a phoneme string [e.g., /ʃʌn/ -> 'shun', 'tion, 'cian']. Similarly, spellers need to know how grammatical forms that are constant across different phonetic contexts are written (e.g., past tense *ed*), and how to spell homophonic words that sound the same. The implications for the assessment and teaching of spelling are considerable as this book clearly demonstrates. Working from the premise that phonological skill provides a foundation for spelling that needs to be secure, the Manual provides a comprehensive guide to the spelling patterns of English with useful recommendations about how to teach them. It also provides lists of words for testing spelling knowledge and for reinforcing spelling concepts, and there is a complete word index for reference. The Manual will be an important resource for teachers of spelling to students at all levels from the beginner to the adult with spelling problems. It will be particularly useful for teachers of people with dyslexia, for those who have English as an additional language and for students who are learning English as a foreign language.

Maggie Snowling
York
June 2003

Preface

This manual has been produced to provide teachers of English, teachers of English as a foreign or additional language and literacy specialists with a tool for developing the spelling skills of their pupils, across the age range and at every level of attainment.

English has one of the most complex orthographic systems of all the alphabetic languages. Although sounds are related to letters, their relationship is far from consistent. Languages such as Spanish, Italian, and even German, have much more "transparent" systems, so once they have learned how letters are related to sounds, children are not likely to have enormous difficulty with spelling. In German, for example, the /sh/ sound is consistently written as *sch,* whereas in English there are 11 possible ways of spelling this sound. There are some 160 ways of representing all the vowel sounds in writing, and over 100 ways of representing the consonant sounds. Furthermore, many spelling patterns are based on morphology, that is the grammatical structure of words. For example, *-ed* forming the past tense (*changed, waited*), *-ly* forming adverbs from adjectives (*badly, wrongly*).

Spelling difficulties may relate to sound–symbol correspondence, to a lack of explicit knowledge of common letter sequences, or to lack of awareness of the way words are formed to take account of their grammatical function. Other major challenges to the student of English spelling are homophones (*their/there, see/sea*), which are numerous, and words whose spelling contains unexpected "silent" letters.

Despite the frustrating complexity of English spelling, there is a need for teachers of this subject to find some order in the chaos. It makes sense to teach the spelling of words according to shared patterns, and if spelling patterns can also be linked to sounds, or to grammatically meaningful units, so much the better.

One of the most challenging and frustrating aspects of teaching spelling is the constant need to think of words that should be taught together, either because they share both sound and spelling pattern, or because they share morphological structure. For example, when teaching the pattern *ci* = /sh/ sound as in *special*, a few words may spring to mind, such as *ancient* and *social*, but though there are many more examples, words tend to be highly elusive when one most needs to bring them to mind. The Manual goes some way towards solving this problem for teachers by providing lists of words that share the same spelling pattern.

Three sections of the Manual (Spelling Vowel Sounds, Spelling Consonant Sounds and Silent Letters and Homophones) are based on the relationship between sounds and letter patterns. The last section (Word Structure) groups words according to shared suffixes, prefixes, plural forms and other grammatically related categories. All four of these "resource" or reference sections provide teachers with lists of words to use in teaching. The first section (Testing Spelling) enables them to establish the needs of their learners through very finely graded testing.

The linking of letter patterns to speech sounds raises the issue of regional accent. This is particularly pertinent to the vowel system in English, as it is here that most regional differences in pronunciation arise.

The Vowel and Consonant sections of the Manual are based on the Received Pronunciation of English (RP), as this is the dialect most widely recognised, if not most widely spoken. However, teachers will find that there is little problem in substituting other sound correspondences for those of RP, as, for the most part, these are likely to be consistent.

For example, the New Zealand pronunciation of the RP /ɪ / sound in *pig* is more like the /ə / sound in *the*. This applies to all the spelling alternatives for this sound: *myth, pretty, busy, build* etc. Teachers will need to take account of these differences, exercising particular caution when their learners' accents are different from their own. For example, *bath, fast,* and *laugh* are listed as having the same vowel sound as *yard,* and *heart,* according to RP. However, in the Midlands and the northern half of Britain, all three would be pronounced with a short /a/ as in *cat.*

The International Phonetic Alphabet (IPA) is used to represent English speech sounds. The symbols for vowel sounds are listed on page 57, and those for consonant sounds are listed on page 123, each with words containing the symbolised sound.

We have tried to make it easy for teachers to find their way around the manual, by giving page references in every section, and listing all words covered in the index. Although it is designed to provide the basis of a teaching programme, it is hoped that teachers will also find it useful as a reference text. It is not intended that the manual will meet all the resource needs of teachers, but it should provide them with the information they require to create worksheets and exercises to support their teaching.

Guide to the Manual

The Manual is divided into five main sections, each of which is outlined in the box below, then described in detail with guidance for use:

SECTION 1: Testing

There are two graded sets of test words. The first set is for identifying spelling patterns and words that need to be taught; the second is for re-testing to monitor progress. The section starts with a short screening test to help teachers to establish an appropriate starting point for the more detailed testing provided by the test words.

SECTION 2: Spelling Vowel Sounds

This section provides the teacher with groups of words that share the same vowel sounds and the same spelling of those sounds, so that words can be taught according to both sound and spelling pattern.

SECTION 3: Spelling Consonant Sounds

This section covers all the consonant sounds in English with their various spelling alternatives, and is set out in the same way as the vowel section.

SECTION 4: Homophones and Silent Letters

This section covers two categories of spellings in which errors are commonly made.

SECTION 5: Word Structure and Grammar

Many spelling patterns and rules, such as those governing prefixes and suffixes, are related to grammar. This section covers these rules, explaining them in relation to grammar, and provides sets of words for use in teaching.

Teaching Spelling

The main body of the Manual comprises lists of words with common spelling patterns related to sound, and spelling rules related to grammar. There are all sorts of possibilities for putting these lists to use, and the manual is designed, not as a prescribed programme with prescribed teaching methods, but as a tool for teachers to use according to their individual needs and experience.

The development of spelling skills, general principles in teaching spelling, and suggested teaching methods, are covered in an introductory chapter. Sound/letter correspondence, high frequency and "key words", using syllables for spelling, regular spelling patterns, and grammar-related rules are covered.

Section 1: Testing Spelling

Standardised spelling tests may, if errors are analysed, provide an indication of the spelling strategies a child is using. They also give a standardised score, enabling teachers to compare a learner's performance with that of his/her peers. However, these tests are not sufficiently comprehensive to provide the teacher with the necessary information to devise a full teaching programme.

Masterson and Apel (2000) state that, for the purpose of assessment of spelling there is to their knowledge "no single comprehensive list that can be used to gather all pertinent data". This is indeed a tall order, but perhaps it is almost achieved in this section.

The Testing section of the Manual provides teachers with two very finely graded, parallel lists of words, from simple Consonant Vowel Consonant words such as *pig*, and very high frequency words such as *if* and *me*, to complex spellings for the most ambitious learner (*phoenix, amoeba, mnemonic*). Grading takes into account both Age of Acquisition (Morrison, Chappell and Ellis 1997) and complexity of spelling, and the high and medium frequency words from the National Literacy Strategy are all included. Because the lists are so comprehensive, they are also very long (400 words each). For ease of reference, words are set out, and numbered, in groups of ten.

It is not intended that the 400 words should be given as a test. The idea is that teachers find an appropriate starting point in Test Words 1, and test the learner(s) on about 20 to 30 words.

As an aid to establishing a suitable starting point in the test words, there is a short screening test. It takes only a few minutes to administer, so it is recommended that, for all but the most advanced learners, the whole test be given. Depending on errors made, teachers are guided to the appropriate starting point in the Test Words. This is only a rough guide, and it is important to take into account information about the learner's knowledge-base gained from other sources, such as free writing, standardised spelling tests and samples of unaided written work.

The plan for teaching spelling can then be based on errors made. Alongside each word in the test lists are page references to the part of the manual where the word is listed with others sharing the same spelling pattern or rule. For example, if the learner spells *guitar* as *gitar*, the page reference for a list of words with the *gu+e/i/y* pattern (*guilty, guide* etc) is given. Each test word is included in a phrase, this will clarify the meaning of the word and prevent confusion, particularly with words that are homophones. After reading the phrase, it is important to repeat the test word, for a second time, to ensure that the target word is written and not the last word heard in the phrase.

It is important to take account of the nature of errors made in the test words. For example, if *thanked* is written as *thaked,* the error is in the root word rather than in the suffix, and so teaching should focus on the *–ank* pattern, linking it with *-onk, -ink* etc. Only if the error is in the *-ed* suffix should the teacher refer to the Word Structure section for teaching. Page references correspond to the anticipated error, so teachers will need to take account of this.

Some words are marked with an asterisk to identify them as "key words". These are words of high frequency, many of which do not conform to a regular spelling pattern. It is suggested that the spelling of these words be taught individually (for teaching methods, see Spelling of Key Words in the Teaching section). Because of their high frequency, hence importance, these words appear in both Test Words 1 and Test Words 2.

The parallel Test Words 2 is primarily intended for use in monitoring progress following teaching. The same spelling patterns, prefixes, suffixes and key words are covered in the same order as in Test Words 1, so by administering the same groups of words in Test Words 2, it is possible to evaluate consolidation of spelling knowledge.

Test Words 2 may also play a role in the initial testing stage: it is often the case that learners' knowledge of spelling is word-specific, in that they might be unable to generalise a particular spelling pattern to other words. The parallel word from the same section in the second list may be given, in addition, as a probe. The numbering of the Test Words in groups of ten allows for easy transfer between the two lists.

For learners at the most basic level, it may become apparent, after using the first set of test words, that assessment of sound/letter correspondence is needed. A suggested method for doing this is given at the beginning of the Testing section, and the teaching of sound/letter correspondence is covered in the Teaching section.

Section 2: Spelling Vowel Sounds

Section 3: Spelling Consonant Sounds

At the beginning of the Vowel section, all the English vowel sounds are listed, each with a word in which the sound appears, and with its International Phonetic Alphabet symbol. For the purpose of linking sounds with spellings, some sounds are included that are made up of two phonemes (individual sounds): the vowel sound in *use* (ju) is included as a single unit, as is the vowel sound in *pure* (/juə/). All the spelling alternatives for each sound are then listed, with examples. For each spelling alternative, a page reference is given to the relevant word list. For example:

/e/ as in bed	Page
ten	67
head	68
many	68
bury	68
said	68
friend	68
leisure	69
leopard	69

If, having used the test lists, or through observation of a learner's writing, the teaching of the spelling pattern *ea* as in *bread* was identified as a need, you would turn to page 78, where words with /ɛ/ (as in red) spelled as *ea* are listed:

> *already bread breast breath dead deaf death head ready spread etc.*

The spelling of consonant sounds is treated in the same way. All the English consonant sounds are listed at the beginning of the Consonant section. The sounds represented by the letter "x" (/ks/ and gz) are listed separately from their component parts /k/, /s/, /g/ and /z/, because of their correspondence to one alphabetic symbol. Likewise /kw/ represented by "qu" is listed in addition to /k/ and /w/. There are thus more sounds listed that appear in the usual list of phonemes for English. Spelling variants for all the sounds are then given, as in the example below.

/ʃ/ as in *shed*	**Page**
shed	159
sure	160
opera**ti**on	160
an**ci**ent	161
mi**ssi**on	161
pen**si**on	162
bro**ch**ure	162
o**ce**an	162
con**sci**ous	163
an**xi**ous	163

On page 162, for example, words with /ʃ/ spelled as *ch* will be listed:

> *brochure chalet champagne chateau chauffeur chef machine etc.*

It is immediately apparent that, where a large number of words is given, the spelling pattern can be considered "regular", and conversely, if, as happens not infrequently, only one or two words are given (e.g. /ɛ/ spelled ie in *friend*), the pattern can be considered irregular. Words such as this are labelled "sole items". Regularity is thus viewed as a continuum, rather than as an absolute concept.

The lists of the more basic spelling patterns are graded according to difficulty, and patterns found in more complex words are in alphabetical order. Teachers will need to take into account the vocabulary level of their learners and to use the lists selectively. Many simple CVC words such as *ban* and *hem* are of such low frequency that they would be perceived as nonsense words by many younger children.

After most word lists there are one or two dictation sentences. These have been devised so that they do not include words or spelling patterns that occur at a higher level in the test lists than the target words. They are intended for use after teaching has taken place.

It is most important to note that the sets of word lists do not appear in the Manual in order of difficulty, but follow the order of the vowel or consonant sounds as listed in the section index. Some spelling alternatives for each sound will be simple (e.g. *sh* for /ʃ/ as in *shed*), and others will be more complex (e.g. *ssi* for /ʃ/ as in *session*). It is therefore not intended that teachers work through these sections of the Manual in sequence. The test lists at the beginning of the Manual, which **are** graded, should be used to establish the state of the learners' particular spelling knowledge, and lists should be selected accordingly to support teaching. Alternatively, teachers may already have identified a spelling pattern they wish to teach, and can find the appropriate list through one of the indices.

As page references are given with the Test Words, at the beginning of each section and in the Word Index it is always easy to find the group of words you are looking for.

Section 4: Homophones and Silent Letters

A large percentage of spelling errors are made in words that sound the same, but have different spellings (homophones). In this section, homophones are listed by either vowel sound or consonant sound, depending on where the spelling discrepancy lies. For example, *pain, pane/weigh way* are grouped under /ɛɪ/ (vowel sound); **bole** and **whole** are grouped under /**h**/ (consonant sound). When they appear in the Test Words, homophones are identified, and a page reference for this section is given. Dictations are included as one means of monitoring learning.

Another major source of spelling errors is "silent letters". These appear in a number of common spelling patterns. For example, **kn** *(know, knee)*, *-mb (lamb, limb)*. These patterns are incorporated into the vowel and consonant sections (2 and 3). In this section, the more unusual silent letter words (e.g. *answer, debt*) are listed so that they can be given special attention. Teachers will be directed to this section through errors made in the Test Words, in which examples of all the silent letter patterns appear.

Section 5: Spelling Related to Word Structure and Grammar

Mastery of the complex relationship between sounds and letters will not, alone, lead to proficiency in English spelling. It is essential in learning to spell, to have developed an awareness of the way in which words are structured, and this extends beyond the level of sequences of sounds, or phonemes. For example, the word *wanted* can be broken into two parts: *want + ed*. The suffix *-ed* is added to the verb to denote the past tense. It is useful to be aware of this, so as to avoid confusion with words such as *stupid*, where the *–id* denotes an adjective ending rather than a verb suffix.

In this fifth section of the Manual, the grammatical concepts required to make full use of the word lists are explained in some detail. Spelling rules for adding suffixes or endings (doubling, dropping "e", changing y to i etc.) are covered with numerous examples. There are lists of words with spelling patterns related to nouns, verbs, adjectives, and adverbs, for example, adding endings to form plurals, common adjective endings (*-ant, - ent* etc.), common adjective endings (*-ance, -ence* etc.)

Words in this section are listed in alphabetical order, so that they can be found easily. Sets of words are also listed in alphabetical order, for example, adjective endings *-able, -al, -an* to *ous, -some, -y.*

The Word Index

To find a word list quickly, or to check whether a particular word has been included in the Manual, the index at the back of the book can be used. Every page where a particular word appears is listed. Many words will appear in more than one word list. For example, *front* is in the initial consonant cluster (fr) list, and in the list of words in which the /ʌ/ sound, as in *mug,* is spelled "o" (*month, son* etc).

Teaching Spelling

The Development of Spelling Skills

In an alphabetic language, in which there is a relationship between speech sounds and the symbols used for writing them, a prerequisite skill for reading and spelling is phonological awareness. This is an ability to reflect on, and manipulate the sounds in words, independently of their meaning (Bradley and Bryant 1983, Goswami and Bryant 1990, Caravolas, Hulme and Snowling 2001). An awareness of syllables, of rhyme, and of phonemes (individual speech sounds) informs children's early attempts to spell.

The skills needed for reading and spelling are inextricably linked, with constant interaction at all stages of the process. However, there is evidence that reading and spelling do not develop in parallel. Uta Frith (1985) describes how, in learning to read and spell single words, either reading or spelling acts as pacemaker for the further development of the other.

According to Frith, children start by recognising a few whole words, simply through awareness of their overall shape. At this stage, they may recognise their own name, the logos on cars, and some of the frequently used words in their environment, or the flash cards and reading books they encounter when they first go to school. They are said to be using *logographic* strategies, as they are not aware of the relationship between individual sounds and letters.

At this early stage, children will be unable to write the words they can read. They then begin to make links between sounds and letters, and it is in their writing that they first put this knowledge into practice. They are now using *alphabetic* strategies, and it is at this stage that writing paves the way for reading. There is often a period of time in which children are able to produce a piece of writing by sounding out words as they write, but when asked to read their writing, they are unable to do so (Bryant and Bradley 1980). Through writing, children develop the ability to use phonic strategies in reading, and are hence able to decode unfamiliar, simple, regular words.

Gradually, through reading experience and phonic teaching, an implicit awareness of more complex spelling patterns develops, and certain letter strings such as -ssion, -ately become familiar. At this stage, children are no longer dependent solely on logographic and alphabetic strategies, as they can now draw on *othographic* strategies. At this stage, reading paves the way for spelling. When awareness of spelling patterns becomes explicit, orthographic strategies are said to be applied to spelling.

At each stage of development, however, children draw on a range of strategies for reading and spelling, and the stages described by Frith are not considered discrete. Ehri (1991, 1992) recognises the interaction between strategies throughout the developmental process. The very complex combinations of strategies which together lead to literacy are illustrated by connectionist models (Hulme, Snowling and Quinlan 1991, Brown and Watson 1991).

The study conducted by Caravolas et al. (2001) supports the independent development of the interdependent skills of reading and spelling observed by Bryant and Bradley (1980) and described by Frith (1985). In a three-year longitudinal study of 153 British children, they found that phoneme segmentation (breaking words into individual sounds), and letter knowledge, led to phonological (alphabetic) spelling skills. These then combined with reading to promote the development of higher-level orthographic skills. As described by Frith, reading appears to become more important as an aid to spelling after children have learned to make explicit links between sounds and letters.

Children who have a weakness in phonological awareness are likely to encounter problems breaking words into sounds and relating sounds to letters. They are likely to make non-phonetic spelling errors, in which the sound sequence of the target word is not accurately represented. For example, they might spell *help* as *blep*, or *region* as *regonin*. A large body of research evidence has identified a weakness in this cognitive function as the core deficit in dyslexia (Stanovich and Siegel 1994, Snowling 2000).

Training in phonological awareness, linked with letter knowledge, has been shown to be particularly effective in promoting competence in reading and early spelling at the alphabetic stage, (Bradley and Bryant 1983, Ehri, Nunes, Willows, Schuster, Yaghoub-Zadeh and Shanahan 2001, Hatcher, Hulme and Ellis 1994, Wagner and Torgesen 1987). However, a weakness in phonological awareness is often persistent (Bruck 1992) and it may be very difficult for some children to acquire the alphabetic principle.

Even once the alphabetic principle has been mastered, problems may arise in acquiring orthographic strategies, in which awareness of morphology (meaning-related word structure, e.g. *walk, walks, walking, walked*) and etymology of words (their origin, e.g. *ambi* meaning *both*) play as important a part as does phonological awareness in the early stages of spelling. Having learned, through great effort, to spell according to sound, students with dyslexia may continue to rely on sound-based spelling, failing to take account of morphology or etymology. For example, they may not be aware that the *-ed* suffix, denotes past tense (*waited*), whereas the *-id* ending is not a suffix but is usually found in adjectives (*horrid*). This aspect of the development of spelling skills has been relatively little researched, because of the much greater focus on links between phonological awareness and literacy.

The significance of morphological awareness is now receiving an increasing amount of attention. The impact of developing morphological awareness on spelling skills has been traced by Nunes, Bryant and Bindman (1997), and the reciprocal relationship between morphological awareness and spelling is demonstrated by Masterson and Apel (2000): spelling experience leads to understanding of morphological structures, which in turn leads to more accurate spelling.

It is almost impossible to become skilled at spelling in English without some understanding of the links between parts of words, such as suffixes, and their grammatical function. For many people, this understanding is implicit, and spelling correctly comes naturally to them. Skilled readers, while recognising familiar words as whole units, are also implicitly aware of the detail of letter sequences as they read. This enables them to identify typing and spelling errors automatically, and to reproduce in their writing the spelling patterns they have observed through reading. However, for people with dyslexia, this cross-over from reading to writing may not take place without explicit teaching, and even when this is provided, they make continue to fail to make the link between what they see and what they write.

The underlying cause of dyslexia is usually a weakness in phonological awareness. A lack of attention to the detail of letter sequences when reading is often a consequence of such a weakness. This can lead to inaccuracy in reading in the form of substitution of visually similar words (e.g. *included* for *induced*, *grasp* for *gasp*), or omissions and insertion of small function words (*and, to, of*) and morphemes (plural *-s*, past tense *-ed*). This lack of awareness of detail when reading leads to difficulty in applying orthographic strategies to spelling. It may lead to word boundary errors (*from my angle > fromy angel*), morphological errors (*wanted > wantid*), or errors in common letter sequences (*attraction > atracshun*).

In summary, competent spelling in English is dependent on the gradual acquisition of a range of skills. These include the ability to segment words into individual sounds, the ability to make links between speech sounds and letters, and the ability to use reading skills to support developing awareness of the wide range of alternative ways of spelling individual sounds (e.g. the sound /ɛɪ/ as spelled in *hate, day, rain* etc.). The skilled speller also needs knowledge (either implicit or explicit) of the way words are formed to play a role in sentences (Moats 1994).

Ultimately, skilled spellers are able to access the correct spelling of words automatically using rapid simultaneous phonological and morphological processing, without the need for the specific application of rules. (Rittle-Johnson and Siegler 1999). A deficit in phonological processing will adversely affect the development of all of these underpinning skills.

For students of English as a foreign language there are different challenges. Most other alphabetic languages have more consistent, or transparent, orthographic systems than English; in some alphabetic systems (e.g. Arabic and Hebrew) vowel sounds are not generally recorded in writing, leading to difficulties in the perception of vowel sounds in English, and students whose first language has a logographic, rather than an alphabetic, writing system (e.g. Chinese, Japanese) need to become familiar with letter/phoneme correspondence, as the basic building block of spelling in an alphabetic language.

General Principles in Teaching Spelling

Spelling and the National Literacy Strategy

Teachers working within the British primary education system will need to be aware of the expected attainment levels for spelling for Years R (reception, age 5) to 6 (key stage 2, age 11). In the National Literacy Srategy (1998) (NLS) a list of 45 high frequency words for "sight recognition" are listed for Year R, and a further 150 words are listed for Year 1 and Year 2. A longer list of medium frequency words is given for Years 4 and 5. Although it is not stipulated that these words should be known for spelling as well as reading, word recognition will be improved through use in writing. All these words are included in the Manual.

Alphabetic knowledge

The NLS suggests an order for teaching spelling patterns during years R, 1 and 2. Teaching order will fall into place naturally if the test lists from this Manual are used. As a general rule, and depending on the pupil's prior knowledge, the short vowel sounds should be taught first, usually within a rime unit: *hat, cat, mat,/ wet, pet, set / hot, cot, got* etc. In this way, the consonant letters are also taught. Consonant digraphs, where more than one letter is used to represent a single sound (such as *sh, ch, th* and *–ck*) and consonant clusters (*bl, cr, sc* etc.), first in initial then in final position (*-mp, -nt* etc), follow. Next, according to the NLS, come the many vowel digraphs (*ee, ea, oa* etc.).

Prefixes

In Year 3 Term 1, the NLS suggests that children should be taught how to use prefixes to generate new words from root words, and they should be able to spell prefixes such as *un, de, dis, re* and *pre*. Spelling patterns such as lit**tle**, mu**ddle**, bot**tle** are introduced at this stage.

Suffixes

In the second term of Year 3, common suffixes are introduced, as are rules for adding *-y, est* and *er*. Silent letters (e.g. *knee, gnat*), and the use of apostrophe for contraction are taught at this stage. Knowledge of prefixes and use of the apostrophe for contraction is extended in term 3.

Root words and their variations

In Year 4, pupils should be taught how to convert nouns and adjectives into verbs, using suffixes, and during the course of the year, some of the more complex letter sequences are taught (*-ible, -able, -ive, -sion* etc.) Diminutive endings such as *–ling* are also introduced.

By the end of Year 6, before transferring to secondary school, it is expected that children will be able to use root words, with a wide range of prefixes and suffixes as a support for spelling. They should be able to distinguish between homophones, should know the correct use and spelling of possessive pronouns, linked to grammar, and should be able to apply a range of spelling rules. Children should also be familiar with the technical vocabulary used to describe language.

It is thus envisaged that, by following the NLS, on entering secondary school, children will have acquired, not only orthographic competence, but considerable explicit knowledge about the way words work.

Multi-sensory Teaching

The rationale for multi-sensory teaching comes from the literature, and the experience of specialist teachers of learners with specific literacy difficulties, such as dyslexia (Rack and Hatcher 2002). There is no doubt that learning is facilitated when more than one, and preferably three, sensory channels are activated. The well-known "look, cover, say, write, check" spelling method uses simultaneous visual, auditory and kinaesthetic feedback, in an endeavour to support memory and lead to automaticity in producing particular letter sequences.

Three multi-sensory study techniques for memorising spellings of words are summarised by Scott (2000). All are based on looking, speaking, writing, and repetition, sometimes additionally using tracing and colour. One of the routines outlined is an eight-step method for practising spellings using a computer. Another multi-sensory technique is described in detail in the section below, "Teaching Key Words".

Metacognitive Skills

The development of explicit awareness and knowledge is important at all stages of the learning process. Learners should be encouraged to observe patterns of letter sequences for themselves, and to make observations about the contexts in which these patterns occur. This applies at all levels of attainment and developmental stages. Thinking and talking about spelling is as important as practising writing words correctly; metacognitive techniques should be used in conjunction with multi-sensory teaching methods. This concept is particularly relevant when teaching grammatically related spelling patterns such as suffixes (see Teaching Word Structure below).

Throughout the word lists in the Manual there are short notes to promote discussion about spelling. Some relate to etymology (the origin of words), and some to the contextual restriction of particular spelling patterns. Furthermore, in the Word Structure section, links are made to equivalent word endings in other languages, especially French. The enormous influence of French on English becomes very clear when looking through that section.

The benefit of becoming aware of these cross-language links is twofold: it promotes the development of explicit awareness of spelling patterns, and the many secondary school pupils in Britain who learn French as a second language will find a means of extending their French vocabulary quite dramatically. For example, almost every English word ending in *-ity* (*university, city, facility*) converts directly to French *-ité* (*université, cité, facilité*). Students of English as a foreign language who have knowledge of French will also find these links useful.

For effective learning to take place, learners need to be actively involved in every stage of the process. They need to be aware of the nature of their difficulty (if indeed spelling is a problem for them); they need to be encouraged to talk about why spelling is important; they need to be helped, through teaching, to gain insight into why spelling in English is so difficult. The priorities for learning, and individual perspectives, particularly of older learners, ought to be taken into account when planning teaching. To ensure that learning has taken place, pupils can be encouraged to play the role of teacher, and to explain how particular spelling patterns work. They can also be asked for feedback about their learning, so that teaching can be modified to individual needs.

Overlearning

For new spelling knowledge to become properly assimilated, especially in the case of learners with dyslexia, much overlearning and practice is required. Teaching needs therefore to be *structured*, in that there should be a clear rationale for the content of lessons and the order in which material is taught. Teaching should be *sequential,* with a clear progression from one target to the next, and it must be *cumulative,* ensuring that new information is only introduced when previously taught material has been fully absorbed.

To ensure that knowledge is secure, much overlearning and on-going assessment will need to take place. It is not sufficient simply to check the previous week's material, but reference needs to be made, on an on going basis, to all work covered, until it is clear that this has been fully accommodated. Pupils may be successful in their spelling when tested, but they may not be able to spell the same words correctly in a less structured format such as free writing. It is important to verify that learning has taken place first at the word level, through short tests; then at sentence level, perhaps through dictation; and then at text level, through observing spelling in free writing. Spelling patterns can be considered properly learned when they are consistently applied in writing outside spelling lessons.

It is important to limit the introduction of new information to a pace that will not cause confusion. Generally, it is not a good idea to teach more than one spelling pattern or rule in a lesson. It is also important not to teach easily confusable spelling patterns together, for example, *ee* as in *keep,* and *ea* as in *reach*; this may be a useful technique when teaching pupils whose literacy skills are developing normally – however, it can lead to confusion for those pupils experiencing difficulty. Some suffixing rules are likely to take three or four lessons to complete.

Word, Sentence and Text Level Teaching

This is a Manual full of individual words, and most spelling books are firmly centred on word-level study. Naturally some teaching will be focused at word level, and on units within words such as sounds, letters, syllables, suffixes etc. This aspect of learning, based on building larger units (words, phrases etc.) from smaller units (letters, sounds etc.), and where the focus is at word level or below (e.g. sound, syllable), is known as "bottom-up" processing. It is necessary for decoding new words, and is applied in learning about letter sequences in words.

Literacy also involves "top-down" processing, in which learners draw on higher-level skills, such as semantic and syntactic context and their general knowledge. Top-down processing is therefore associated with higher-level language skills, and, in the domain of literacy development, with text rather than word-level activities. The integration of bottom-up and top-down processing, of word level and text level teaching, is essential if learning is to be applied outside the spelling lesson, and generalised to a range of contexts.

Integrating Spelling with Reading

The skills involved in learning to read and spell are related but different, in that reading primarily involves recognition of whole words and of letter sequences, whereas spelling demands specific, explicit knowledge. However, there is constant interaction, and much overlap between the two sets of skills, which can be used to good effect in teaching. As children in the very early stages of learning to read tend to rely on recognising whole words (in the absence of effective decoding strategies) their spelling is unlikely to improve through "noticing", for example, consonant clusters (*st, pl*) or vowel digraphs (*ai, oy*) while reading. They are more likely to gain explicit awareness of these basic phonic principles through the act of writing, and so, in the early stages of literacy development (and reflecting Frith's 1985 model), spelling should be the starting point.

An implicit awareness of more complex spelling patterns appears to develop as a result of reading experience. Through this implicit awareness, students may know that they have spelled a word incorrectly, simply because it doesn't "look right". This awareness can be made more explicit through teaching. Particular letter sequences (e.g. *-ssion, -tion*) can be pointed out in texts, and later elicited from the learner. Once recognition becomes more explicit, this knowledge can be transferred to writing. There is thus a complex interplay between the apparently more passive activity of reading, and the more demanding, or more explicit activity of writing. It is through the integration of these two sets of skills that higher-level literacy is ultimately achieved.

Teaching Letter Names, the Alphabet and Sound–Letter Correspondence

Common Problems in the Early Stages

Confusion of letter names with sounds

If a learner spells the word *arm* as *rm*, it is likely that he/she thinks the letter *r* says /*ar*/. While some letter names start with the sound that is associated with them: b, d, j, k, p, t, v, z, others end with their sounds: **f** = /ɛf/, **l** = /ɛl/, **m** = /ɛm/, **n** = /ɛn/, **s** = /ɛs/, **x** = /ɛx/. Worse still, some letters don't have the sound in the name at all: **h**, **w**, **y**, so it is easy to see why confusion arises.

Confusion of letter orientation

In the Roman alphabet, orientation is a distinguishing feature in some letters, but not in others, and this is likely to cause confusion in the early stages of learning: b/d, p/q, m/w, n/u, t/f.

Letters that represent more than one sound and sounds that represent more than one letter

Children are taught to associate each letter with a particular sound, but this is an over-simplification of a much more complex set of correspondences. All the vowel letters represent more than one sound (at the simplest level, each has a short and a long form (*hat/hate, pet/Pete, hid/hide, rod/rode, cut/cute*), as do some consonant letters, for example, c can represent /k/ or /s/, and g represents both /g/ and /dʒ/. Sometimes two letters are used to represent one sound, for example *sh, ch, -ng,* and *th.*

Restricted knowledge of alphabetical order

Children may have been taught to recite, or sing the alphabet, using a mnemonic rhyme or tune, but they may not really know the order of individual letters. For example, in one popular alphabet song, the letters *l m n o p* are usually run together to such an extent that it is not clear where one letter ends and the next begins. Is it *ellem   enno p*, or *el, emmen, opee*? When the alphabet is learned as a long string of letters, children may not be aware of where a particular letter fits into the sequence without reciting the whole string. Their ability to make use of alphabetical order is thus very limited.

Teaching the Alphabet/Letter Names

The focus here is on letter names, the shapes that these names relate to, and the order in which they should be learned.

Plastic letters are useful, as these can be manipulated, arranged in sequence and combined to form words. They can also be rotated to show how orientation may be important. For small group teaching, large plastic letters can be used on a communal table or on a floor mat.

Set out the plastic letters in alphabetical order in an arc, with the help of the learner/s, naming the letters at the same time. Talk about the first letter and the last letter, and note the position of others (e.g. m in the middle) count the letters together and talk about the fact that all the hundreds of thousands of words in English can be written with just these few letters. Recite the alphabet slowly with the learner/s, pointing at each letter in turn. See if they can recite the alphabet, again pointing at the letters. Watch out for the muddle when at LMNOP, and practise reciting this letter sequence slowly.

Find the middle letter (m), and divide the arc into four "chunks" – A–E, F–M, N–S and T–Z. Recite the letters in these chunks, so that learners become aware of the letters that are near the beginning of the alphabet, near the end, or in the middle. This will be useful for locating words in a dictionary or for using reference books.

Talk about alphabetical order. Why is it useful? Where do the learners' surnames come in the alphabet? Does the teacher call the register in alphabetical order? How are dictionaries, telephone directories arranged?

Ask the learner/s to close their eyes while you remove a letter, or turn one upside down, or transpose two letters. See how quickly they can discover what you have done. Let them try the same test on you. Once the alphabet is learned, use a stopwatch to time the learners setting out the plastic letters in order, and practise spelling words using letter names, rather than letter sounds.

Sound–Letter Correspondence

The focus here is on linking sounds with the names and shapes of letters. Because of the likelihood of confusing names with sounds (e.g. thinking that the letter y has the sound /w/), it is important to make a clear distinction between the names of letters and the sounds they represent.

The ability to reflect on and manipulate the sound structure of words independently of meaning (phonological awareness) is known to be a crucial prerequisite skill in literacy development. As the majority of learners with dyslexia have a weakness in this cognitive function, they may therefore experience difficulty relating sounds to letters.

In the same way as for learning about the alphabet, plastic letters are very useful for teaching sound–letter correspondence.

Talk about the fact that we use the 26 letters for different sounds. Ask learners to point to some letters and make the sounds, then ask them to think of words starting with particular sounds.

It is important to teach the difference between vowel and consonant letters, because many spelling conventions are based on this distinction. At a very basic level, the letters *a e i o u* and *-y* represent vowel sounds; sounds in which there is vibration of the vocal folds (voicing) and in the production of which the passage of air is not impeded. In the production of consonant sounds, there is always some "blockage" to the airway, whether through closure or partial closure /p/, /b/, /w/, friction /f/, /s/, /v/, /z/ or nasal articulation /m/, /n/, /ŋ/.

Learners may already know the names of the vowel letters, and may also have heard that there is a vowel letter in every word. Demonstrate why this is so by trying to read a word (the name of the school, names of learners) in which the vowel letters have been omitted. This is almost impossible.

When teaching the consonant sounds, it is important to avoid inserting the unstressed /ə/ **sound** as in the: /bə/, /fə/, /mə/, as this will lead to difficulties in blending sounds to make words. It may also lead to spelling errors (*letter* may be spelled *let* as in /l/ /ɛ/ /tə/).

As awareness of rhyme generally precedes awareness of individual sounds (phonemes), it is generally more effective, rather than teaching individual letter/sound correspondences, to teach at the level of onset and rime, e.g. *-at*. Remove from the letter arc, and set out the *a* and *t*. Add different onsets, selected by the child from the arc. Read the resulting "words" aloud, and ask the child if they are real words. Put non-word onsets back into the arc. The child can then write the "set" of real words: *bat, cat, fat, hat, mat, pat, rat, sat*. This exercise alone gives practice in sound/symbol correspondences for reading, manipulating sounds and letters, and writing, in addition to oral practice for the non-word onsets.

Teaching Spelling Patterns (regular words)

Spellings are considered regular if they have a letter and sound sequence that is shared by a large number of words. For example, *-ck* after a short vowel, *-ight* and *wa*/*squa* as in *wash, squash*. In this manual, words are only grouped together if they share both sound structure and letter pattern, so, for example, *rough* and *tough* are placed together in a separate group from *fought, bought* and *thought*.

The simplest regular patterns include CVC words, and words with initial consonant digraphs (*sh, ch, th*), final consonant digraphs (*-ng, -ck, -sh, -ch*), initial consonant clusters (*sp, tr*) and final consonant clusters (*-nt, -mp*). When introducing these to younger learners, the use of plastic letters as outlined above, is generally effective, as it promotes phonemic awareness through working with different combinations of sounds and letters. The spelling pattern is introduced through reading and manipulating the letters.

The recognition stage can be further exploited before there is any need to start writing. The teacher and pupil can talk about the letter sequence, repeatedly naming the relevant letters in a group of words, e.g. *night* IGH, *sight* IGH, *tight* IGH etc. This will lead to auditory reinforcement of the letter sequence, so that errors such as *nihgt* are less likely to occur.

Examples of particular spelling patterns can also be looked for in texts, and again, the relevant letter sequence can be named or highlighted. Teachers may wish to use the word lists in this manual to create sentences or stories that include examples of a particular spelling pattern. At this point, it is important to be aware of the vocabulary level of pupils, as some uncommon words have regular spelling patterns, and will thus have been included in the word lists. It is best to avoid working with words that are not in the pupil's spoken vocabulary. Pupils can track through sentences or stories you have composed, looking for the target words and highlighting them as they name the letter sequence.

When pupils are familiar with the letter pattern, and are able to identify it in text, they should start to write the words that share the pattern. To maximise kinaesthetic feedback, the words should first be copied as a list. The next stage of the writing process is word by word dictation, followed by dictation within sentences. Next, sentences or short stories that contain as many as possible of the target words can then be composed and written by pupils. If the stories are slightly implausible, so much the better. It is likely that pupils will already know how to spell some of the words. New spellings will be learned by semantic association, for example, *The knight with tight trousers had a fight last night in the moonlight.* It is thus important to move from word level to sentence and text level as soon as possible. The correct use of taught patterns should be monitored in pupils' writing in contexts other than within the spelling lesson.

The concept of regularity in spelling is by no means simple in English, hence the more frequent use of the term "pattern" in this manual. Some patterns, such as *bought, fought, nought* etc. are relatively small in scope, but are also quite important. Where there is a group of words like this, it is useful to use the methods above, promoting the generalisation of any word-specific knowledge the pupil may have.

It is all too easy to become so absorbed in the issue of spelling that the meaning of words is quite forgotten. When reading words and focusing on the spelling, meaning should also be discussed and clarified when necessary. Word level practice of spelling can become very mechanical, hence the importance of promoting spelling awareness at text level. The latter will also aid the development of decoding strategies for reading unfamiliar words.

Spelling "Key" Words

Some words will need to be taught individually, and not as part of a sound-based spelling programme. These include words of very high frequency such as *was, in, of, me, because.* Most of these words do not have a regular spelling pattern, yet because of their importance, they need to be taught early. The words listed below are incorporated into the test words, and marked with an asterisk to indicate that they should be taught as individual items. Other high frequency words not identified in this way (such as *then, that*) have regular spelling patterns, and are incorporated into the manual with their "partner" words. However, these also may well need to be taught as individual items. As they are so important, the key words listed below appear in both sets of test words.

Key Words Identified in the Test Word Lists

TEST WORDS 1		**TEST WORDS 2**	
a	her	a	her
I	off	I	would
if	could	if	our
the	our	the	because
of	because	of	friend
do	friend	to	school

be	school		me	there
no	there		on	before
as	before		is	their
was	their		was	where
by	here		my	here
going	people		going	people
said	were		said	were
you	who		you	who
they	buy		they	buy
where	does			does
are	beauty		are	beauty
put	through		put	through
one	straight		once	straight
out			out	

Other words that may need to be taught as "key words" include personal words (names of school, friends and family, names of streets etc.), and topic, subject, or work-related vocabulary.

Teaching Techniques for Key Words

Simultaneous Oral Spelling (SOS)

The multi-sensory method described below has been developed from Bradley's (1981) adaptation of the Gillingham and Stillman method (1956).

Materials: a spiral-bound notebook (top binding)
                    pencil

- a word to learn is selected
- the teacher prints the word at the bottom of the page
- the learner is shown the word (visual input)
- the teacher reads the word which the learner repeats (auditory input)
- the teacher names the letters (using letter grouping and exaggerated intonation if the spelling pattern lends itself to this, e.g. *fr- ie- nd*)
- the learner copies the word (in print) above the teacher's writing (kinaesthetic feedback)
- and simultaneously names each letter (oral and auditory feedback)
- the learner says the word again
- and checks that it has been written correctly (visual feedback)
- the word is covered by folding the page over at the bottom
- the learner says the word again
- the learner prints the word again, naming the letters
- and checks that it is correct

- if the word is written correctly, the page is folded over again and the word is written again
- the word should be written at least three times
- the same process should be practised between lessons

Printing, rather than cursive script, is used in order to focus on individual letters in sequence. Letter names are used, rather than letter sounds, because many words taught in this way do not have clear grapho-phonic correspondence. Care should be taken not to teach confusable words too close together, e.g. *where, when, were.*

This method is not suitable for long words, as too great a load would be placed on auditory memory. It is ideal for words of up to 6 or 7 letters. Lynette Bradley suggests that the method can be used as a starting point for learning, not just irregular or "key" words, but words whose spelling patterns and sounds generalise to others. This generalisation should then be taught (see Teaching Spelling Patterns, above). *Words in Words* (Brooks 1995).

The technique of looking for words within words can be effective for older learners with a relatively strong visual memory. It is also useful for spelling longer words. This strategy suits some learners whose phonological difficulties are such that they cannot make progress with a phonic-based approach.

Examples:
- *piece*:   a PIEce of pie
- *comparison*:   comPARISon
- *business*:   I get the BUS to business
- *mystery*:   I've lost MY STEREO. It's a mystery
- *pirates*:   piRATES don't pay RATES
- *familiar*:   famiLIAR
- *believe*:   I don't beLIEve a lie
- *secretary*:   the SECRETary keeps a secret

Pupils should be involved in creating these mnemonics for themselves, as they will be less likely to remember the words within words if they have been presented to them "ready made".

Initial Letter Mnemonics

This technique involves making up a sentence, the initial letters of which spell the key word. For example: **B**ig **E**lephants **C**an **A**dd **U**p **S**o **E**asily = *because*. This technique helps some learners, but if children's spelling is very weak, they are prone to forget which word the mnemonic was supposed to help them to spell: "I know how to spell *beauty* – It's **B**ig **E**lephants **C**an **A**dd **U**p... etc."

Initial letter mnemonics work better if there is a clear semantic link between the sentence and the word. For example: **D**ashing **I**n **A** **R**eal **R**ush, **H**urry **O**r **E**lse **A**ccident = *diarrhoea* – an effective way of remembering the spelling of a particularly troublesome word.

As for words within words, it is important to involve the pupil in the creation of these mnemonics. This technique is probably more useful for learning material such as the sequence of the names of the planets or of the cranial nerves than for learning how to spell, but it is worth bearing in mind.

Spelling and Syllable Structure

An awareness of syllable structure in speech is a useful tool in learning to spell. The first step in spelling long words is the ability to reflect on and represent the syllable structure. Errors such as *atshun* for *attention* are barely decipherable, because the middle syllable is not recorded. *Atenshun*, although incorrect, is at least decipherable.

Awareness of syllables is more useful for spelling than for reading, because spelling is a sequential process that necessitates writing words bit by bit. Rather than writing letter by letter, it is often more effective to write in small "chunks", and one very useful type of chunk is the syllable.

English is a "stress-timed" language, in which some syllables are stressed more than others, and in multi-syllabic words, some syllables are so weak that they are barely represented in speech. For example, in *photography* the first "o" and the "a" both have the neutral, unstressed /e/ sound, and in words like *Tottenham, Arsenal* and *family*, the middle syllable has all but disappeared in spoken form. In the early stages of syllable awareness training, words such as the latter three should be avoided.

Teaching methods for syllable awareness

- explain what a syllable is: a burst of sound, a "beat" or a chunk of a word, produced on one push of air
- say some words – e.g. your name, the pupil's name, breaking them into syllables, and clapping on each syllable: *te- le- vi- sion* (4), *football* (2), *en- thu- si- as- tic* (5)
- look round the room and name objects, clapping out the syllables
- graduate to tapping out the syllables with a finger (as this can be done more discreetly than clapping)
- identify the number of syllables in the words
- gradually move on to longer and longer words – 4, 5, 6 syllables
- explain that there is almost invariably a vowel letter in every syllable – it is usually the vowel that provides the "burst" of sound in the push of air

- try writing words of up to three syllables to reflect the syllable structure, remembering that each syllable needs a vowel letter – leave a big space between each syllable
- gradually introduce longer words for writing
- write multisyllabic words without leaving a space between the syllables, but with articulation of each syllable

There is a popular myth that syllables in spoken words can be identified by placing the fingers on one's chin while articulating a word. The idea is that the chin drops for each syllable. It is certainly not the case that the chin drops in this way during normal speech, and to perform the exaggerated chin movement necessary to make this method work, you need to know about syllable structure in the first place. The "chin-drops" method of teaching syllable awareness is, therefore, not advocated.

The objective for spelling, with this technique, is simply successful representation of syllables in writing, so it does not really matter if, at first, words are not correctly spelled – the goal is readability.

It does not really matter in the initial stages, where the syllable break is made. There is much confusion about this issue, because linguistic and phonological study of the syllable is based on spoken English, and the educational focus is on written English. For example, the word *button* would be split by the phonologist as /bʌ tən/ (no double "t" in the spoken form), and by the spelling teacher as but/ton.

Written representation of syllables

Knowledge about the way in which spoken syllables are represented in writing can provide learners with a useful strategy for spelling new words, but the categorisation of syllables into "types" is actually an over-simplification of a complex system.

Many resources refer to six kinds of syllables in written English. These are closed and open syllables (described below), syllables in which a vowel is followed by a consonant letter, which in turn is followed by –e (*bite*, in/**bale**), vowel digraph syllables, in which more than one letter represents the vowel sound (*coat*, *day*), consonant + *le* syllables (*bot/**tle***, *ta/**ble***), and "r-controlled syllables", in which the vowel sound is followed by the letter *r* (*arm, form, turn*).

Although knowledge of these types of syllable can aid spelling, English orthography is so complex that over-reliance on these syllable patterns can be misleading. For example, many words that might sound as if they should be spelled with a vowel + consonant + e are spelled differently (*sight*, *de/rail*); by no means all words ending in a consonant + /l/ are spelled consonant –le (*camel, chapel, funnel*).

Of these syllable types, the distinction between open and closed syllables is probably the most useful for spelling, once the concept has been fully understood. A closed syllable has a vowel, which may be long or short, followed by a consonant (VC). It may also start with a consonant (CVC) or with a consonant cluster (CCVC). It may also end with a consonant cluster (CVCC). The important thing is that it ends with a consonant (the consonant "closes" it). It may form part of a word or it may be a word on its own: e.g. *up, but, spot, bend, boot, ab/(sent), but/(ress), bend/(ing)*.

An open syllable ends in a vowel (V, CV, CCV), and the vowel is usually long: *o/pen, a/pron, cra/zy*.

An awareness of open and closed syllables, and an ability to determine whether the vowel they contain is long or short, is helpful in making sense of the rules for doubling consonants.

Raising awareness of stress in words

There is a very useful spelling rule that relates to the stress pattern of words of two or more syllables ending with a single consonant letter (see Word Structure section of this Manual, page 237): If the stress is on the final syllable, you double the final consonant before adding a vowel ending (*begin, beginning, admit, admitting*). If the stress is on the first syllable, you do not double the final consonant (*orbit, orbiting, target, targeting*). This is all very well if one has an awareness of where the stress falls in words, but this is often a complete mystery to those who are trying to learn spelling rules. Here is a tip for identifying the stressed syllable in words.

Imagine you are standing at a table, giving a very animated speech; that you are desperately trying to convey your strong opinions on a particular subject, perhaps to a slightly unresponsive audience. You feel the need, now and then in the course of your speech, to thump the table, in order to give more weight to your very important point.

You want to know whether the first or the second syllable of *begin* is stressed; imagine that, while articulating this word in your animated speech, you feel the need to thump the table, "I cannot be**gin** to imagine…". The thump will have happened to coincide with the stressed syllable. What about *gallop*?: "You want the poor horse to **gall**op?" (thump) – and it is clear that the stress falls on the first syllable. This method works well, as it is almost impossible to do the table-thumping on an unstressed syllable. However, it is important to let go of self-consciousness and act the part.

Teaching Homophones

Many spelling errors arise from the confusion of words that sound the same but are spelled differently.

One technique for distinguishing between these pairs of words is to link some aspect of the word's meaning to the form of the word. For example, *bury* = to dig a hole and put something in it. Imagine that the letter U is a deep pit with something sitting at the bottom about to be covered. There is really no need then to devise a technique for remembering *berry* (it's simply "the other one" and it's more regular).

Another technique is to make a semantic link with a word that is already known, and that shares the same spelling pattern:

(here)	*hear*:	you h**ear** with your **ear**
(none)	*nun*:	the **nun** had a **gun**
(pane)	*pain*:	his **sprain** caused him **pain**
(fare)	*fair*:	she has **fair hair**
(see)	*sea*:	the **seal** is in the **sea**

Some words do not evoke a strong visual image, and so these semantic-based strategies will not be successful:

whose	*who's*
your	*you're*
their	*there*
its	*it's*

These pairs of words need to be distinguished through understanding of context, and this is covered in the manual in the Apostrophe and Possessive Pronoun sections of Word Structure.

The dictations in the homophone section place both words of the pair in one sentence. These should be used to check understanding and consolidation of knowledge after teaching has taken place.

Teaching Silent Letters

Learners are likely to have in their sight vocabulary for reading a large number of words with silent letters. They may not, however, have explicit awareness of these strange spelling patterns. It is a good idea to raise awareness of these, through recognition (reading) before applying knowledge to writing.

One idea is to present, on flash cards, a number of words with silent letters, for example, *answer, sword, miniature, parliament*. The learner is first asked to read the word aloud, then to read it again slowly, running a finger under the letters, pronouncing every one. The "silent letter" can then be identified and highlighted in a bright colour. The words can then be written, with the "silent letters" written in a different colour.

Probably more effective than these visually-based techniques is an "auditory-feedback" approach. The silent letter is taken out of obscurity and pronounced: ***mini-ature, parli-ament, k-not, lam-b, Wed-nes-day***. This "literal" pronunciation should be practised simultaneously with writing to promote learning through a range of sensory modalities.

In the same way as for homophones, the dictation sentences included in the manual are intended for use in monitoring learning after teaching has taken place.

Spelling Rules

The word "rule" should be taken with a pinch of salt when applied to the spelling of English. The best known so-called rule: *I before E except after C,* is probably one of the least useful, as there are so many exceptions. Even if the rule is modified to read "When writing the "ee" sound, I before E except after C" there are still exceptions like *protein, caffeine* etc.

Some so-called spelling rules are really reading rules (c + e, i, y = /s/) – this is a very consistent rule, but it only guides reading. If you encounter a word with c followed by e, i or y, it will be pronounced /s/ –(*cell, city, cycle*) but if you want to write the /s/ sound with e, i or y, you have to choose between the letters "s" and "c", "s" being the more common representation.

Another example of a so-called spelling rule being more useful for reading is the well-known "silent e". The pattern CVCe (*hate, like, hope, cute*) or CCvCe (*spike, drape*) is frequently used. For reading, the letter to sound conversion is consistent. With the exception of *have, come and some*, words with this spelling pattern have a long vowel sound. However, as there are many alternative spelling patterns (*wait, fight, coat, feud*), this rule is not very useful for spelling. The terms "spelling conventions" or "spelling guidelines" are probably more appropriate than "rules" when applied to English. Among the spelling patterns discussed above are some that apply relatively consistently, and behind which there is some sort of rationale. It is therefore useful to talk about that rationale when teaching, to promote metacognition.

Listed below are some of these patterns, and as the focus here is on spelling rather than on reading, they are described with the sound as the starting point: i.e. to spell a word that sounds like …, you would use… letters.

- the sound /s/, after certain vowel sounds: after /a/, /ɛ/, /ɪ/, /ɔ/, /ʌ/, and /ɑ/, double "s" is usually used, as in *mass, mess, bliss, loss, fuss,* and *class,* .
- the sound /f/ after certain vowel sounds: after /ɑ/, /ɪ/, /ɔ/, /ʌ/, double "f" is usually used, as in *staff, cliff, off, bluff.*
- the sound /l/, after certain vowel sounds: after /ɑ/, /ɛ/, /ɪ/, /ɔ/, /o/, /ʌ/, /u/, double "l" is usually used, as in *ball, well, fill, doll, roll, dull, full*
- the sound /ɔɪ/, at the end of a word, is spelled -*oy*, and at the beginning or in the middle of a word it is spelled *oi*-.
- the sound /ɑs/ as in *mast*, the /ɑf/ sound as in *raft*, and the /ɑθ/ sound as in *path*, are written without the letter "r" generally associated with this sound (*car, farm, hard*)

- the sound /dʒ/ at the end of a word is spelled *-ge*, and the letter "j" is never used at the end of words
- the /dʒ/ sound after the five short vowel sounds /a/, /ɛ/, /ɪ/, /ɔ/, /ʌ/, is spelled *-dge*, as in *badge, hedge, ridge, lodge, fudge.* The "d" serves to keep the vowel short. It would otherwise be affected by "silent e" (*cadge > cage*)
- the sound /ch/ after the five short vowel sounds /a/, /ɛ/, /ɪ/, /ɔ/, /ʌ/ is usually spelled *-tch* as in *catch, fetch, stitch, notch, hutch* (*such, much, rich and which* are exceptions)
- the sounds /wɔ/ and /skwɔ/ are usually written as *wa,* and *squa,* as in *wash, squash*
- the sound /wɛ:/ is usually written *wor* as in *worm, word*
- the sound /wɑ/ is usually written *war* as in *war, ward*
- the sounds /gɪ/ and /gɛ/ are often written as *gui* and *gue,* as in *guitar* and *guest.* This is because the *ge* and *gi* letter sequence usually represents a /dʒ/ sound, as in *gentle, giant.* The letter "u" serves to mark the "hard" g sound

Where these patterns appear in the Manual, there is a note about their use and consistency.

Teaching Word Structure Related to Grammar

The "real" spelling rules can be found in the Word Structure section of the Manual. They are more satisfactory than the patterns observed above, because they apply relatively consistently, when adding prefixes and suffixes to words – they can be thought of as "transformational" rules, because they involve a change from one word to another grammatically related word:

bad	+	ly	=	badly
happy	+	ly	=	happily (y changes to -i)
like	+	ing	=	liking (drop e)

It is in the domain of grammatically related word structure that metacognitive teaching is most important. It is very helpful, in developing spelling knowledge, to be aware of the way in which words are related to one another, and the function of the various prefixes and suffixes. Sometimes, because of the stress patterns of English speech, the links between words are obscured:

pho**to**	ec**o**nomy	ge**o**graphy
photo**graph**	econ**o**mics	geo**gra**phic
pho**to**graphy		

In the examples above, the spelling of different parts of the words is evident in speech. If learners are encouraged to relate to one another words in this way, they will find this helpful for spelling.

In the examples below, words are grouped with the focus on the root word, showing various possible additions in terms of prefix and suffix. In the Word Structure section, all these inflections (additional parts of words) are covered and related to syntactic function (in the case of suffixes) and meaning (in the case of prefixes). Sets of words such as those below can be elicited from learners. They should be given the "focus" or "root" word, then asked to think of any variations. Responses can be encouraged by asking targeted questions:

focus word: *courage*

If you are keen for someone to do something, you … (*encourage*) them

A brave person is… (*courageous*)

The concept of linking words should be approached orally first, and then transferred to writing.

	courage		
en	**courage**		
dis	**courage**		
	courage	ous	
	courage	ous	ly
en	**courage**	ment	
dis	**courage**	ment	

			count	
		ac	**count**	
		dis	**count**	
		ac	**count**	able
			count	less
			count	ed
un	mis		**count**	ed
		ac	**count**	able
		ac	**count**	ant

			vantage	
	ad		**vantage**	
dis	ad		**vantage**	
	ad		**vantage**	ous
dis	ad		**vantage**	ous

	differ	
	differ	ent
	differ	ence
	differ	ing
in	**differ**	ent
in	**differ**	ence
	differ	entiation

	finite	
de	**finite**	
in	**finite**	
de	**finite**	ly
in	**finite**	ly

	special	
	special	ise
	special	ly
	special	ity
e	**special**	ly

Linking words according to their root develops understanding of the meaning of the associated words. For example, the words *definite* and *definitely* are of very high frequency in speech. Yet the "root" word *finite* is seldom explicitly recognised as such. The meaning of the root words should be explored, using a dictionary, and the derivations can then be interpreted more literally.

finite (OED)   =   limited, bounded, not infinite

infinite   =   not limited, bounded

definite   =   having clear, definable limits (from *define*)

This exploration of words serves the dual purpose of increasing general knowledge about words, and leading to better spelling. Once the link with *finite* is made, spelling errors such as *definatly* are less likely to occur.

If the word *differ* is recognised as the stem from which *different* derives, the spelling error *diffrent* (in which syllable structure reflects pro-nunciation) is less likely to occur.

In addition to making links at the level of the root word, links should be made between word endings and the syntactic categories with which they are associated. For example, words ending in *-tion* are always nouns, the ending *-id* (*solid, horrid, rapid*) almost always appears in adjectives, as do the endings *-ous,* and *-al.*

An awareness of the syntactic structure of sentences is beneficial in the acquisition of higher-level spelling skills.

Take the sentence:

I was very impressed by the man's generous and candid offer of employment.

The potential for spelling errors is great:

I was very imprest by the man's genrus and canded offer of employmint.

Knowledge of *-ed* as a past tense/past participle verb inflection, of *-ous* and *-id* as adjective endings, and *-ment* as a noun ending may, if not eliminate, then lessen such confusion. To make use of such strategies, the syntactic categories will need to be taught. The most important, as far as spelling is concerned, are Nouns, Verbs, Adjectives, Adverbs and Possessive Pronouns. These are all covered in the Word Structure section, and David Crystal's *Rediscover Grammar* (1996) is highly recommended as an accessible route to grammatical understanding.

When teaching spelling rules related to suffixes (doubling conso-nants, keeping or dropping "e", changing "i" to "y"), it is tempting to adopt an exclusively exercise-based "drill" approach. While the completion of work sheets full of word sums, such as *sad + est = (saddest)*, demon-strates understanding at a certain level, it is important to move from this very circumscribed word-level practice, to more general application at text level. There is otherwise a strong likelihood that the use of the desired spelling rule will be confined to exercises of this type. Once such practice ceases, so may the use of the rule.

As an additional resource, *Solving Language Difficulties* (1988), a workbook by Steere, Peck and Kahn, provides exercises for students based on metacognitive principles. Users are invited to reflect on etymology, syllable structure and the morphological structure of words.

Section 1

Testing Alphabetic Knowledge and Sound–Symbol Correspondence

The Alphabet

- can the learner recite the alphabet?
- can he/she start halfway through, or from a given letter?
- is he/she reliant on singing the alphabet, or using a rhyme?
- does he/she know any uses of alphabetical order?
- can he/she arrange plastic letters in alphabetical order?
- does he/she place the letters in the correct orientation?

Use a table such as the one below to record

- knowledge of individual letter names
- knowledge of letter sounds
- ability to think of a word that starts with that sound (or in the case of "x", ends with it)
- ability to write the letter to dictation (it is not intended that the learner write the whole word, just the relevant letter)
- knowledge of lower and upper case letters

Notes:

When asked for the sounds of the letters c and g, the learner may respond with the "soft" /s/ and /dʒ/. These are correct responses, and should be acknowledged, but knowledge of the "hard" /k/ and /g/ correspondences should also be ascertained.

It is difficult to make the **/ks/** sound (as in bo**x**) in isolation – easier in a word such as *fox, mix.*

Encourage learners to pronounce the sounds without an accompanying /ə/ sound, i.e. /s/ and /f/, rather than /sə/ and /fə/, as this will facilitate the blending and segmenting of sounds for reading and spelling.

As it would be extremely time-consuming and tedious to gather all this information in one sitting, this can be done over time, and evidence of sound–symbol knowledge from other sources (school work etc) should be taken into account.

Chart for recording sound-symbol knowledge

letter	name	sound	word	write L/C	write U/C
a					
b					
c					
d					
e					
f					
g					
h					
i					
j					
k					
l					
m					
n					
o					
p					
q(u)					
r					
s					
t					
u					
v					
w					
x					
y					
z					

Digraphs	sound	word	write
sh-			
ch-			
th-			

SCREENING TEST

As an aid to establishing a suitable starting point in the test lists, this short screening test can be administered. The test is made up of two spelling patterns from each of the forty word groups in the test lists. The test should be administered from left to right, in pairs of words, e.g. *mat, pen – ship, chin – drum, step* etc. As the test takes only a few minutes to administer, it is recommended that, for all but the most advanced learners, the whole test be given. The numbers in brackets following each pair of words refers to the suggested starting point in the test word lists, should an error be made. For example, if a learner spells *step* incorrectly, it is recommended that the teacher start the more detailed testing from list one. However, should the first error be made in *frown,* test word list six might be a more appropriate starting point. This is only a rough guide, and it is important to take into account information about the learner's knowledge base gained from other sources.

mat	ship	drum	bang	camp
pen (1)	chin (1)	step (1)	lamp (1)	of (1)
name	brain	might	girl	fall
rock (3)	float (3)	spell (3)	frown (6)	crook (6)
blast	fridge	running	lying	thread
gold (6)	match (6)	hiding (9)	should (9)	knob (9)
money	wanted	group	married	reward
ginger (11)	wished (11)	pointless (11)	topic (11)	guitar (11)
squat	babies	deceive	taught	finally
doctor (15)	different (15)	appoint (15)	limb (15)	echoes (15)
castle	contour	photograph	lecture	pension
double (20)	bruise (20)	fraction (20)	energetic (25)	fought (25)
irrelevant	boulder	fabulous	grotesque	million
astrology (25)	leisure (25)	calibre (25)	electrify (25)	access (25)
partial	experience	adjective	spontaneous	anaemic
hyperbole (25)	chalet (25)	ricochet (25)	psychiatry (25)	neural (25)

Test Words 1

* Key words see page 19   **Pages**

1.1

in	he was **in** the kitchen	i: 69	n: 144	
cap	put on your **cap**	c: 135	a: 66	p: 130
mug	a **mug** of tea	m: 142	u: 74	g: 139
ten	count to **ten**	t: 132	e: 67	n: 144
pig	a **pig** is a farm animal	p: 130	i: 69	g: 139
but	you can, **but** be careful	b: 131	u: 74	t: 132
fat	cut off the **fat**	f: 149		
let	**let** me go first	l: 172		
sad	she cried because she was **sad**	s: 153	d: 134	
run	can you **run** fast?	r: 176		

1.2

bo**x**	you can put things in a **box**	o: 72	x: 170
kid	a **kid** is a young goat	k: 136	
van	he drove a red **van**	v: 151	
a*	it was **a** nice day	a: 112	
I*	**I** am hungry	I: 88	homophone: 201
shed	I have a **shed** in the garden	sh: 159	
chip	I don't want to **chip** this cup	ch: 165	
then	he had a drink, **then** he went to bed	th: 153	
if*	wear gloves **if** it is cold	if: 149	
the*	**the** weather is good	the: 153	

1.3

trap	don't **trap** your fingers	tr: 183
drip	the tap began to **drip**	dr: 183
pram	the baby was in a **pram**	pr: 183
plum	a **plum** is a fruit	pl: 185
clap	**clap** your hands	cl: 185
flag	fly the **flag**	fl: 186
spin	**spin** round and round	sp: 186
slip	don't **slip** on the ice	sl: 186
stem	the flower had a long **stem**	st: 186
snap	**snap** your fingers	sn: 187

1.4

swim	he knew how to **swim**	sw: 188	
gift	a **gift** is a present	-ft: 192	
jump	**jump** in the air	j: 167	-mp: 192
of*	a cup **of** tea	of: 72	
do*	**do** you like cake?	do: 96	
be*	**be** careful!	be: 81	homophone: 200
no*	say yes or **no**	no: 144	
as*	she dressed up **as** Cinderella	as: 158	
was*	she **was** here	was: 73	
ri**ng**	**ring** the bell	-ng: 147	

1.5

bank	she got money from the **bank**	nk: 191
lo**st**	she **lost** her purse	-st: 190
by*	she sat **by** the fire	by: 87 homophone: 201
going*	where are you **going**?	going: 90
said*	she **said,** "Thank you"	said: 68
you*	did **you** go out?	you: 95
they*	**they** had a good time	they: 80/153
send*	**send** a letter	-nd: 191
day	**day** and night	ay: 79
thin	the dog was very **thin**	th: 152

1.6

strap	put on your **strap**	str: 189
split	**split** it in two	spl: 188
can't	I **can't** do my homework	-': 292
gi**ve**	**give** it to me	ve: 151
ba**ck**	he went **back** home	ck: 137
are*	we **are** going out	are: 100
shrub	plant the **shrub** in the garden	shr: 189
n**o**t**e**	he had a **note** book	o-e: 91
m**a**k**e**	I will **make** the tea	a-e: 77
t**i**m**e**	can you tell the **time**?	i-e: 87 homophone: 201

1.7

c**u**b**e**	a **cube** is a shape	u-e: 94
put*	**put** on your coat	put: 100
c**ar**d	he got a birthday **card**	ar: 100
b**ee**n	it has **been** snowing	ee: 82 homophone: 200
h**ea**t	the **heat** of the sun	ea: 83
one*	it is **one** o'clock	one: 179 homophone: 199
tr**ai**n	the **train** is at the station	ai: 79
b**oa**t	I can row the **boat**	oa: 92
b**oy**	the **boy** kicked the ball	oy: 109 homophone: 206
out*	he went **out** of the house	out: 108

1.8

m**oo**n	we see the **moon** at night	oo: 96
queen	the **queen** wore a crown	qu: 141
l**ow**	is it high or **low**?	ow: 92
her*	she lost **her** book	her: 164
f**ear**	you have nothing to **fear**	ear: 113
se**ll**	will you **sell** your car?	ll: 173 homophone: 208
dre**ss**	she got a new **dress**	ss: 154
off*	she fell **off** her chair	off: 149
f**igh**t	the brothers like to **fight**	igh: 88
could*	**could** you show me the way?	could: 100

1.9

b**or**n	where were you **born**?	or: 102
c**o**m**e**	**come** here!	o-e: 75
d**ow**n	it rolled **down** the hill	ow: 108
f**i**nd	can you **find** a pen?	i+CC 89

our*	we lost **our** way	our: 119	homophone: 205
pie	a slice of apple **pie**	ie: 89	homophone: 201
bird	a crow is a **bird**	ir: 106	
toe	I stubbed my **toe**	oe: 93	homophone: 202
because*	I'm going to sleep **because** I'm tired	because: 74	
friend*	she is my best **friend**	friend: 68	

1.10

school*	where do you go to **school**?	school: 138	
boy's	that is the **boy's** jumper	's: 294	
dogs'	the **dogs'** names were on their collars	s': 294	
call	can you **call** me tomorrow?	a+ll: 173	
zoo	we saw elephants at the **zoo**	z: 157	
cats	he had three **cats**	plural s: 236	
walk	**walk**, don't run!	al: 104	
there*	look over **there**!	there: 115	homophone: 205
book	read your **book**	oo: 99	
two	he had **two** brothers	wo: 97	homophone: 202

1.11

before*	wash your hands **before** eating	before: 103	
their*	they lost **their** football	their: 115	homophone: 205
hold	**hold** my hand	o+CC: 90	
eye	he shut one **eye**	eye: 89	homophone: 201
month	January is a **month**	o: 75	nth: 196
baby	the **baby** is crying	-y: 83	
pull	**pull** your socks up	u: 100	
fast	the car was very **fast**	a+CC: 101	
key	unlock it with a **key**	ey: 84	homophone: 201
new	is it old or **new**?	ew: 94	homophone: 202

1.12

term	it is the end of **term**	er: 106	
here*	can you come **here**?	ere: 114	homophone: 204
coin	he has a silver **coin**	oi: 110	
much	how **much** does it cost?	ch: 165	
want	I **want** a new bike	(w)a: 73	
catch	**catch** the ball	tch: 166	
bridge	the **bridge** crossed the river	dge: 168	
house	where is your **house**?	ou: 109	
path	stay on the **path**	a: 101	
more	do you want any **more**?	ore: 103	homophone: 203

1.13

people*	we saw lots of **people** in the town	people: 85	
bigger	an elephant is **bigger** than a mouse	gg + er: 224	
bleeding	his cut finger was **bleeding**	-ing: 226	
mixing	I am **mixing** a potion	-ing: 227	
taking	are you **taking** me to school?	-ing: 230	
swimming	I went **swimming** today	-ing: 225	
carrying	she was **carrying** a heavy bag	-ing: 234	
loose	the knot was **loose**	oo-e: 97	
sew	**sew** on a button	ew: 92	homophone: 202
lose	don't **lose** your purse	o-e: 96	

1.14

idea	it was a good **idea**	-ea: 114
see**ing**	are you **seeing** your friend today?	-ing: 232
tying	he was **tying** his laces	-ing: 232
o**dd**	he wore **odd** socks	dd: 135
e**gg**	she had a boiled **egg**	gg: 140
kind**ness**	he treated her with **kindness**	-ness: 250
were*	**were** you away?	were: 108
where*	**where** is my jumper?	where: 115/179
who*	**who** is that girl?	who: 96/165
lit**tle**	I have a **little** sister	-tle: 174

1.15

gr**ew**	the boy **grew** very quickly	ew: 97	
goodb**ye**	remember to say **goodbye**	ye: 89	
h**ea**d	put your hands on your **head**	ea: 68	
fl**oor**	it fell on the **floor**	oor: 104	
ni**ce**	it was a **nice** day	ce: 155	
knife	cut the bread with a **knife**	kn: 145	
f**ear**	he had a **fear** of spiders	ear: 113	
buy*	remember to **buy** some milk	buy: 90	homophone: 201
pure	it is **pure** gold	ure: 120	
nu**r**se	the **nurse** worked in a hospital	ur: 107	

1.16

bu**s**y	the road was very **busy**	u: 71	
br**o**ther	my **brother** is called Tom	o: 75	
does*	how much **does** it cost?	does: 76	
p**oor**	the **poor** man hurt his leg	oor: 117	
ewe	a **ewe** is a female sheep	ewe: 95	homophone: 202
Sat**ur**day	I am going out on **Saturday**	ur: 112	
Thomas	his name is **Thomas**	th: 134	
giant	he was a friendly **giant**	gi: 168	
bott**le**	a **bottle** of milk	-le: 174	
f**au**lt	it was all your **fault**	au: 105	

1.17

ev**er**	have you **ever** been here before?	er: 110	
ch**air**	sit on your **chair**	air: 115	
d**eer**	a **deer** has antlers	eer: 113	homophone: 204
sh**o**n**e**	the sun **shone** all day	o-e: 73	
fi**ng**er	I have a swollen **finger**	ng: 148	
b**ear**	he had a teddy **bear**	ear: 116	homophone: 204
play**ed**	he **played** with his train set	-ed: 234	
wait**ed**	he **waited** for a bus	-ed: 255	
sav**ed**	she **saved** the boy's life	-ed: 230	
help**ed**	she **helped** me do my work	-ed: 256	

1.18

lik**ed**	I **liked** meeting you	-ed: 257
hopp**ed**	he **hopped** on one foot	-ed: 224
hope**ful**	don't be too **hopeful**	-ful: 270
m**a**ny	have you **many** hobbies?	a: 68

hope**less**	she was **hopeless** at spelling	-less: 273	
claw	the eagle's **claw** was sharp	aw: 104	
sou**p**	she had tomato **soup**	ou: 98	
four	he had **four** sisters	our: 105	homophone: 203
ru**de**	he was **rude** to the teacher	u-e: 99	
tru**th**	tell me the **truth**	u: 98	

1.19

pretty	it was a **pretty** dress	e: 70	
rare	I have a **rare** coin	are: 116	
hurri**ed**	we **hurried** to catch the train	ied: 233	
slep**t**	she **slept** all night	-t: 257	
cycle	do you **cycle** to school?	cy: 156	
whole	I ate a **whole** pizza	wh: 165	homophone: 207
mag**ic**	he did a **magic** trick	ic: 168	
wor**d**	can you spell that **word**?	or: 107	
beauty*	the racehorse was a **beauty**	beauty: 95	
guilty	he felt very **guilty**	gu: 140	

1.20

sw**ar**m	there was a **swarm** of bees	ar: 104	
bury	he wanted to **bury** the treasure	u: 68	homophone: 199
drag**on**	the **dragon** breathed fire	on: 146	
org**an**	he played the **organ**	an: 146	
through*	she walked **through** the tunnel	through: 98	homophone: 202
fire	they lit a **fire**	ire: 117	
tune	she could play a **tune** on the piano	t: 166	
half	it is **half** past six	al: 101	
music	the **music** was very loud	u: 95	
blue	the sky is **blue**	ue: 97	homophone: 202

1.21

ghost	she thought she saw a **ghost**	gh: 141	
st**ea**k	**steak** and chips	ea: 79	homophone: 200
squash	don't **squash** me!	(qu)a: 73	
abb**ey**	an **abbey** is a church	ey: 84	bb: 132
tim**id**	the mouse was very **timid**	m: 143	id: 272
resc**ue**	come to the **rescue**	ue: 94	
fact**or**	it was an important **factor**	or: 250	
roar	the lion started to **roar**	oar: 105	homophone: 203
sh**oe**	I lost my **shoe**	oe: 98	homophone: 202
power	plug it in the **power** point	ower: 119	

1.22

island	he lived on a desert **island**	silent s: 215
box**es**	they packed the **boxes** with books	-es: 237
wolv**es**	**wolves** live in packs	-es: 238
berri**es**	the birds ate **berries**	-ies: 239
church**es**	there were three **churches** in the town	-es: 237
earth	planet **Earth**	ear: 107
th**ough**	we went even **though** we didn't want to	ough: 93
confid**ent**	he was **confident** that he had passed	-ent: 267
enjoy**ment**	the music added to the **enjoyment**	-ment: 249
appear	I **appear** to have lost my way	ap-: 284

1.23

van**ish**	the magician made the rabbit **vanish**	-ish: 262
sure	are you **sure** you like it?	s: 160 homophone: 203
c**ei**ling	the **ceiling** is white	ei: 84 homophone: 200, 208
sad**ly**	she looked on **sadly**	-ly: 225/275
quick**ly**	see how **quickly** you can run	-ly: 275
wash**es**	he **washes** his clothes everyday	-es: 258
begin**n**ing	start at the **beginning**	-ing: 227
gallop**ed**	the horse **galloped** in the field	-ed: 227
notice**able**	there was a **noticeable** improvement	-able: 231
piano**s**	he owned two **pianos**	-(o)s: 240

1.24

inst**ant**	it was ready in an **instant**	-ant: 265
fin**al**	it was the cup **final**	-al: 265
safe**ly**	he arrived **safely**	-ly: 231
c**augh**t	she **caught** the ball	augh: 105 homophone: 203
b**ui**ld	he tried to **build** a sandcastle	ui: 71
f**ol**k	he played **folk** music	ol: 93
cli**mb**	**climb** the mountain	mb: 143
bl**oo**d	the doctor took a **blood** sample	oo: 76
athl**e**t**e**	she was an excellent **athlete**	e-e: 85
happ**en**	when will it **happen**?	-en: 146

1.25

laz**ily**	she dozed **lazily** in the sun	-ily: 276
simp**ly**	it **simply** can't happen	-ly: 277
fatal**ly**	he was **fatally** wounded	-ly: 276
historic**ally**	the facts were **historically** correct	-ally: 278
ex**c**ept	I eat anything **except** fish	xc: 171
tomato**es**	**tomatoes** are red	-(o)es: 239
br**ie**f	it was a **brief** visit	ie: 84
e**x**act	have you the **exact** money?	x: 171
r**ei****gn**	how long was the king's **reign**?	ei: 80 gn: 145 homophone: 200
r**ou-e**	he took the direct **route**	ou-e: 98 homophone: 202

1.26

m**ayor**	he was the **mayor** of the town	-ayor: 116 homophone: 204
de**s**ert	the Sahara **desert**	s: 158
y**ou**ng	she is very **young** for her class	ou: 76
adult**hood**	you reach **adulthood** at eighteen	-hood: 247
m**y**th	is it a **myth** or a legend?	y: 70
cell**ar**	the **cellar** was full of cobwebs	ar: 111 homophone: 208
pr**ayer**	they said a **prayer** in the mosque	ayer: 116
li**st**en	**listen** to me!	st: 156
a**ch**e	his head began to **ache**	ch: 138
advi**se**	can you **advise** me?	se: 158

1.27

ber**et**	he wore a green **beret**	-et: 81
d**iar**y	she wrote her **diary** every day	iar: 118
w**o**men	the two **women** went home	o: 71
de**ss**ert	I will not **desert** you	ss: 158

heart	your **heart** pumps blood	ear: 102
duty	the doctor was on night **duty**	d: 169
gr**ey**	he wore a **grey** suit	ey: 80
fr**ui**t	an orange is a **fruit**	ui: 98
t**our**	they went on a **tour** of the city	our: 117
f**ue**l	the car ran out of **fuel**	ue: 176

1.28

wrist	he broke his **wrist**	wr: 177
autu**mn**	leaves fall in **autumn**	mn: 143
opera**tion**	she had an **operation** on her knee	tion: 160
aunt	**aunt** and uncle	au: 102
anim**al**	a dog is an **animal**	-al: 175
sword	the **sword** was sharp	silent w 215
dram**a**	she belonged to the **drama** club	a: 112
phone	the **phone** was ringing	ph: 150
either	you can have **either** red or blue	ei: 90
horr**ible**	don't be **horrible**	-ible: 271

1.29

honest	be **honest** and tell the truth	ho: 213
pic**ture**	draw me a **picture**	ture: 252
cap**able**	he is very **capable**	-able: 264
straight*	draw a **straight** line	straight: 80 homophone: 200
free**dom**	he loved the **freedom** of having a car	-dom: 245
artist**ic**	she was very **artistic**	-ic: 136
act**ive**	owls are **active** at night	-ive: 273
Feb**r**uary	**February** is the second month	silent r 214
bus**iest**	rush hour is the **busiest** time of day	-iest: 233
We**d**nesday	I'm going out on **Wednesday**	silent d 212

1.30

barg**ain**	she got a **bargain** in the sale	ain: 147
televi**sion**	he likes watching **television**	sion 163
trave**ll**er	the **traveller** toured Europe	ll + er: 229
br**ough**t	she **brought** an umbrella	ough: 106
l**ei**sure	he went to the **leisure** centre	ei: 69
s**ie**ve	**sieve** the flour	ie: 71
stat**us**	what is his **status** in the company?	us: 153
mod**ern**	**modern** art	ern: 147
c**ough**	he had a **cough**	ou: 74 gh: 150
optim**ist**	he is an **optimist**	-ist: 248

1.31

forgive	can you **forgive** me?	for-: 289
oce**a**n	Atlantic **Ocean**	ce: 162
bio**logy**	**biology** is a science	-logy: 168
address	what is your **address**?	ad-: 283
real**ise**	do you **realise** how late it is?	-ise: 261
immoral	it is **immoral** to steal	im-: 279
irregular	it was an **irregular** pattern	ir-: 279
illegal	it is **illegal** to drive without a licence	il-: 280
forehead	he had freckles on his **forehead**	fore-: 286
discomfort	he was in a lot of **discomfort**	dis-: 281

1.32

aeroplane	the **aeroplane** landed smoothly	aer-: 116
su**gg**est	can you **suggest** a good place to eat?	gg: 169
ton**gue**	I bit my **tongue**	gue: 148
dissolve	sugar will **dissolve** in tea	dis-: 281
sh**ou**lder	the parrot sat on her **shoulder**	ou: 93
ga**u**ge	it is difficult to **gauge** its weight	silent u 215
v**io**lent	it was a **violent** film	io: 119
harb**our**	the boats were in the **harbour**	-our: 112/251
mea**su**re	can you **measure** the size of the room?	-su: 163
saus**age**	he ate **sausage** and chips	-age: 169/243

1.33

picnick**ing**	they were **picnicking** by the river	-ing: 229
v**ei**l	the bride wore a **veil**	ei: 80 homophone: 200
fib**re**	a balanced diet includes **fibre**	re: 111
m**ere**	it was a **mere** coincidence	ere: 114
ridicul**ous**	don't be **ridiculous**	-ous: 273
pl**ough**	**plough** the field	ough: 109
f**ier**y	she had a **fiery** temper	ier: 118
pl**ai**t	**plait** your hair	ai: 67
w**eir**d	he had a **weird** experience	eir: 114
choir	she sings in a **choir**	ch: 138

1.34

brew**ery**	a **brewery** makes beer	-ery: 246
ques**tion**	he asked me a **question**	tion: 167
forf**ei**t	you will **forfeit** your privileges	ei: 71
p**ier**	a **pier** juts into the sea	ier: 114 homophone: 204
de**bt**	he paid his **debt**	silent b 211
advi**ce**	he gave good **advice**	ce: 155
grotes**que**	the monster looked **grotesque**	que: 138
gnome	the **gnome** was in the garden	gn: 145
ma**tt**	the paint was **matt** not shiny	tt: 133 homophone: 209
clar**ify**	could you **clarify** this for me?	-ify: 261

1.35

l**eo**pard	a **leopard** has spots	eo: 69
divis**ible**	nine is **divisible** by three	-ible: 270
leaf**let**	she gave him a **leaflet**	-let: 249
serv**ice**	the shop provided a good **service**	-ice: 247
a**cc**ident	she broke it by **accident**	cc: 171 ac-: 284
cheet**ah**	a **cheetah** is the fastest cat	ah: 113
notori**ety**	his gained **notoriety** as a criminal	-ty: 252
opin**io**n	it is a matter of **opinion**	io: 180
e**xc**ept	I eat everything **except** fish	xc: 171
Euro	the **Euro** is the currency of Europe	eur: 120

1.36

q**ueue**	he waited in the **queue**	eue: 95 homophone: 202
fact**ory**	they visited a chocolate **factory**	-ory: 250
fr**eigh**t	it was a **freight** train	eigh: 80
par**ti**al	there was a **partial** eclipse of the moon	ti: 160
impud**ent**	he was cheeky and **impudent**	-ent: 267

lyre	a **lyre** is a stringed instrument	yre: 118 homophone: 205
apostrophe	remember where to put the **apostrophe**	-e: 82 ph: 150
quay	the ship docked at the **quay**	ay: 85 homophone: 201
clerk	he was the office **clerk**	er: 102
informant	the **informant** gave secret information	-ant: 265

1.37

hindrance	it was more of a **hindrance** than a help	-ance: 243
independence	**Independence** Day	-ence: 245
science	physics is a **science**	sc: 156
theory	the **theory** of relativity	eor: 114
journey	they went on a long **journey**	our: 108
account	can you **account** for this mistake?	ac-: 284
mission	his **mission** was to reach Mars	ssi: 161/251
singeing	he kept **singeing** his hair	ing: 232
ancient	this is an **ancient** monument	ci: 161
pension	he collected his **pension**	si: 162/251

1.38

twelfth	L is the **twelfth** letter	silent f 212
activity	netball was a new school **activity**	-ity: 248
anxiety	her level of **anxiety** increased	x: 159
salmon	a **salmon** is a fish	silent l 213
exhaust	the **exhaust** fell off the car	silent h: 213
adjective	an **adjective** describes a noun	dj: 169 ad-: 283
rhinoceros	the **rhinoceros** comes from Africa	rh: 178
brochure	she read the travel **brochure**	ch: 162
adequate	there was **adequate** space in the car	-ate: 266/283
precarious	it was a **precarious** journey	-ious: 272

1.39

thorough	give it a **thorough** cleaning	-ough: 112
prestige	he gained **prestige** from his expeditions	ge: 164
acquire	she wanted to **acquire** more paintings	cq: 142 ac-: 284
indict	**indict** means accuse	silent c 212
engineer	he was an electrical **engineer**	-eer: 245
instantaneous	he made an **instantaneous** decision	-eous: 268
psychic	she had **psychic** powers	ps: 157
conscious	he was **conscious** of being watched	sc: 163
miniature	she had a **miniature** poodle	silent i: 213
colloquial	**colloquial** English is conversational	col: 282

1.40

neutral	it was a **neutral** colour	eu: 95
phoenix	the **phoenix** rose from the ashes	oe: 86
eyrie	an **eyrie** is an eagle's nest	eyr: 114 homophone: 204
seizure	he suffered an epileptic **seizure**	z: 164
maestro	the **maestro** conducted the orchestra	ae: 90
anaemic	he became very **anaemic**	ae: 86
diaphragm	the **diaphragm** is a strong muscle	silent g: 212
mnemonic	the **mnemonic** helped him remember	silent m: 214
pneumonia	he was ill with **pneumonia**	silent p: 214
bankruptcy	he was discharged from his **bankruptcy**	cy: 244

Test Words 2

* Key words		Pages

2.1

it	do you like **it**?	i: 69	t: 132	
hat	the witch wore a **hat**	h: 164	a: 66	t: 132
bug	the **bug** was on a leaf	b: 131	u: 74	g: 139
bed	she slept in a **bed**	e: 67	d: 134	
pit	he fell in a **pit**	p: 130	i: 69	
cut	you **cut** with scissors	c: 135		
gap	mind the **gap**	g: 139	p: 130	
log	put a **log** on the fire	l: 172	o: 72	
set	we **set** off on a walk	s: 153	homophone: 209	
ran	she **ran** all the way home	r: 176	n: 144	

2.2

fo**x**	a **fox** has a bushy tail	f: 149	x: 170
kit	he wore his football **kit**	k: 136	t: 132
vet	take the dog to the **vet**	v: 151	
a*	can I have **a** biscuit?	a: 112	
I*	**I** am hot	I: 88 homophone: 201	
di**sh**	the soup is in a **dish**	sh: 159	
chop	**chop** the wood	ch: 165	
this	what is **this**?	th: 153	
if*	I'll eat **if** I'm hungry	if: 149	
the*	where is **the** book?	the: 153	

2.3

trim	**trim** the hedge	tr: 183
drum	beat the **drum**	dr: 183
prop	**prop** it up	pr: 183
plot	the story had a clever **plot**	pl: 185
clip	hair **clip**	cl: 185
flat	the car had a **flat** tyre	fl: 186
spit	it is rude to **spit**	sp: 186
slam	don't **slam** the door	sl: 186
stop	**stop** at the red light	st: 186
snip	**snip** with the scissors	sn: 187

2.4

swam	he **swam** in the sea	sw: 188	
lo**ft**	the **loft** is dusty	-ft: 192	
just	he was **just** in time	j: 167	-st: 190
of *	a cup **of** tea	of: 72	
to*	go **to** bed	to: 96	homophone: 202
me*	can you help **me**?	me: 81	
on	put **on** a hat	on: 144	
is*	he **is** happy	is: 158	
was *	when **was** your birthday?	was: 73	
lo**ng**	a swan has a **long** neck	-ng: 147	

2.5

ta**nk**	the goldfish is in a **tank**	-nk: 191
re**st**	have a **rest** in bed	-st: 190
m**y***	this is **my** house	my: 87
going*	I am **going** out	going: 90
said*	she **said** "hello"	said: 68
you*	what are **you** doing?	you: 95
they*	**they** went to school	they: 80/153
po**nd**	a fish **pond**	-nd: 191
w**ay**	which **way** do we go?	-ay: 79
think	I **think** that's a good idea	th: 152

2.6

strip	she tore off a **strip** of paper	str-: 189
splash	**splash** in the puddle	spl: 188
don'**t**	**don't** shout	-': 292
ha**ve**	do you **have** a dog?	-ve: 151
pi**ck**	**pick** up the litter	-ck: 137
are*	when **are** you coming home?	are: 100
three	they have **three** children	thr: 190
h**o**p**e**	I **hope** you get better soon	o-e: 91
g**a**m**e**	they played a **game**	a-e: 77
r**i**d**e**	can you **ride** a bike?	i-e: 86

2.7

c**u**t**e**	puppies are **cute**	u-e: 94
put*	**put** on your gloves	put: 100
h**ar**d	she worked very **hard**	ar: 100
f**ee**l	I **feel** happy	ee: 82
s**ea**t	take a **seat**	ea: 83
once*	**once** upon a time	once: 179
dr**ai**n	the water went down the **drain**	ai: 79
c**oa**t	you will need a **coat**	oa: 92
t**oy**	the baby had a new **toy**	oy: 109
out*	they went **out** for a walk	out: 108

2.8

s**oo**n	I am going **soon**	oo: 96
quote	it was a well-known **quote**	qu: 141
r**ow**	**row** the boat	ow: 92 homophone: 202
her*	do you like **her**?	her: 164
n**ear**	he lived **near** the town	ear: 113
we**ll**	I am very **well**	-ll: 173
pre**ss**	**press** the button	-ss: 154
cli**ff**	we walked along the edge of the **cliff**	-ff: 149
s**igh**t	it was an amazing **sight**	igh: 88 homophone: 201
would*	what **would** you like to do?	would: 100 homophone: 205

2.9

f**or**m	fill in the **form**	or: 102
d**o**n**e**	have you **done** your homework?	o-e: 75
t**ow**n	he went shopping in **town**	ow: 108

mind	**mind** the step!	i + CC: 89
our*	we lost **our** cat	our: 119 homophone: 205
tie	**tie** up your laces	ie: 89
girl	boy or **girl**	-ir: 106
toe	I stubbed my **toe**	oe: 93 homophone: 202
because*	I'm frightened **because** it's dark	because: 74
friend*	she saw her best **friend**	friend: 68

2.10

school*	they worked hard at **school**	school: 138
girl's	he broke the **girl's** glasses	's: 294
cats'	she filled the **cats'** feeding bowls	s': 294
ball	throw me the **ball**	a: 173 homophone: 203
zip	do up the **zip**	z: 157
hands	remember to wash your **hands**	-s: 236
talk	the baby was learning to **talk**	al: 104
there*	put it over **there**	there: 115 homophone: 205
look	**look** at that	oo: 99
two	he ate **two** biscuits	wo: 97 homophone: 202

2.11

before*	brush your teeth **before** bedtime	before: 103
their*	they left **their** books at school	their: 115 homophone: 205
told	I **told** him a story	o + cc: 90
dye	I am going to **dye** my hair	ye: 89 homophone: 201
front	she was at the **front** of the queue	o: 75
lady	the **lady** wore a hat	-y: 83
bull	the **bull** charged at the red flag	u: 100
last	they went for the **last** time	a + CC: 101
key	unlock it with a **key**	-ey: 84 homophone: 201
few	there are only a **few** left	ew: 94

2.12

herb	parsley is a **herb**	er: 106
here*	come **here**	here: 114 homophone: 204
oil	fry it in **oil**	oi: 110
such	it was **such** a mess	-ch: 165
wash	**wash** your hands	(w)a: 73
fetch	can you **fetch** me some milk?	tch: 166
fridge	keep it in the **fridge**	dge: 168
mouse	the **mouse** lived in a hole	ou: 109
bath	**he put bubbles in the bath**	a: 101
sore	her leg was very **sore**	ore: 103 homophone: 203

2.13

people*	we invited lots of **people**	people: 85
fatter	the piglet was getting **fatter**	tt: 234
needing	he was always **needing** help	-ing: 226
rowing	they were **rowing** down the river	-ing: 227
making	what are you **making**?	-ing: 230
clapping	everyone started **clapping**	-ing: 224
flying	the birds were **flying**	-ing: 234
goose	the **goose** was on the pond	oo-e: 97

sew	**sew** on the button	ew: 92	homophone: 202
move	can you **move** over, please	o-e: 96	

2.14

id**ea**	what a good **idea**	-ea: 114	
flee**ing**	they chased the **fleeing** man	-ing: 232	
ly**ing**	she was **lying** on the bed	-ing: 232	
a**dd**	can you **add** two and two?	-dd: 135	
e**gg**	can I have a fried **egg**?	-gg: 140	
sad**ness**	he cried with **sadness**	-ness: 250	
were*	what **were** you doing?	were: 108	
where*	**where** is it?	where: 115/179	
who*	**who** is at the door?	who: 96/165	
lit**tle**	can I have a **little** more?	-tle: 174	

2.15

dr**ew**	she **drew** a lovely picture	ew: 97	
goodb**ye**	she waved **goodbye**	ye: 89	
bread	**bread** and jam	ea: 68	
d**oo**r	shut the **door**	oor: 104	
mi**ce**	there were white **mice** in the cage	ce: 155	
knit	**knit** a jumper	kn: 145	
n**ear**	I live **near** the shops	ear: 113	
buy*	I need to **buy** some milk	buy: 90	homophone: 201
c**ure**	the doctor found a **cure**	ure: 120	
p**ur**se	put the money in a **purse**	ur: 107	

2.16

min**u**te	I'll be ready in a **minute**	u: 71	
an**o**ther	I'd like **another** slice of cake	o: 75	
does*	how much **does** it cost?	oe: 76	
m**oor**	the wild horses lived on the **moor**	oor: 117	homophone: 203
ewe	a **ewe** is a female sheep	ewe: 95	homophone: 202
m**ur**mur	there was a **murmur** from the crowd	ur: 112	
thyme	**thyme** is a herb	th: 134	homophone: 201
gentle	there was a **gentle** breeze	ge: 168	
sing**le**	he counted every **single** one	-le: 174	
l**au**nch	they decided to **launch** the rocket	au: 105	

2.17

nev**er**	I have **never** been there	er: 110	
h**air**	she had long **hair**	air: 115	homophone: 204
st**eer**	**steer** carefully round the corner	eer: 113	
g**o**n**e**	where have you **gone**?	o-e: 73	
a**ng**er	she shouted in **anger**	ng: 148	
p**ear**	a **pear** is a fruit	ear: 116	homophone: 205
stay**ed**	we **stayed** near the seaside	-ed: 234	
hunt**ed**	the lion **hunted** the deer	-ed: 255	
lov**ed**	she **loved** her doll	-ed: 230	
thank**ed**	he **thanked** them for the present	-ed: 256	

2.18

hop**ed**	he **hoped** the weather would be good	-ed: 257	

stopped	the car **stopped** suddenly	-ed: 225	
careful	be **careful** when you cross the road	-ful: 270	
any	are there **any** left?	a: 68	
safety	he was very **safety**-conscious	-ty: 231	
raw	the meat was **raw**	aw: 104	homophone: 203
group	there were six people in the **group**	ou: 98	
four	it is **four** o'clock	our: 105	homophone: 203
flute	she played the **flute**	u-e: 99	
truth	remember to tell the **truth**	u: 98	

2.19

pretty	she is very **pretty**	e: 70	
care	take **care** when you cross the road	are: 116	
married	they got **married** on Saturday	-ied: 233	
crept	she **crept** along the corridor	-t: 257	
circle	draw a **circle**	c: 155	
whole	he ate a **whole** box of chocolates	wh: 165	homophone: 207
logic	there was **logic** in her answer	ic: 168	
work	this is very hard **work**	or: 107	
beauty*	the racehorse was a **beauty**	beauty: 95	
guess	**guess** what time it is	gu: 140	

2.20

ward	she visited the children's **ward**	ar: 104	
bury	dogs like to **bury** bones	u: 68	homophone: 199
lemon	**lemon** is a citrus fruit	on: 146	
human	**human** being	an: 146	
through*	he walked **through** the gap	through: 98	homophone: 202
wire	the fence was made of **wire**	ire: 117	
Tudor	Henry VIII was a **Tudor** king	t: 166	
calf	a young cow is called a **calf**	al: 101	
tunic	he wore a leather **tunic**	u: 95	
true	it was a **true** story	ue: 97	

2.21

ghastly	it was a **ghastly** experience	gh: 141	
great	we had a **great** time	ea: 79	homophone: 200
squat	**squat** on the floor	(qu) a: 73	
valley	a river **valley**	ey: 84	
solid	it was a **solid** block	id: 272	
subdue	he tried to **subdue** the crying child	ue: 94	
actor	he was a famous **actor**	or: 250	
board	she dived off the high **board**	oar: 105	homophone: 203
canoe	the **canoe** went down the rapids	oe: 98	
flower	a rose is a **flower**	ower: 119	homophone: 205

2.22

island	he lives on a desert **island**	silent s: 215	
foxes	there were three **foxes** in the wood	-es: 237	
shelves	put them on the book **shelves**	-ves: 238	
babies	the **babies** were crying	-ies: 239	
branches	the **branches** had lost all their leaves	-es: 237	
learn	you must **learn** your tables	ear: 107	

d**ough**	you make bread from **dough**	ough: 93 homophone: 202
differ**ent**	he wore a **different** tie every day	-ent: 267
orna**ment**	she put the **ornament** on the table	-ment: 249
appeal	she will **appeal** against her sentence	ap-: 284

2.23

fin**ish**	what time does the film **finish**?	-ish: 262 homophone: 207
sugar	do you have **sugar** in your tea?	s: 160
rec**ei**ve	did you **receive** my letter?	ei: 84
bad**ly**	he did **badly** in his exams	-ly: 225/275
silent**ly**	he crept **silently** along the passage	-ly: 275
catch**es**	he always **catches** the ball	-es: 258
admitt**ed**	she **admitted** she had broken the cup	-ed: 227
happen**ed**	what **happened** to you?	-ed: 228
trace**able**	the number plate made the car **traceable**	-able: 231
radio**s**	he had two **radios**	-s: 240

2.24

vac**ant**	the room was **vacant**	-ant: 265
brut**al**	it was a **brutal** attack	-al: 264
late**ly**	I haven't seen him **lately**	-ly: 231
daughter	my **daughter** is called Sarah	augh: 105
b**ui**lt	he **built** a house	ui: 71
y**o**lk	egg **yolk** is yellow	o: 93 homophone: 202
la**mb**	a **lamb** is a young sheep	mb: 143
fl**oo**d	the **flood** ruined the carpet	oo: 76
concr**e**t**e**	**concrete** is very strong	e-e: 85
rott**en**	the apple was completely **rotten**	-en: 146

2.25

happ**ily**	they played **happily** on the swings	-ily: 276
gent**ly**	rock the baby **gently**	-ly: 277
mental**ly**	he was **mentally** very quick	-ly: 276
artistic**ally**	he painted **artistically**	-ally: 278
e**x**pect	what time do you **expect** to arrive?	x: 170
potato**es**	peel the **potatoes**	-s: 239
sh**ie**ld	he had a metal **shield**	ie: 84
e**x**am	when is your next **exam**	x: 171
fei**gn**	to **feign** illness	ei: 80 gn: 145
r**ou**t**e**	take the quick **route**	ou-e: 98 homophone: 202

2.26

m**ayor**	the **mayor** visited the school	-ayor: 116 homophone: 204
mi**s**er	the **miser** counted his money	s: 158
t**ou**ch	don't **touch** the animals	ou: 76
child**hood**	he had a happy **childhood**	-hood: 247
Egyp**t**	the pyramids are in **Egypt**	y: 70
coll**ar**	his **collar** was too tight	ar: 111
l**ayer**	she put the top **layer** on the cake	ayer: 116
ca**st**le	the **castle** was on a hill	st: 156
e**ch**o	you could hear the **echo** in the cave	ch: 138
choo**se**	**choose** which one you want	se: 158

2.27

chale**t**	a **chalet** is a wooden house	-et: 81
l**iar**	I thought he was a **liar**	iar: 118 homophone: 205
w**o**men	the **women** wore hats	o: 71
pos**se**ss	I don't **possess** any money	ss: 158
h**ear**th	the dog sat by the **hearth**	ear: 102
during	It rained **during** the match	d: 169
ob**ey**	**obey** the rules	ey: 80
j**ui**ce	do you want some orange **juice**?	ui: 98
cont**our**	he put **contour** lines on the map	our: 117
d**ue**l	they fought a **duel** at dawn	ue: 176

2.28

wrap	**wrap** up the present	wr: 177 homophone: 208
sole**mn**	it was a **solemn** event	mn: 143
elec**tion**	there was a general **election**	tion: 160
l**augh**	the joke made him **laugh**	au: 102 gh: 150
penc**il**	I sharpened my **pencil**	-il: 176
an**sw**er	what is the right **answer**?	silent w: 215
cinem**a**	we went to the **cinema**	-a: 112
photo	he took a good **photo**	ph: 150
n**ei**ther	**neither** of them knew the way	ei: 90
ed**ible**	is that mushroom **edible**?	-ible: 271

2.29

honour	it is a great **honour**	ho: 213
cap**ture**	he tried to **capture** a butterfly	-ture: 252
lov**able**	the kitten was very **lovable**	-able: 264
straight*	draw a **straight** line	straight: 80 homophone: 200
wis**dom**	he shared his **wisdom**	-dom: 245
domest**ic**	she studied **domestic** science	-ic: 136
mass**ive**	he drove a **massive** lorry	-ive: 273
lib**r**ary	he returned the book to the **library**	silent r: 214
bus**iest**	it was the **busiest** time of year	-iest: 233
We**d**nesday	I'm going out on **Wednesday**	silent d: 212

2.30

curt**ain**	it was a blue **curtain**	-ain: 147
revi**sion**	he finished his **revision**	-sion: 163
pedall**ing**	she was **pedalling** very fast	ll + ing: 229
th**ough**t	I **thought** we should go home	ough: 106
h**ei**fer	a **heifer** is a young cow	ei: 69
s**ie**ve	**sieve** the flour	ie: 71
foc**us**	the picture was out of **focus**	-us: 153
cav**ern**	a **cavern** is like a cave	-ern: 147
tr**ough**	the horse drank from a **trough**	ou: 74 gh: 150
pessim**ist**	he was a **pessimist**	-ist: 248

2.31

forget	try not to **forget**	for: 289
o**ce**an	the Pacific **Ocean**	ce: 162
geo**logy**	he had a degree in **geology**	-logy: 168
addition	subtraction and **addition**	ad-: 283

organ**ise**	he will **organise** a school trip	-ise: 261
immature	her behaviour was very **immature**	im-: 279
irrational	he used an **irrational** argument	ir-: 279
illegible	her handwriting was **illegible**	il-: 280
forecast	listen to the weather **forecast**	fore-: 286
dislike	do you **dislike** him?	dis-: 281

2.32

aerosol	he used an **aerosol** spray	ae: 116
exa**gg**erate	don't **exaggerate**	gg: 169
merin**gue**	lemon **meringue** pie	gue: 148
dissuade	try to **dissuade** him from doing that	dis-: 281
b**ou**lder	the **boulder** rolled down the hill	ou: 93
ga**u**ge	can you **gauge** its weight?	silent u: 215
v**io**let	**violet** is a shade of purple	io: 119
arm**our**	the knight wore **armour**	our: 112/251
ca**su**al	it was **casual** not formal	su: 163
cour**age**	she showed great **courage**	-age: 168/243

2.33

panick**y**	he felt **panicky**	-y: 229
v**ei**n	take blood from a **vein**	ei: 80 homophone: 200
lit**re**	he drank a **litre** of water	re: 111
sev**ere**	he had a **severe** headache	ere: 114
tremend**ous**	it was a **tremendous** idea	ous: 273
b**ough**	a **bough** is a branch	ough: 109 homophone: 204
fi**er**y	he had a **fiery** personality	ier: 118
pl**ait**	you can **plait** long hair	ait: 67
w**eir**	the water cascaded over the **weir**	eir: 114
choir	she sang in a **choir**	ch: 138

2.34

nurs**ery**	**nursery** school	-ery: 246
sugges**tion**	it was a good **suggestion**	-tion: 167
surf**ei**t	there was a **surfeit** of grain	ei: 71
t**ie**r	they kept the top **tier** of the cake	ie: 114 homophone: 204
dou**bt**	there is no **doubt**	silent b: 211
dev**ice**	it is a clever **device**	-ice: 155
anti**que**	it was a valuable **antique**	-que: 138
si**gn**	he put up a "For Sale" **sign**	gn: 145
wa**tt**	it was a sixty **watt** bulb	tt: 133 homophone: 209
qual**ify**	she will **qualify** as a teacher	-ify: 261

2.35

j**eo**pardy	he was placed in **jeopardy**	eo: 69
permiss**ible**	it was not **permissible** for him to leave	-ible: 270
brace**let**	she had a silver **bracelet**	-let: 249
prejud**ice**	it might **prejudice** his chances	-ice: 247
suc**c**ess	it was a great **success**	cc: 171
cheet**ah**	a **cheetah** is a member of the cat family	ah: 113
certain**ty**	she did it with absolute **certainty**	-ty: 252
mill**io**n	he won a **million** pounds	io: 180

excite	try to **excite** the pupil's interest	xc: 171	
Europe	he travelled to **Europe**	eur: 120	

2.36

qu**eue**	wait in the **queue**	eue: 95	homophone: 202
hist**ory**	he wrote a **history** essay	-ory: 250	
n**eigh**bour	we have a new **neighbour**	eigh: 80	
ini**ti**al	she made an initial inquiry	ti: 160	
confid**ent**	he was very **confident**	-ent: 267	
b**yre**	a **byre** is a barn	-yre: 118	
catastro**phe**	it was a complete **catastrophe**	-e: 82	ph: 150
qu**ay**	the ship docked at the **quay**	ay: 85	homophone: 201
cle**rk**	he was an office **clerk**	er: 102	
igno**rant**	she was **ignorant** of the facts	-ant: 265	

2.37

eleg**ance**	she was known for her **elegance**	-ance: 243
evid**ence**	he gave **evidence** in court	-ence: 245
de**sc**ent	he began his **descent**	sc: 156
the**or**em	he worked out the **theorem**	eor: 114
j**our**nal	she read a **journal** every day	our: 108
accord	they agreed with one **accord**	ac-: 284
se**ssi**on	what time does the next **session** start?	ss: 161/251
sing**eing**	she was always **singeing** her hair	-ing: 232
spe**ci**al	it was a **special** occasion	ci: 161
man**si**on	they lived in a **mansion**	si: 162/251

2.38

twel**f**th	he was **twelfth** in the queue	silent f: 212	
celeb**ri**ty	she was a **celebrity** film star	-ity: 248	
xylophone	he played the **xylophone**	x: 159	
as**th**ma	she had an **asthma** attack	silent th: 215	
ex**h**ibit	there was a new **exhibit** in the museum	silent h: 213	
a**dj**ust	can you **adjust** the picture?	dj: 169	ad-: 283
rhubarb	I made a **rhubarb** crumble	rh: 178	
para**ch**ute	the **parachute** broke his fall	ch: 162	
fortun**ate**	she was **fortunate** to be alive	-ate: 266	
cur**ious**	he was **curious** about the stranger	-ious: 272	

2.39

thor**ough**ly	she was **thoroughly** fed up	ough: 112	
regi**g**e	it was a strict **regime**	g: 164	
a**cq**uit	they might **acquit** him of the crime	cq: 142	ac-: 284
recei**p**t	the cashier gave her a **receipt**	silent p: 214	
mountain**eer**	she was a skilled **mountaineer**	eer: 245	
spontan**eous**	it was a **spontaneous** decision	eous: 268	
psychology	**psychology** is the study of behaviour	ps: 157	
uncon**sc**ious	the boxer was knocked **unconscious**	sc: 163	
parl**i**ament	they visited the Houses of **Parliament**	silent i: 213	
colleague	he was a **colleague** as well as a friend	col: 282	

2.40

feud	they had a family **feud**	eu: 95
amoeba	an **amoeba** has only one cell	oe: 86
panacea	a **panacea** is a cure	-a 114
azure	**azure** is the colour of a clear blue sky	z: 164
minutiae	he paid close attention to **minutiae**	ae: 90
paediatric	the doctor worked on a **paediatric** ward	ae: 86
paradigm	a **paradigm** is a pattern or model	silent g: 212
silhouette	he drew a **silhouette**	silent h: 213
pneumatic	they used a **pneumatic** drill	silent p: 214
mortgage	she paid off the **mortgage** on her house	silent t: 214

Section 2

English Vowel Sounds

IPA

(International
Phonetic Alphabet)   **Page**

1.	/æ/	as in *sad*	58
2.	/ɛ/	as in *ten*	58
3.	/ɪ/	as in *pig*	58
4.	/ɔ/	as in *box*	58
5.	/ʌ/	as in *mug*	58
6.	/ɛɪ/	as in *make*	59
7.	/iː/	as in *me*	59
8.	/aɪ/	as in *kite*	59
9.	/əʊ/	as in *no*	60
10.	/ju/	as in *cube*	60
11.	/uː/	as in *moon*	60
12.	/ʊ/	as in *put*	61
13.	/ɑː/	as in *yard*	61
14.	/ɒː/	as in *born*	61
15.	/ɜː/	as in *bird*	61
16.	/aʊ/	as in *clown*	62
17.	/ɔɪ/	as in *coin*	62
18.	/ə/	as in *the*	62
19.	/ɪə/	as in *fear*	62
20.	/ɛə/	as in *chair*	62
21.	/ʊə/	as in *poor*	63
22.	/aɪə/	as in *fire*	63
23.	/aʊə/	as in *our*	63
24.	/juə/	as in *pure*	63

Spelling Alternatives for Vowel Sounds

1.	/ae/	**as in sad**	**Page**
1:1	a	*sad*	66
1.2	ai	*plait*	67

2.	/ε/	**as in ten**	**Page**
2.1	e	*ten*	67
2.2	ea	*head*	68
2.3	a	*many*	68
2.4	u	*bury*	68
2.5	ai	*said*	68
2.6	ie	*friend*	68
2.7	ei	*leisure*	69
2.8	eo	*leopard*	69

3	/ɪ/	**as in pig**	**Page**
3.1	i	*pig*	69
3.2	y	*myth*	70
3.3	e	*pretty*	70
3.4	u	*busy*	71
3.5	ui	*build*	71
3.6	o	*women*	71
3.7	ie	*sieve*	71
3.8	ei	*forfeit*	71

4	/ɔ/	**as in box**	**Page**
4.1	o	*box*	72
4.2	a	*want*	73
4.3	o – e	*shone*	73
4.4	ou	*cough*	68
4.5	au	*because*	74
4.6	eau	bur*eau*cracy	74

5	/ʌ/	**as in mug**	**Page**
5.1	u	*but*	74
5.2	o – e	*come*	74
5.3	o	*brother*	75
5.4	ou	*young*	76
5.5	oe	*does*	76
5.6	oo	*blood*	76

6	/ɛɪ/	**as in *make***	**Page**
6.1	a – e	*make*	77
6.2	ai	*train*	78
6.3	ay	*way*	79
6.4	ea	*steak*	79
6.5	ey	*grey*	80
6.6	aigh	*straight*	80
6.7	ei/ei(gn)	*vein*	80
6.8	eigh	*freight*	80
6.9	ae	*gaelic*	81
6.10	et	*beret*	81

7	/iː/	**as in *me***	**Page**
7.1	e	*me*	81
7.2	ee	*feel*	82
7.3	ea	*heat*	83
7.4	-y	*baby*	83
7.5	ey	*key*	84
7.6	ie	*brief*	84
7.7	ei	*ceiling*	84
7.8	e – e	*athlete*	85
7.9	eo	*people*	85
7.10	ay	*quay*	85
7.11	ae	*anaemic*	86
7.12	oe	*phoenix*	86

8	/aɪ/	**as in *kite***	**Page**
8.1	i – e	*kite*	86
8.2	y	*my*	87
8.3	igh	*fight*	88
8.4	eigh	*height*	88
8.5	i	*find*	88
8.6	ie	*pie*	89
8.7	ye	*eye*	89
8.8	uy	*buy*	90
8.9	ei	*either*	90
8.10	ae	*maestro*	90

9	**/əʊ/**	**as in *no***	**Page**
9.1	o	*hold*	90
9.2	o – e	*note*	91
9.3	oa	*boat*	92
9.4	ow	*low*	92
9.5	ew	*sew*	92
9.6	oe	*toe*	93
9.7	ough	***though***	93
9.8	ou	*shoulder*	93
9.9	eo	*yeoman*	93
9.10	ol	*yolk*	93
9.11	eau	*bureau*	93

10	**/ju/**	**as in *cube***	**Page**
10.1	u – e	*cube*	94
10.2	ue	*due*	94
10.3	ew	*few*	94
10.4	ewe	***ewe***	95
10.5	u	*music*	95
10.6	eue	*queue*	95
10.7	eau	*beautiful*	95
10.8	eu	*neutral*	95
10.9	you	***you***	95

11	**/uː/**	**as in *moon***	**Page**
11.1	o	*do*	96
11.2	o – e	*lose*	96
11.3	oo	*moon*	96
11.4	oo – e	*choose*	97
11.5	wo	*two*	97
11.6	ue	*true*	97
11.7	ew	*grew*	97
11.8	oe	*shoe*	98
11.9	ou	*soup*	98
11.10	ough	*through*	98
11.11	u	*truth*	98
11.12	ui	*fruit*	98
11.13	u – e	*rude*	99
11.14	eu	*sleuth*	99

12	/ʊ/	as in *book*	Page
12.1	oo	*book*	99
12.2	u	*put*	100
12.3	ou	*could*	100

13	/ɑː/	as in *yard*	Page
13.1	are	*are*	100
13.2	ar	*card*	100
13.3	a	*fast*	101
13.4	al	*half*	101
13.5	ear	*heart*	102
13.6	au	*laugh*	102
13.7	er	*clerk*	102

14	/ɒː/	as in *born*	Page
14.1	or	*born*	102
14.2	a	*call*	103
14.3	ore	*sore*	103
14.4	oor	*floor*	104
14.5	ar	*swarm*	104
14.6	aw	*claw*	104
14.7	al	*walk*	104
14.8	our	*four*	105
14.9	oar	*roar*	105
14.10	augh	*caught*	105
14.11	au	*fault*	105
14.12	ough	*brought*	106

15	/ɜː/	as in *bird*	Page
15.1	ir	*bird*	106
15.2	er	*term*	106
15.3	ur	*nurse*	107
15.4	or	*word*	107
15.5	ear	*earth*	107
15.6	our	*journey*	108
15.7	olo	*colonel*	108
15.8	ere	*were*	108

16	/aʊ/	**as in _clown_**	**Page**
16.1	ow	_down_	108
16.2	ou	_house_	108
16.3	ough	_plough_	109

17	/oi/	**as in _coin_**	**Page**
17.1	oy	_boy_	109
17.2	oi	_coin_	110

18	/ə/	**as in _the_**	**Page**
18.1	er	_ever_	110
18.2	e	_the_	111
18.3	ar	_cellar_	111
18.4	or	_factor_	111
18.5	re	_fibre_	111
18.6	our	_harbour_	112
18.7	ur	_murmur_	112
18.8	ough	_thorough_	112
18.9	a	_drama_	112
18.10	ah	_cheetah_	113

19	/ɪə/	**as in _fear_**	**Page**
19.1	ear	_fear_	113
19.2	eer	_deer_	113
19.3	ere	_here_	114
19.4	eir	_weird_	114
19.5	ier	_pier_	114
19.6	eor	_theory_	114
19.7	eyr	_eyrie_	114
19.8	ea	_idea_	114

20	/ɛə/	**as in _chair_**	**Page**
20.1	ere	_where_	115
20.2	air	_chair_	115
20.3	eir	_their_	115
20.4	are	_rare_	116
20.5	ear	_bear_	116
20.6	ayor	_mayor_	116
20.7	ayer	_prayer_	116
20.8	aer	_aeroplane_	116

21	/ʊə/	as in *poor*	Page
21.1	oor	*poor*	117
21.2	ure	*sure*	117
21.3	our	*tour*	117

22	/aɪə/	as in *fire*	Page
22.1	ire	*fire*	117
22.2	ia	*diary*	118
22.3	yr	*lyre*	118
22.4	oir	*choir*	118
22.5	ier	*fiery*	118
22.6	io	*violent*	119

23	/aʊə/	as in *our*	Page
23.1	our	*our*	119
23.2	ower	*power*	119

24	/juə/	as in *pure*	Page
24.1	ure	*pure*	120
24.2	eu	*Europe*	120

Vowel word lists

1   /a/ as in *sad*

spelling alternatives: a, ai

1.1   **a:** test words *sad, bat*

-at	-an	-ap	-ag	-ad	-am	-ab
cat	ban	cap	bag	bad	am	cab
mat	can	gap	hag	Dad	ham	jab
sat	Dan	lap	lag	had	Sam	tab
rat	fan	map	nag	sad	jam	dab
hat	man	nap	rag	pad	Pam	
pat	pan	rap	tag	mad	ram	
bat	ran	sap	wag	lad		
vat	tan	tap				
	van	yap				
		zap				

-ash	-and	-ant	-amp	-ang	-ank	sta-
ash	and	ant	damp	bang	bank	stab
bash	band	pant	camp	fang	dank	stag
cash	hand	rant	lamp	pang	lank	
dash	land		ramp	rang	rank	
gash	sand		vamp	sang	sank	
lash				tang	tank	
mash						
rash						
sash						

spa-	fla-	sna-	tra-	bra-	cla-	cra-
spam	flab	snag	tram	brag	clam	crab
span	flat	snap	trap	bran	clan	crag
spat	flap			brat	clap	cram

Dictation:
A fat cat sat on the mat.
Dan ran to the van.
He had damp sand on his hand.
He went to the bank with the cash.

ai: test word *plait*   1.2

```
plait
plaid
```

Dictation:
She wore her hair in two long plaits.

/ɛ/ as in *ten*   2

spelling alternatives: e, ea, a, u, ai, ie, ei, eo

e: test words *ten, bed*   2.1

-et	-en	-ed	-eg	-em
bet	Ben	bed	beg	hem
get	den	fed	leg	gem
jet	hen	led	peg	stem
let	men	red		
met	pen	wed		
net	ten	sped		
pet		sled		
set		bled		
vet		fled		
wet				
fret				

-st	-sk/-ld	-nd	-nt	-lp/-lf
best	desk	bend	bent	help
lest		fend	dent	
pest	held	lend	lent	elf
rest		mend	rent	self
test		rend	sent	
vest		send	tent	
west		tend	went	
		wend		

Dictation:
Let the pet get on the bed.
Ben led Len to the wet den.
The elf can help to mend the tent.

2.2   **ea:** test words *bead*, *bread*

head	breath	leather	meadow
dead	breast	heather	peasant
lead	sweat	feather	pleasure
read	sweater	heaven	measure
deaf	threat	heavy	treasure
bread	thread	health	stealth
ready	steady	wealth	weapon
spread	meant	instead	dreamt
death	weather	jealous	

Dictation:
Put the spread on the bread.
He wore a heavy sweater in the cold weather.
She found treasure in the heather meadow.

2.3   **a:** test words *many, any*

any
many
Thames

Dictation:
How many boats are on the Thames?

2.4   **u:** test word *bury* (**sole item**)

Dictation:
The dog will bury the bone.

2.5   **ai:** test word *said** (**sole item** and "**key word**" see page 19)

Dictation:
Tom said he was going home.

2.6   **ie:** test word *friend* (**sole item**)

friend* "**key word**" see page 19

Dictation:
Pam is my best friend.

ei: test words *leisure, heifer* (sole items) 2.7

Dictation:
He likes to visit the leisure centre.
A heifer is a young cow.

eo: test words *leopard, jeopardy* (sole items) 2.8

Dictation:
The leopard was in jeopardy when it climbed the tree.

/ɪ/ as in *pig* 3

spelling alternatives: i, y, e, u, ui, o, hi, ie, ei

i: test words *in, it, pig, pit* 3.1

-ip	-ig	-it	-in	-id	-im	-ib
dip	big	it	in	bid	dim	bib
hip	dig	bit	bin	did	him	fib
kip	fig	fit	din	hid	rim	nib
lip	jig	hit	fin	kid	Tim	rib
nip	pig	kit	gin	lid		
pip	rig	lit	pin	rid		
rip	wig	pit	sin			
sip		sit	tin			
tip		wit	win			
zip						
snip	twig	spit	spin	slid	slim	crib
slip	prig	slit	skin	grid	swim	
skip		flit	thin		skim	
trip			chin		trim	
drip			shin		prim	
clip					brim	
grip						
flip						

(contd)

3.1 (contd)

-st	-sp	-sk	-nd	-nt	-sh	-ch
fist	lisp	risk	wind	dint	dish	rich
list				hint	fish	
mist				lint	wish	
				mint		
				tint		

-nk	-ng	-mp	-ft
kink	king	limp	lift
link	ring		gift
pink	sing		rift
rink	wing		sift
sink			
wink			

Dictation:
Did the lid fit on the bin?
Tim hid the pig in the pit.
Did Sid sit on a pin?

3.2   y: test words *myth, Egypt*

This spelling pattern comes from Greek

hymn	bicycle	lynx	sycamore	antonym
myth	typical	symbol	syringe	synonym
Egypt	physics	syllable	crystal	homonym
syrup	mystery	symptom	hypnosis	
gypsy	oxygen	system	abyss	
cygnet	pyramid	symmetry	hypocrite	
crypt	sympathy	pygmy	hysterics	

Dictation:
The gypsy knew a myth about the pyramids in Egypt.
Sympathy has three syllables.
The physics syllabus covers oxygen and crystals.

3.3   e: test word *pretty*

pretty
England

Dictation:
England can be pretty cold.

u: test words *busy, minute*   3.4

> busy
> lettuce
> minute
> business

Dictation:
He was so busy he didn't have a spare minute.
She was in the lettuce business.

ui: test words *build, built*   3.5

> build   biscuit
> built   guilt
> builder   guild
> building   circuit

Dictation:
The builder built a big building.

o: test word *women* (sole item)   3.6

Dictation:
There were three women at the bus stop.

ie: test word *sieve* (sole item)   3.7

Dictation:
Remember to sieve the flour.

ei: test words *forfeit, surfeit* (sole items)   3.8

Dictation:
If you lose there will be a forfeit.
There was a surfeit of information.

4 /ɔ/ as in *box*

spelling alternatives: o, a, o-e, ho, ou, au, eau

4.1 **O:** test words *box, fox, of*, off**

-ot	-op	-og	-ob	-od	-om / -on / -of
dot	cop	bog	Bob	god	Tom
got	hop	dog	fob	nod	from
hot	lop	fog	hob	pod	
jot	mop	hog	job	rod	
cot	pop	jog	lob	sod	
lot	sop	log	rob		
not	top		sob		on
pot					
rot					
tot					
	stop	smog	blob	trod	of*
spot	drop	slog		plod	off*
slot	plop	clog		prod	**"key**
Scot	prop	flog	box	clod	**words"**
trot	crop	frog	fox	shod	see page 19
plot	flop				
blot					
clot					
shot					

-st	-ft	-nd	-mp		
cost	loft	bond	romp		
lost	soft	fond	stomp		
		pond			

Dictation:
Bob the dog got hot.
Tom has not got a job.
The fox is in a box

a after w: test words *was, want, wash* 4.2
a after qu: test words *squat, squash*

w + a / wh + a		
was * **"key word"** see page 19		
want	wander	watt
wash	wallet	wattle
wasp	wallow	swan
watch	wan	swap
wand	wanton	swallow

Dictation:
It was a hot day.
I want to watch the swan.
He lost his wallet in the swamp.

qu + a	
quad	squad
qualify	squadron
quality	squabble
quantity	squander
squash	squalor
squat	

Dictation:
He played a high-quality squash game.
The squadron was in the quad.

o – e: test words *shone, gone* 4.3

gone
shone
scone

Dictation:
The sun shone all day.
Where has the scone gone?

4.4   **ou:** test words *cough, trough* (sole items)

Dictation:
He had a bad cough.
The pig's food was in the trough.

4.5   **au:** test word *because**

because* **"key word"** see page 19	
Austria	Australia
sausage	cauliflower

Dictation:
She ate a big meal because she was hungry.
The Austrian ate sausages and cauliflower in Australia.

4.5   **eau:** *bureaucracy* (sole item)

5   /ʌ/ as in *mug*

spelling alternatives: u, o – e, o, ou, oe, oo

5.1   **u:** test words *but, bug*

-ug	-ud	-um	-un	-ub	-us	-up	-ut
bug	bud	bum	bun	cub	us	up	but
dug	cud	gum	fun	hub	bus	cup	cut
hug	dud	hum	gun	pub	pus	pup	gut
jug	mud	Mum	nun	rub			hut
mug		rum	pun	tub			nut
rug		sum	run				rut
tug			sun				
smug	spud	slum	spun	stub			
slug	stud	swum	stun	snub			
plug		scum		club			
glug		drum		grub			

(contd)

5.1 (contd)

-ush	-ust	-usk	-unk	-ung	-mp	-lp	-uch
gush	bust	plum	bunk	bung	bump	gulp	much
hush	gust	glum	dunk	dung	dump		such
lush	lust	busk	hunk	hung	hump		
mush	must	dusk	sunk	lung	jump		
rush	rust	husk		rung	lump		
		musk		sung	pump		
		rusk			rump		
		tusk			thump		

Dictation:
The cub and pup had fun in the hut.
Mum cut us up a bun.

o – e: test words *come, done* 5.2

come	love
some	dove
done	glove
none	above

Dictation:
Come and see some doves above the trees.

o: test words *month, front, brother, another* 5.3

o + n	o + v/th	o + other letters
son	mother	dozen
ton	brother	somersault
won	other	worry
monk	another	amok
front	nothing	
money	smother	
honey	shove	
among	oven	
monkey	cover	
Monday	govern	
London		
month		
wonder		
sponge		

(contd)

5.3 (contd)

o + n		
conjuror		
mongrel		
fishmonger		
amongst		
tongue		

Dictation:
My brother comes to London on the last Monday of the month.
My mother discovered some money hidden in the oven.

5.4   **OU:** test words *young, touch*

young	nourish
touch	flourish
couple	enough
double	rough
country	tough
trouble	southern
cousin	courage

Dictation:
My young cousin got into trouble for touching the plug.

5.5   **OE:** test word *does* **(sole item** and **"key word"** see page 19)**

Dictation:
Where does he live?

5.6   **OO:** test words *blood, flood* **(sole items)**

Dictation:
The river began to flood.
Blood is red.

/ɛɪ/ as in *make*

6

spelling alternatives: a-e, ai, ay, ea, ey, aigh, ei, eigh, ae, au, et

---

Note:

Indefinite article "a" is pronounced /ɛɪ/ in early reading and spelling
See "a" in /ə/ on page 00
This should be taught as a "key word"

---

a – e, aste: test words *make, game, paste*

6.1

-ke	-te	-ne	-le	-me/-pe
bake	ate	cane	ale	dame
cake	date	Dane	bale	fame
fake	fate	Jane	gale	game
hake	gate	lane	hale	lame
Jake	hate	mane	male	name
lake	late	pane	pale	same
make	mate	sane	tale	tame
rake	rate	vane	vale	
sake		wane		gape
take				tape
wake				
				shame
shake	state	plane	scale	blame
stake	slate	crane	stale	flame
snake	skate		shale	frame
drake	plate			
brake	crate			grape
flake	grate			shape
				drape

(contd)

6.1 (contd)

-ge	-ce	-ve/-fe	-de	-ze/-se	-aste
age	face	cave	bade	maze	haste
cage	lace	gave	fade	haze	taste
page	mace	pave	made	craze	paste
wage	pace	rave	wade	laze	waste
sage	race	save		daze	chaste
		wave		faze	baste
				gaze	
		safe		raze	
				graze	
				blaze	
				glaze	
stage	space	shave	shade	phase	
	trace	stave	spade	phrase	
	place	slave	trade		
	grace	brave	glade		
		crave			
		chafe			

Dictation:

Make Jane take the tame ape out of the cage.
Kate made a cake and ate it.

6.2   **ai:** test words *train, drain*

-ain	-ail	-aid	-ait	-aim	-aint	-aif/ -aive	aise/ aize aisy
gain	ail	laid	bait	aim	faint	waif	raise
lain	bail	maid	gait	maim	paint		praise
main	fail	paid	wait		quaint	waive	maize
pain	hail	raid			saint		
rain	jail						daisy
again	mail						
	nail						
	pail						liaise
	rail						liaison

(contd)

6.2 (contd)

-ain	-ail *	-aid	-ait	-aim	-aint	-aif/ -aive	aise/ aize aisy
Spain	sail	staid	trait				
stain	tail	braid					
slain	wail						
train	snail						
drain	trail						
plain	grail						
grain	flail						
strain	frail						
sprain	quail						

Dictation:
We had to wait for the train to Spain.
The cat cut his tail on a nail.

-ay: test words *day, way* 6.3

bay	may	stay	away
day	pay	play	today
gay	ray	tray	
hay	say	pray	spray
jay	way	clay	
lay	slay	flay	
	spay		
	sway		

Dictation:
Stay and play with the sand tray.
The stray dog lay in the hay all day.
I may go away today.

ea: test words *great, steak* 6.4

great
break
steak

Dictation:
He had a great big steak in his lunch break.

6.5   ey: test words *they, grey, obey*

they* "**key word**" see page 19	
grey	drey
prey	osprey
obey	convey
whey	survey
fey	

Dictation:
They must obey the rules.
An osprey is a bird of prey.

6.6   aigh: test word *straight** (**sole item** and "**key word**" see page 19)

Dictation:
Draw a straight line.

6.7   ei: test words *veil, vein*
ei (gn): test words *reign, feign*

rein	feint	deign
vein	reindeer	feign
veil	abseil	reign
beige		

Dictation:
She wore a white veil.
Blood is carried in our veins.

6.8   eigh: test words *freight, neighbour*

weigh	freight
neigh	weight
sleigh	neighbour
eight	inveigh

Dictation:
What weight are those eight freight containers?

ae: *reggae, gaelic* (sole items)   6.9

Dictation:
He sang a reggae song in gaelic.

-et: test words ***beret, chalet***   6.10

from French

ballet	cachet	ricochet
beret	chalet	sachet
bouquet	crochet	soubriquet
buffet	croquet	tourniquet
cabaret	gourmet	valet

Dictation:
The valet will wear a beret at the ballet.
We had a buffet in the chalet.

/i/ as in *me*   7

spelling alternatives: e, ee, ea, y, ey, ie, ei, e – e, eo, ay, ae, oe

e: test words ***be*, me****   7.1
apostrophe, catastrophe

Basic Level "key words" see page 19

me*	he
be*	we
	she

Dictation:
He had to be up at ten.

Higher Level

Most of these words come from Greek

acne	posse
anemone	recipe
apostrophe	simile
catastrophe	synecdoche
hyperbole	ukulele
karate	vigilante
machete	

in this final, unstressed position, the sound is shorter and more neutral

Dictation:

It is a catastrophe to put an apostrophe in the wrong place.

7.2   ee: test words *been, feel*

-ee	-een	-eep	-eet	-eed	-eek	-eem	-eech	-eel
bee	been	deep	feet	deed	leek	deem	beech	eel
see	seen	jeep	meet	feed	meek	seem	leech	feel
fee	teen	keep		heed	peek	teem		heel
lee		peep		need	seek			keel
tee		seep		reed	week			peel
wee		weep		seed				reel
				weed				
tree	sheen	sheep	sheet	speed	sleek		speech	
glee	preen	steep	sleet	breed	Greek		breech	kneel
flee	green	sleep	sweet	creed				steel
free	queen	sweep	greet	greed				
three		bleep	fleet	screed				
spree		creep	street					

Dictation:

I can see a bee on the green tree.

The queen will make a speech this week.

ea: test words *beat, seat*   7.3

-ea	-eat	-ean	-eam	-ead	-eap	-each	-eaf	-eak	-eal
sea	eat	bean	beam	bead	heap	each	leaf	beak	deal
pea	beat	dean	ream	lead	leap	beach		leak	heal
tea	feat	lean	seam	mead	reap	peach		peak	meal
	heat	mean	team	read		reach		teak	peal
	meat	wean				teach		weak	seal
	neat	Jean							teal
	peat								weal
	seat								
	teat								
flea	wheat	clean	steam	knead		bleach		speak	steal
	treat	glean	dream					sneak	
	bleat		bream					tweak	
			cream					bleak	
			gleam					creak	
								freak	

Dictation:
It is a treat to eat lean meat.
We had a feast on the beach by the sea.

Consonant + y: *baby, lady*   7.4

any	family	greedy	carry
many	party	holy	happy
army	clumsy	lucky	jelly
baby	early	only	lady
body	easy	ready	pretty
city	fancy	funny	silly

in this final, unstressed position, the sound is shorter and more neutral

Dictation:
The lady and the baby had jelly for tea.
The funny lady had a silly hat.

7.5   -ey: test words *key*
                       abbey, valley

key

money	chimney	valley	attorney
honey	abbey	parsley	barley
donkey	alley	journey	galley
kidney	hockey	chutney	medley
turkey	jockey	trolley	volley
Jersey	storey	pulley	

in this final, unstressed position, the sound is shorter and more neutral

Dictation:
She lost her key.
The jockey in the red jersey rode the donkey in the valley.

7.6   ie: test words *brief, shield*

-ief	-ieve	-iece	-ield	ie + other	-ie
brief	grieve	niece	field	priest	pixie
chief	relieve	piece	shield	shriek	
grief	achieve		wield	siege	
thief			yield	mien	
relief					

Dictation:
The priest said my niece was a thief.
Tom found a piece of a roman shield in the field.

7.7   ei: test words *ceiling, receive*

receive	receipt
deceive	ceiling
conceive	protein
perceive	seize
deceit	caffeine
conceit	inveigle
heinous (also pronounced with /ɛɪ/ vowel)	

Dictation:
She received a receipt for the new ceiling.

e – e: test words *athlete, concrete*   7.8

aesthete	gene
athlete	impede
compete	obsolete
complete	recede
concede	replete
concrete	scene
convene	scheme
effete	serene
eke	stampede
Eve	swede
extreme	these

Dictation:
Pete was a good athlete who liked to compete with others.
The concrete block will impede the stampede.

eo: test word *people** (**sole item** and **"key word"** see page 19)   7.9

Dictation:
There were lots of people at the football match.

-ay: test word *quay* (**sole item**)   7.10

Dictation:
The boat was at the quay.

7.11   **ae:** test words *anaemic, paediatric*

This spelling pattern is from Greek; it appears in many words related to medicine; in American English spelling there is no letter "a" in these words

aegis	Caesar
aeon	anaesthetist
anaemic	haemoglobin
anaemia	leukaemia
paediatric	aesthete
orthopaedic	archaeology

7.12   **oe:** test words *phoenix, amoeba*

This is another spelling pattern from Greek; in American English spelling there is no letter "o" in these words

amoeba
foetus
phoenix
coelacanth

8   /aɪ/ as in *kite*

spelling alternatives: i – e, y, igh, eigh, i, ie, ye, uy, ei, ae

8.1   **i – e:** test words *time, ride*

-ine	-ite	-ide	-ive	-ice
dine	bite	bide	dive	dice
fine	kite	hide	five	lice
line	mite	ride	hive	mice
mine	site	side	jive	nice
pine		tide	live	rice
vine		wide		vice
wine				

(contd)

8.1 (contd)

-ine	-ite	-ide	-ive	-ice
shine	white	chide	skive	spice
whine	spite	slide	drive	splice
spine	smite	bride		price
swine	trite	glide		
twine				
brine				
divine	respite	deride	derive	device
refine	polite			
	appetite			

-ike	-ime	-ipe	-ife	-ile	-ise
bike	dime	ripe	wife	bile	rise
hike	lime	pipe	life	mile	wise
like	mime	wipe	rife	pile	
Mike	time	snipe		rile	
pike		gripe	knife	tile	
		tripe	strife	vile	
		stripe			
		swipe			
spike	grime			while	
				stile	
				smile	
				senile	
	sublime			febrile	

Dictation:
I like to ride my bike.
That kite is mine.

-y: test words ***by*, *my*
        *cycle, thyme***   8.2

Basic Level

my* by* **"key words"** see page 19		
cry	sky	July
dry	sly	reply
fly	spy	style
fry	try	type
pry	why	dyke
shy	guy	

(contd)

8.2 (contd)

Higher Level (*see also -ify in Morphology section on page 261*)

cycle	thyme	dynamo
cyclone	typhoid	hydro
pylon	asylum	hydrant
nylon	dynamite	hygiene
rhyme	dynamic	xylophone

Dictation:
Try not to be shy.
I will fly in the sky.
Why did the spy start to cry?

8.3   **igh:** test words *fight, sight*

This is an Old English/Germanic spelling pattern; the "gh" would once have been pronounced as in Scottish loch (as the "ch" is pronounced in German nicht, nacht)

sigh	fight	flight
high	might	slight
thigh	night	bright
right	tonight	plight
light	knight	delight

Dictation:
The knight might fight tonight.
You might be right, the bright light might give him a fright.

8.4   **eigh:** test word *height*

height sleight *(of hand)*

8.5   **i:** test words I*, *mind, find*

I *(first person singular pronoun)* **"key word"** see page 19

Dictation:
I got a bun.

- ind/-int	-ild	-i final
bind	mild	alibi
find	wild	
hind	child	
kind		
mind		
rind		
wind		
blind		
grind		
behind		
pint		

Dictation:
The child was kind to the blind man.

ie: test words *pie, tie*   8.6

tie
lie
die
pie

Dictation:
You will die if you eat that pie.

-ye: test words *eye, dye*   8.7

goodbye
rye
dye
eye

Dictation:
She got red dye in her eye.

8.8   -uy: test word *buy** (sole item and "key word' see page 19)

Dictation:
He went to buy a dog.

8.9   ei: test words *either, neither* (sole items) (*note: also pronounced "ee"*)

Dictation:
Have either of you been here before?

8.10   ae: test words *maestro, minutiae*

maestro
minutiae

9   /əʊ/ as in *no*

spelling alternatives: o, o–e, oa, ow, ew, oe, ough, ou, eo, ol, eau

9.1   o: test words *going**, no, so, bold, told*

go	hero	old	hold	roll
no	solo	bold	sold	poll
so	tomato	fold	told	
	potato	gold		

going* "**key word**" see page 19

Dictation:
Are you going to the shop?
She sold most of her old gold.
He told her to hold the bolt.
The hero had potato and tomato for lunch.

o – e: test words *note, hope*   9.2

-ole	-ope	-ode	-ome	-ote	-oke
hole	cope	bode	dome	dote	joke
mole	dope	code	home	note	coke
pole	hope	node	Rome	rote	poke
sole	lope	rode	tome	vote	woke
vole	mope				
	pope				
	rope				
stole	slope				spoke
	grope				stoke
					choke
					broke
					bloke

-one	-ose	-oze	-ove	-obe
bone	dose	doze	cove	lobe
hone	hose		rove	
cone	nose		wove	
tone	pose			
	rose			
stone	close		stove	probe
throne			trove	globe
drone			drove	strobe
clone			clove	
			grove	
			strove	

Dictation:
She left him a note in code.
He woke up from his doze.

9.3   **oa:** test words *boat, coat*

-oat	-oak	-oam	-oal	-oan	-oaf/	-oach/	-oap	-oax
oat(s)	oak	foam	goal	loan	**oad**	**oast**	soap	coax
boat	soak	roam	foal	moan	oaf	coach		
coat	cloak	loam	coal	groan	loaf	poach		
goat			shoal					
moat								
float					road	roast		
gloat					toad	coast		
stoat					load	boast		
throat						toast		

Dictation:
The toad and the goat roast toast as they float in the boat.

9.4   **ow:** test words *low, row*

bow	show	own
low	know	bowl
mow	crow	elbow
row	grow	arrow
sow	blow	
tow	glow	
	flow	
	slow	
	stow	
	snow	
	throw	

Dictation:
The wind will blow the snow.

9.5   **ew:** test word *sew* (sole item)

Dictation:
Can you sew on this button?

oe: test word *toe*   9.6

toe	doe	hoe	sloe	roe
Joe	foe	woe	floe	throe

Dictation:
Joe cut his toe with a hoe.

ough: test words *though, dough*   9.7

This spelling pattern has evolved from Old English

though	although	dough

Dictation:
Although the dough was moist the bread was dry.

ou: test words *shoulder, boulder*   9.8

soul	shoulder	boulder
mould	moult	

Dictation:
The poor old soul put a mouldy boulder on his shoulder.

eo: test word *yeoman* (sole item)   9.9

ol: test words *yolk, folk* (sole items)   9.10

Dictation:
The yolk of an egg is yellow.
She likes to sing folk songs.

eau: test word *bureau*   9.11

chateau	plateau	portmanteau	tableau
trousseau			

10   /**ju**/ as in *cube*

spelling alternatives: u–e, ue, ew, ewe, u, eue, eau, eu, y + ou

10.1   **u – e:** test words *cube, cute*

use	abuse	altitude
tube	amuse	magnitude
cube	refuse	platitude
cute		
dune	accuse	attitude
fuse		
mule	excuse	ridicule
muse		
mute		
nude		

Dictation:
Put a fuse in the plug.
A cube and a tube are shapes.
Please excuse his bad attitude.

10.2   **ue:** test words *rescue, subdue*

due	rescue
	subdue
	residue

Dictation:
The rescue team was due to arrive soon.

10.3   **ew:** test words *new, few*

new	nephew
few	askew
dew	curfew
pew	view
knew	pewter
stew	
skew	

(contd)

Dictation:
He knew he had to sit on the new pew.
She asked her nephew for more stew.

---

ewe: test word *ewe* (sole item) 10.4

---

u: test words *music, tunic* 10.5

funeral	cucumber
music	cubicle
tunic	Cuba
puny	cupid
	*a common spelling error is to substitute the letter **Q** for **cu***

---

eue: test word *queue* (sole item) 10.6

Dictation:
Take your place in the queue.

---

eau: test word *beauty** (**sole item** and **"key word"** see page 19) 10.7

Dictation:
The model was famous for her great beauty.

---

eu: test words *neutral, feud* 10.8

Apart from feud (Middle English), these words all come from Greek

feud	pneumatic	eulogy
neuter	pneumonia	euphoria
neutral		euthanasia
neutron		euphonium
deuce		eucalyptus
Teutonic		Eucharist
		eugenic

---

y + ou: test word *you**: (sole item) 10.9

you* **"key word"** see page 19

Dictation:
Did you go to the shop?

11   /**u:**/ as in *moon*

spelling alternatives: o, o–e, oo, oo–e, wo, ue, ew,
oe, ou, ough, u, u–e, ui, ou–e, eu

11.1   **O:** test words *do, to, who*

> do* to* who* **"key words"** see page 19

Dictation:
I do not run to the shed.

11.2   **O–e:** test words *lose, move*

> lose
> move
> prove
> whose

Dictation:
Whose books did we lose after the move?

11.3   **OO:** test words *moon, soon*

-oon	-oot	-oom	-ood	-oop	-oof/ooth	-ool
boon	boot	boom	food	hoop	hoof	fool
moon	hoot	doom	mood	loop	roof	cool
noon	loot	loom		coop		pool
soon	moot	room			tooth	tool
	root					
croon	shoot	broom	brood		proof	drool
spoon	scoot	groom				spool
swoon		bloom		troop		stool
		gloom		droop		school
				stoop		
				scoop		
				snoop		
				swoop		
				sloop		
				whoop		

(contd)

Dictation:
We will soon see the moon.
The groom sat on a stool eating his food with a spoon.

oo–e: test words *loose, choose*   11.4

noose	choose
moose	ooze
goose	booze
loose	snooze

Dictation:
The goose and the moose will choose where to snooze.

wo: test word *two* **(sole item)**   11.5

Dictation:
He will be two in May.

ue: test words *blue, true*   11.6

blue	accrue
clue	
true	
glue	
Sue	
flue	
rue	

Dictation:
Sue had some blue glue.

ew: test words *grew, drew*   11.7

blew	shrew
drew	shrewd
flew	lewd
grew	screw
chew	strew
crew	threw
Jew	

(contd)

Dictation:
The wind blew the crew on the ship.

11.8   oe: test words *shoe, canoe* (sole items)

Dictation:
He left his shoe in the canoe.

11.9   ou: test words *soup, group*

ou–e: test word *route* (French)

you	wound	route
soup	coupon	
group	ghoul	

Dictation:
Will you give the group some soup?

11.10 ough: test word *through** (sole item and "key word" see page 19)

Dictation:
He walked through the tunnel.

11.11 u: test word *truth*

truth
Ruth

Dictation:
Ruth could never tell the truth.

11.12 ui: test words *fruit, juice*

bruise	juice	pursuit
cruise	sluice	nuisance
fruit	suit	recruit

Dictation:
We drank fruit juice on the cruise.

u–e: test words *rude, flute*   11.13

rude	ruse	delude
crude	flume	include
flute	June	intrude
jute	brute	juvenile
Luke	lute	recluse

Dictation:
Luke was rude to June when she played the flute.

eu: test word *sleuth*   11.14

ieu: test word *lieu* (sole item)

sleuth
rheumatic
leukaemia

/ʊ/ as in *book*   12

spelling alternatives oo, u, ou

OO: test words *book, look*   12.1

book	good	took
hook	hood	shook
cook	wood	crook
look	foot	stood
nook	rook	brook

Dictation:
The cook took a good look at the book.
He put a hook in the wood.
He stood with one foot in the brook.

12.2 u: test word *put** "**key word**" see page 19

put*	full
	bull
	pull

Dictation:
Pull the bull and put him in the field.

12.3 ou: test words *could, would*

could*	
would*	
should*	"**key words**" see page 19

Dictation:
Would you go to the party if you could?

13   /ɑ:/ as in yard

spelling alternatives: are, ar, a, al, ear, au, er

13.1 are: test word* *are* (**sole item** and "**key word**" see page 19)

13.2 ar: test words *card, hard*

-ar	-ark	-ard	-art	-arn
bar	ark	bard	art	barn
car	bark	card	cart	darn
far	dark	hard	fart	yarn
jar	hark	lard	part	
par	lark	yard	tart	
tar	mark			
	park	shard	start	
spar				
star	shark			
scar	stark			

-arp	-arb	-arm	-arch	-arsh
carp	barb	arm	arch	harsh
harp	garb	farm	larch	marsh
			march	
sharp			parch	
			starch	

Dictation:

Park the car in the dark farmyard.

Start to march to the park.

a: test words *fast, last*   13.3

-ask	-ast	-asp	-ath	-aft/-aff	-ance
ask	fast	gasp	bath	aft	dance
bask	cast	rasp	path	daft	
cask	last			raft	
mask	mast				
task	past				
	vast				
flask	blast	grasp	father	shaft	France
basket	plaster	clasp	rather	craft	chance
	master		lather	after	trance
	nasty				stance
	fasten			staff	advance
	castle				
	rascal				

Dictation:

Fasten the clasp on the basket.

The master ran fast after the nasty rascal.

His father lived in a castle in France.

al: test words *half, calf*   13.4

half	alm(s)
calf	balm
calm	psalm
palm	qualm
	almond
	embalm

(contd)

Dictation:
The calf was very calm.
We only sang half the psalm.

13.5   ear: test words *heart, hearth* (sole items)

Dictation:
The heart pumps blood round the body.

13.6   au: test words *aunt, laugh*

aunt
laugh
draught

Dictation:
My aunt started to laugh at the joke.

13.7   er: test word *clerk*

clerk
sergeant
Berkshire
Hertford

Dictation:
The sergeant sent the clerk to Berkshire.

14   /ɒː/ as in *born*

**spelling alternatives: or, a, ore, oor, ar, aw, al, our,
oar, augh, au, ough, hau**

14.1   or: test words *born, form*

-or	-orn	-ort	-orm	-ord	-ork	-orth	other
or	born	fort	form	cord	fork	north	horse
for	corn	port	norm	lord	pork	forth	Norse
nor	horn	sort					gorse

(contd)

14.1 (contd)

-or	-orn	-ort	-orm	-ord	-ork	-orth	other
	torn worn						force
	shorn scorn sworn	short sport snort	storm	sword	stork		porch scorch
	corner morning	forty					

Dictation:
The horse was born in the morning.
The storm came from the north.

a(l): test words *call, ball* 14.2

all	mall	stall	halt	bald	appal
ball	pall	small	malt	scald	
fall	tall	salt			
gall	wall				
hall					

Dictation:
The small ball hit the wall.
Call the tall boy into the hall.

ore: test words *more, sore, before** 14.3

bore	tore	shore	before* **"key word"** see page 19
core	wore	chore	
gore	fore	spore	
more	ore	store	
pore	yore	score	
sore	lore	snore	
		swore	
		explore	

Dictation:
There was more food in the store.
She wore her new coat at the sea shore.

14.4   **oor:** test words *floor, door* (sole items)

Dictation:
The door fell on the floor.

14.5   **ar (after w and qu):** test words *swarm, ward*

war	swarm	quart
warm	reward	quarter
ward	dwarf	
warn	towards	
warp		
wart		

Dictation
The swarm of bees went towards the house.
The nurse was rewarded for her work on the ward.

14.6   **aw:** test words *claw, raw*

law	thaw	dawn	bawl	awful
paw	draw	lawn	shawl	awkward
raw	claw	fawn	crawl	dawdle
saw	flaw	pawn	trawl	
	straw	prawn		
	gnaw	spawn		

Dictation:
I saw the awful claws on the tiger's paws.
The lawn looked like straw.

14.7   **al:** test words *walk, talk*

talk
walk
chalk
stalk

Dictation:
We had a long talk on the walk.

our: test words *four, pour* 14.8

four	court
pour	course
	mourn

Dictation:
Pour out four cups of tea.

oar: test words *roar, board* 14.9

oar	board
roar	coarse
soar	hoarse

Dictation:
The oar was on board the boat.
The lion's roar made him hoarse.

augh: test words *caught, daughter* 14.10

caught	slaughter
taught	naughty
fraught	haughty
daughter	distraught
onslaught	

Dictation:
He taught my naughty daughter.

au: test words *fault, launch* 14.11

haul	daunt	August	bauble	haunch
Paul	haunt	autumn	caution	dinosaur
laud	vaunt	author	clause	thesaurus
fault	jaunt	auction	launch	taut
fraud	flaunt	astronaut	laundry	
vault	saucer	nautical	saunter	

Dictation:
Paul went to an auction in August.
The author wrote about an astronaut.

14.12 **ough:** test words *brought, thought*

ought	thought
bought	brought
nought	sought
fought	wrought

Dictation:
I bought some wrought iron and brought it home.

15 /3ː/ as in *bird*

spelling alternatives: ir, er, ur, or, ear, our, olo

15.1 **ir:** test words *bird, girl*

fir	gird	birth
girl	first	circle
stir	skirt	circus
bird	shirt	flirt
dirt	third	swirl
firm	thirty	twirl
	thirteen	whirl

Dictation:
The girl got dirt on her shirt and skirt.
Thirty birds sat on the fir tree.

15.2 **er:** test words *term, herb*

term	person	hermit
herb	verse	
verb	serve	
kerb	berth	
fern	expert	
stern	certain	
Perth	kernel	

(contd)

Dictation:
The stern shepherd lived in Perth.
We did verbs at school this term.

ur: test words *nurse, purse* 15.3

curb	curve	disturb	urgent	turtle
burp	urge	further	burden	turbine
burn	burst	gurgle	burglar	purchase
urn	church	Thursday	curtain	
hurt	spur	turkey	surface	
hurl	spurn	murder	surplus	
lurk	churn	surname	surprise	
	murmur	survive		
nurse	suburb	urchin		
purse	purpose	turnip		
curse	furnish	purple		
burr	purr	demur		

Dictation:
The nurse lost her purse in the church on Thursday.
The police surprised the burglar as he surfaced from the tunnel.

or (after w): test words *word, work* 15.4

word	world
work	worse
worm	worship
worth	

Dictation:
The bird ate the worm.
His work took him all over the world.

ear: test words *earth, learn* 15.5

earn	heard
learn	search
early	earnest
earth	hearse
pearl	rehearse
earl	

(contd)

Dictation:
I heard he searched the earth for the black pearl.
Learn your lines for the rehearsal.

15.6   **our:** test words *journey, journal* (sole items)

Dictation:
He wrote a journal on the long journey.

15.7   **olo:** test word *colonel* (sole item)

15.8   **ere:** test word *were*

were* **"Key word"** see page 19

16   /aʊ/ as in *clown*

spelling alternatives: oe, ou, ough

16.1   **ow:** test words *down, town*

cow	down	crowd
bow	frown	growl
how	crown	howl
now	drown	fowl
row	powder	town
sow		
vow		
wow		

Dictation:
The crowd ran down to see the clown.
The dog started to howl and growl.

ou: test word *out** "Key word" see page 19   16.2
ou-e: test words *house, mouse*

bout	clout	bound	douse	ouch	mouth
gout	flout	found	house		south
lout	grout	hound	mouse	couch	
pout	scout	mound		pouch	foul
rout	snout	pound	grouse	vouch	
	trout	round	spouse		
shout		sound		crouch	
		wound	oust	slouch	
		ground		voucher	

Dictation:
We found the hound behind the house.
The scout found a pound on the ground.

ough: test words *plough, bough* (sole items)   16.3

Dictation:
The plough hit the bough of the tree.

/ɔɪ/ as in *coin*   17

spelling alternatives: oy, oi

oy: test words *boy, toy*   17.1

-oy usually appears in word-final position, or before a suffix

boy	toy	annoy	employ
coy	ploy	enjoy	convoy
joy	cloy	destroy	
Roy			

oy appears initially and medially in a few words

royal	voyage
loyal	oyster

(contd)

Dictation:
Roy is a boy's name.
Joy got a new toy.
The royal prince was loyal to the king.

17.2   oi: test words *coin, oil*

oi appears initially and medially

oil	choice
boil	voice
coil	poise
foil	noise
soil	avoid
toil	point
spoil	joint
coin	poison
join	toilet
void	cloister

Dictation:
She found a coin in the soil.
Boil up some oil in the pan.
Avoid drinking poison.

18   /ə/ as in *the*

spelling alternatives: er, e, ar, or, re, our, ur, ough, a, -ah

18.1   er: test words *ever, never*
(see also -er suffix in Morphology section, page 246)

ever	silver	fester
never	rather	weather
mother	lather	whether
father	leather	over
brother	tether	under
sister	after	linger

Dictation:
My mother gave my father a silver pot and my sister a leather belt.

e: test word *the* (sole item)   18.2

Dictation:
Is the cat on the bed?

ar: test words *cellar, collar*   18.3
(see also -ar suffix in Morphology section, page 244)

altar	pillar	
burglar	popular	calendar
cellar	vinegar	
collar	wizard	
grammar	custard	

Dictation:
The wizard put vinegar in the custard.

or: test words *factor, doctor*   18.4
(see also -or suffix in Morphology section, page 250)

author	monitor	sponsor
castor	motor	opportunity
doctor	tractor	
mirror	emperor	

Dictation:
The tractor had a new motor.
The doctor was a famous author.

re: test words *fibre, litre*   18.5

This is a French spelling pattern

fibre	meagre	lustre
litre	sombre	calibre
acre	spectre	manoeuvre
metre	theatre	massacre
centre	mitre	mediocre
ogre	sabre	sepulchre

Dictation:
The theatre was in the town centre.
The ogre was five metres tall.

18.6   **our:** test words *harbour, armour*
                    (see also -our ending in Morphology section, page 243)

This is related to the French -eur ending (vapeur, humeur etc)

ardour	odour	vapour
armour	harbour	vigour
colour	honour	savour
favour	humour	saviour
flavour	glamour	behaviour
labour	parlour	neighbour
rumour		

Dictation:
The ice cream was a lovely colour and flavour.
The vapour had a strong odour.

18.7   **ur:** test words *Saturday, murmur*

murmur	augur
Arthur	Saturday
femur	jodhpurs
sulphur	

Dictation:
Arthur is going out on Saturday.

18.8   **ough:** test word *thorough* (sole item)

Dictation:
The police carried out a thorough investigation.

18.9   **a:** test words *a* drama, cinema*
       (see also -a plural ending in Morphology, page 240)

a* "key word" see page 19
(/ə/ in continuous speech, but stressed /ɛɪ/ used in early reading and spelling)

agenda	comma	enigma	regatta
cinema	dilemma	era	replica
cobra	diploma	formula	vendetta
coma	drama	quota	veranda

                                                                    (contd)

Dictation:
The escaped cobra caused a drama in the cinema.
He got a diploma for his data about the formula.

ah: test word *cheetah* 18.10

cheetah	pariah
messiah	purdah
Sarah	

/ɪə/ as in *fear* 19

spelling alternatives: ear, eer, ere, eir, ier, eor, eyr, -ea

ear: test words *fear, near* 19.1

ear	near	clear
dear	rear	spear
fear	sear	smear
gear	tear	dreary
hear		
		appear

Dictation:
I can hear you when you speak near my ear.

eer: test words *deer, steer (see also word structure, Noun Endings page 245)* 19.2

beer	queer
deer	steer
jeer	sneer
leer	eerie
peer	
veer	

Dictation:
If you peer over the wall you will see the deer.

19.3   **er (+vowel):** test word *here*

here* **"key word"** see page 19		
era	severe	zero
mere	sphere	period
series	experience	
serial	interfere	
cereal		

Dictation:
Here is my Dad.

19.4   **-eir:** test words *weird, weir* **(sole items)**

19.5   **-ier:** test words *pier, tier*

pier	pierce	brigadier
tier	fierce	cashier
		chandelier
		grenadier

Dictation:
The fierce brigadier had his ears pierced on the pier.

19.6   **eor:** test words *theory, theorem* **(sole items)**

19.7   **eyr:** test word *eyrie* **(sole item)**

19.8   **-ea:** test words *idea, panacea*

idea panacea diarrhoea

Dictation:
He had a good idea.

/ɛə/ as in *chair* 20

spelling alternatives: ere, air, eir, are, ear, ayor, ayer, aer

ere: test words ***there*, where**** (sole items) 20.1

there* where* **"key words"** see page 19

Dictation:
Where is your coat? It is over there.

air: test words ***chair, hair*** 20.2

air	chair	impair
fair	stair	affair
hair	flair	dairy
lair		
pair		

Dictation:
The girl with fair hair sat on the chair.

eir: test word ***their**** 20.3

their* **"key word"** see page 19

their
heir

Dictation:
They left their coats on the bus.
He was heir to the throne.

20.4 **are:** test words *rare, care*

bare	share
care	blare
dare	glare
fare	flare
hare	spare
mare	stare
pare	scare
rare	snare
ware	

Dictation:
We saw a rare hare.
Can you spare some money for my train fare?

20.5 **ear:** test words *bear, pear*

bear
pear
tear
swear
wear

Dictation:
I swear that bear was eating a pear.

20.6 **ayor:** test word *mayor* (sole item)

20.7 **ayer:** test words *layer, prayer* (sole items)

20.8 **aer:** test words *aeroplane, aerosol*

aeroplane
aerosol
aerial
aerate

/ʊə/ as in *poor* 21

spelling alternatives: oor, ure, our

oor: test words *poor, moor* (sole items) 21.1

Dictation:
The poor boy got lost on the moor.

ure: test words *sure* (sole item) 21.2

Dictation:
Are you sure you can swim?

our: test words *tour, contour* 21.3

tour
dour
contour

Dictation:
He went on a tour of the city.

/aɪə/ as in *fire* 22

spelling alternatives: ire, ia, yre, oir, ier, io

ire: test words *fire, wire* 22.1

dire	mire	umpire
fire	sire	
hire	wire	

Dictation:
The wire was on fire.

22.2 ia: test words *diary, liar*

briar	bias	diarrhoea
liar	phial	
diary	trial	
friar		

Dictation:
She wrote in her diary every day.
He said she was a liar.

22.3 yr: test words *lyre, byre*

byre	tyre
lyre	gyrate
pyre	tyrant

22.4 oir: test word *choir*

abattoir
choir

Dictation:
They sang in the school choir.

22.5 ier: test word *fiery*

fiery
pliers

Dictation:
She had a fiery temper.

io: test words *violent, violet*   22.6

violet	prior
violent	riot
violate	iodine

/ɑʊə/ as in *power*   23

spelling alternatives: our, ower

our: test word *our**   23.1

our* **"key word"** see page 19

sour
flour
scour
hour
devour

Dictation:
The flour tasted sour.
Our clock is one hour fast.

ower: test words *power, flower*   23.2

bower	shower
cower	glower
dower	vowel
power	towel
tower	flower

Dictation:
We had a power shower in the bathroom.
Flowers grew up the walls of the tower.

24   /juə/ as in *pure*

spelling alternatives: ure, eur, ue

24.1   **ure:** test words *pure, cure*

cure	mature	spurious
pure	manure	duress
lure	endure	duration
	demure	
	secure	
	obscure	
	urine	

Dictation:
This pure apple drink will cure you.

24.2   **eur:** test words *euro, Europe*

Europe
euro
neuron

Dictation:
He got some euros to spend in Europe.

Section 3

English Consonant Sounds

IPA
(International
Phonetic Alphabet)   **Page**

1.	/p/	as in *pig*	130
2.	/b/	as in *bag*	131
3.	/t/	as in *ten*	132
4.	/d/	as in *dog*	134
5.	/k/	as in *cat*	135
6.	/g/	as in *gap*	139
7.	/kw/	as in *quick*	141
8.	/m/	as in *man*	142
9.	/n/	as in *not*	144
10.	/ŋ/	as in *ring*	147
11.	/f/	as in *fat*	149
12.	/v/	as in *van*	151
13.	/θ/	as in *thin*	152
14.	/ð/	as in *that*	153
15.	/s/	as in *sad*	153
16.	/z/	as in *zoo*	157
17.	/ʃ/	as in *shed*	159
18.	/ʒ/	as in *vision*	163
19.	/h/	as in *heat*	164
20.	/tʃ/	as in *chip*	165
21.	/dʒ/	as in *jump*	167
22.	/ks/	as in *box*	170
23.	/gz/	as in *exact*	171
24.	/l/	as in *let*	172
25.	/ɹ/	as in *rug*	176
26.	/w/	as in *want*	178
27.	/j/	as in *yes*	180

Spelling Alternatives for Each Consonant Sound

1	p	as in *pig*	Page
1.1	p	*pig*	130
1.2	pp	*happy*	130

2.	b	as in *bag*	Page
2.1	b	*bag*	131
2.2	bb	*rabbit*	132

3	t	as in *ten*	Page
3.1	t	*ten*	132
3.2	tt	*matt*	133
3.3	th	*Thomas*	134

4	d	as in *dog*	Page
4.1	d	*dog*	134
4.2	-dd	*add*	135

5	c	as in *cat*	Page
5.1	c	*cat*	135
5.2	k	*kid*	136
5.3	ck	*back*	137
5.4	ch	*ache*	138
5.5	que	*antique*	138
5.6	cc	*account*	138
5.7	qu	*quay*	139
5.8	cqu	*racquet*	139

6	g	as in *gap*	Page
6.1	g	*gap*	139
6.2	gg	*egg*	140
6.3	gu	*guilty*	140
6.4	gh	*ghost*	141

7.	**qu**	as in *quick*	**Page**
7.1	qu	*qu*een	141
7.2	ch	*ch*oir	141
7.3	cqu	ac*qu*ire	142

8.	**m**	as in *man*	**Page**
8.1	m	*m*an	142
8.2	mm	ha*mm*er	142
8.3	mb	la*mb*	143
8.4	mn	autu*mn*	143

9.	**n**	as in *not*	**Page**
9.1	n	*n*ot	144
9.2	nn	fu*nn*y	144
9.3	kn	*kn*ife	145
9.4	gn	*gn*ome	145
9.5	en	happ*en*	146
9.6	on	drag*on*	146
9.7	an	org*an*	146
9.8	ain	barg*ain*	147
9.9	ern	mod*ern*	147

10.	**-ng**	as in *sing*	**Page**
10.1	ng	ri*ng*	147
10.2	n+g	a*ng*er	148
10.3	ngue	to*ngue*	148
10.4	n	a*n*xiety	148

11.	**f**	as in *fat*	**Page**
11.1	f	*f*at	149
11.2	ff	cli*ff*	149
11.3	ph	*ph*one	150
11.4	gh	cou*gh*	150

12	v	as in *van*	Page
12.1	v	*van*	151
12.2	ve	*give*	151

13.	th	as in *thin*	Page
13.1	th	*thin*	152

14	th	as in *that*	Page
14.1	th	*that*	153

15	s	as in *sad*	Page
15.1	s	*sad*	153
15.2	ss	*dress*	154
15.3	se	*house*	154
15.4	ce /ci /cy	*nice*, *city*	155
15.5	st	*listen*	156
15.6	sc	*science*	156
15.7	ps	*psychic*	157

16	z	as in *zoo*	Page
16.1	z	*zoo*	157
16.2	zz	*dizzy*	157
16.3	s	*miser*	158
16.4	ss	*dessert*	158
16.5	x	*anxiety*	159

17	sh	as in *shed*	Page
17.1	sh	*shed*	159
17.2	s	*sure*	160
17.3	ti	*operation*	160
17.4	ci	*ancient*	161
17.5	ssi	*mission*	161
17.6	si	*pension*	162
17.7	ch	*brochure*	162
17.8	ce	*ocean*	162
17.9	sci	*conscious*	163
17.10	xi	*anxious*	163

18	/zh/	as in *vision*	Page
18.1	si	*vision*	163
18.2	su	*measure*	163
18.3	ge	*prestige*	164
18.4	z	*seizure*	164

19	h	as in *beat*	Page
19.1	h	*beat*	164
19.2	wh	*whole*	165

20	ch	as in *chip*	Page
20.1	ch	*chip*	165
20.2	tch	*hutch*	166
20.3	tu	*tutor/picture*	166
20.4	ti	*question*	167

21	j	as in *jump*	Page
21.1	j	*jump*	167
21.2	dge	*hedge*	168
21.3	g+e/i/y	*magic*	168
21.4	gg	*exaggerate*	169
21.5	d	*duty*	169
21.6	dj	*adjective*	169

22	x	as in *box*	Page
22.1	x	*box*	170
22.2	xc	*excess*	171
22.3	cc	*access*	171

23	gz	as in *exact*	Page
23.1	x	*exact*	171

24	l	as in *let*	Page
24.1	l	*let*	172
24.2	ll	*grill*	173
24.3	le	*single*	174
24.4	al	*animal*	175
24.5	el	*duel*	176
24.6	il	*pencil*	176

25	r	as in *run*	Page
25.1	r	*run*	176
25.2	rr	*carry*	177
25.3	wr	*wrap*	177
25.4	rh	*rhinoceros*	178

26	w	as in *want*	Page
26.1	w	*want*	178
26.2	wh	*where*	179
26.3	o	*one*	179
26.4	u	*suede*	179

27	y	as in *yes*	Page
27.1	y	*yes*	180
27.2	i	*opinion*	180

Consonant word lists

1   /**p**/ as in *pig*

spelling alternatives: p, pp

1.1   **p:** test words *pig, pit, cap*

For "p" clusters see pages 183 and 185

initial		final		
pat	pig	cap	dip	hop
Pam	pin	gap	lip	mop
pad	pip	lap	hip	top
pan	pit	map	nip	pop
		nap		
peg	pod	pip	rip	cup
pen	pet	tap	sip	pup
	pot	yap		
	pop	tip		

Dictation:
The pet pig is in the pen.

1.2   **pp** (following a short vowel)

For double p + le (apple), see page 174
For doubling rule (hopping) see Word Structure, page 224

happy	poppy	puppy	copper
hippo	hippy	dipper	kipper

Dictation:
Poppy the hippo had a kipper.

Note:
single p following short vowel

topic
rapid
tropic
chapel

/**b**/ as in *bag*   2

spelling alternatives: b, bb

test words ***but, bug***   2.1

initial	final				
bad	big	bud	cab	bib	Bob
bag	bin	bug	dab	fib	job
ban	bit	bum	lab	nib	lob
bat	bib	bun	tab	rib	mob
bap		bus	fab		rob
	bog	but	jab		sob
bed	Bob				
beg	bop		web		pub
Ben	box				cub
bet					rub
					tub

Dictation:
Bad Ben bit Bob.
The bat is on the bed.

2.2   **bb** (following a short vowel)

For double b + le (bubble), see page 00
For doubling rule (rubbing) see Word Structure, page 224

ebb	
abbey	rabbit
bobbin	ribbon
cabbage	rubbish
gibbon	Sabbath
hobby	shabby

Dictation:
The gibbon and the rabbit ate cabbage.

Note: *single b following a short vowel*

baboon	rabid
cabin	rebel
habit	robin

3   /t/ as in ten

spelling alternatives: t, -tt, th

3.1   **t:** test words *ten, bat*

For "t" clusters see pages 183 and 185

initial			final		
tap	Tim	tub	bat	it	but
tab	tin	tug	cat	bit	gut
tan	tip		fat	fit	hut
tag			hat	hit	nut
	Tom		pat	kit	rut
ten	top		rat	lit	cut
Ted			sat	pit	jut
				sit	
				wit	

(contd)

3.1 (contd)

final	
bet	dot
get	got
let	hot
met	lot
net	not
pet	pot
set	rot
wet	
yet	

Dictation:

Tim got a pet cat.

Tom met a fat rat.

-tt: test words *matt, watt*   3.2

For double t + le (battle), see page 174

For doubling rule (wetting) see Word Structure, page 000

butt	butter
putt	batter
matt	mattress
watt	fetter
	tattoo

Dictation:

A badger lives in a sett.

Note: *single t following short vowel*

metal	satin
city	fetid
petal	baton
pity	British

3.3   **th:** test words *Thomas, thyme*

> Esther
> Thomas
> thyme
> Thames
> Thailand

Dictation:
Thomas and Esther went to the Thames.

4   /**d**/ as in *dog*

spelling alternatives: d, dd

4.1   **d:** test words *sad, bed*

For "d" clusters see pages 183 and 185

initial		final		
Dad	dog	Dad	did	cod
dab	dot	bad	hid	god
Dan		had	bid	nod
	dug	lad	lid	pod
den	dub	mad	rid	
	dud	sad		bud
did		bed		dud
dig		fed		mud
dim		led		
din		wed		
dip				

Dictation:
A mad dog hid in a bed.
Dan is a bad lad.

-dd: test words *odd, add*   4.2

For double d + le (middle), see page 174
For doubling rule (budding) see Word Structure, page 224

odd	adder
add	shudder
	sudden
	fodder
	Yiddish

Note: *single d following a short vowel*

medal	widow
body	shadow
adult	modern
pedal	radish
study	bodice
model	

Dictation:
The widow had a modern study.

/k/ as in *cat*   5

spelling alternatives: c, k, ck, ch, que, cc, qu

c (+a, o, u,): test words *cap, cut*   5.1

For "c" clusters see pages 184 and 185

cab	cod	cub
can	cog	cup
cap	con	cut
cat	cop	
	cot	

Dictation:
A cat can sit in a cot.

-ic (words of more than one syllable)
see also Morphology section –ic nding page 271

2 syllable	3 syllable	4 syllable
comic	elastic	economic
magic	artistic	scientific
panic	athletic	ergonomic
tonic	Atlantic	esoteric
topic	electric	
frantic	heroic	
picnic	historic	
public	magnetic	
plastic	terrific	
traffic	domestic	
tragic	fantastic	
attic	republic	

Dictation:
The public were frantic with panic when they saw the fantastic magic.

5.2   k: test words *kid, kit*

Initial (before e/i)	Final -k	- ke (see vowels)	-nk
Ken	ask	bake	bank
keen		take	rank
	look	lake	sank
kid	book	fake	tank
kin	cook	cake	thank
kit	took	make	stank
kill	rook	wake	blank
kiss	hook		drank
kind	nook	bike	plank
king		hike	flank
		like	
		Mike	ink
		pike	kink
		spike	link
			pink
			rink
			sink

(contd)

5.2 (contd)

		-ke (see vowels)	-nk
		joke poke smoke	wink think shrink stink slink drink junk trunk bunk

Dictation:
Ken had a kid.
Mike, take a look at the pink book.

-ck (after a short vowel): test words *back, pick*   5.3

a	e	i	o	u
back	deck	kick	rock	duck
sack	neck	lick	lock	luck
rack	peck	pick	sock	muck
pack	fleck	sick	dock	suck
lack	speck	Dick	cock	
tack	wreck	Mick	hock	buck
hack		tick	mock	tuck
Jack	check	wick		
		rick	shock	chuck
shack				
whack		chick	block	cluck
		thick	clock	stuck
black			flock	truck
crack		quick	knock	pluck
track		stick		
smack		prick		
snack		crick		
quack		brick		
knack				

(contd)

Dictation:
Jack can pack his sock in the black sack.
The hen went cluck and the duck went quack.

5.4   **ch:** test words *school* ache, echo*

This spelling pattern comes from Greek

school* **"key word"** see page 19

Christmas	character	architect	technical
Christopher	chemist	archaeology	schedule
Christine	chronicle	archive	scheme
choir	echo	mechanic	schizophrenia
chorus	ache	orchestra	stomach
chaos	anchor	parochial	technique

Dictation:
The school choir and orchestra gave me a headache.
Christine and Christopher caused chaos at Christmas.

5.5   **-que:** test words *grotesque, antique*

This spelling pattern comes from French

unique	Mozambique	critique
cheque	baroque	mystique
antique	brusque	physique
technique	clique	arabesque
oblique	opaque	burlesque
picturesque	pique	statuesque
grotesque	boutique	mosque

Dictation:
The unique antique in the mosque was very picturesque.

5.6   **cc:** test words *account, accord*

(See also prefixes in Morphology section, page 278)

occur	succulent	broccoli	impeccable
occupy	succumb	raccoon	hiccup
occasion	succour	desiccated	
occult		buccaneer	

qu: test words *quay, queue*   5.7

This spelling pattern comes from French

quay	mosquito
quiche	tourniquet
conquer	masquerade
queue	exchequer
liquor	croquet
tequila	marquee

Dictation
There was a queue for the ferry on the quay.

-cqu-: test words *racquet, lacquer* (sole items)   5.8

/g/ as in *gap*   6

spelling alternatives: g, gg, gu, gh, and doubling (page 140)

g: test words *mug, gap, bug*   6.1

For "g" clusters see pages 184 and 185

initial			final		
gap	gum	get	bag	big	jog
gas	gun	gear	gag	dig	log
gag	gut		hag	fig	bug
		gift	lag	gig	but
go		give	nag	jig	dug
god		girl	rag	pig	hug
got		gill	tag	wig	jug
gone			wag	bog	lug
			beg	dog	mug
			leg	fog	rug
			Meg	hog	tug
			peg		

(contd)

Dictation:
Meg got a big bag.
The dog had a jog in the fog.

6.2   **-gg:** test word *egg*

For double g + le (wiggle), see page 174
For doubling rule (wagging) see Word Structure, page 224

egg	buggy
	nugget
	maggot
	luggage

Note: *single g following a short vowel*

dragon	sugar
flagon	rigour
figure	vigour
wagon	frigate

6.3   **gu (before e/i/y):** test words *guilty, guess, colleague*

+ e	+ i/ y	final -gue (from French)	gu + a (exceptions)
guess	guide	vague	guard
guest	guilt	vogue	guarantee
guerrilla	guile	plague	
Guernsey	guild	rogue	
	guinea-pig	league	
	guitar	fugue	
	guillotine	fatigue	
		prologue	
	guy	epilogue	
		catalogue	
		colleague	
		dialogue	
		synagogue	
		demagogue	

(contd)

Dictation:
Guy was my guest in Guernsey.

gh: test words *ghost, ghastly*   6.4

Afghan	ghost
aghast	ghoul
dinghy	spaghetti
ghastly	

Dictation:
We saw a ghastly ghost in the dinghy.

/kw/ as in *quick*   7

spelling alternatives: qu, cqu, ch(oir)

qu: test words *queen, quote*   7.1

quack	quest	square	conquest
queen	quad	squash	inquire
quick	quilt	squeak	request
quiet	quake	squeal	require
quite	quill	squirm	
question	quid	squire	
queer	quaint	squat	
quiver	quip	squalid	
quote	quota		

Dictation:
The quarrel with the queen made him quake and quiver.

ch: test word *choir* (sole item)   7.2

7.3   cqu: test words *acquire, acquit*

> acquaintance
> acquire
> acquit
> acquiesce

8   /m/ as in *man*

spelling alternatives: m, mm mb, mn (and doubling page 224)

8.1   m: test words *mug, me*

initial		final	
mad	mob	ham	Tom
man	mop	jam	
map		Pam	bum
mat	mug	Sam	hum
	mud		sum
me		dim	
Meg	my	him	
men		rim	
met			
		Tim	

Dictation:
My mum had jam and Tom had ham.

8.2   mm: test word *hammer*

For doubling rule (humming) see Word Structure, page 00

hammer	summit
Mummy	lemming
tummy	
summer	

Note: *single m following short vowel*

timid	camel	damage	lemon
image	woman	women	tremor
chemist	promise	homage	glamour
famish			

Dictation:
The timid woman rode the camel.

-mb: test words *climb, lamb*   8.3

bomb	numb
climb	tomb
comb	thumb
dumb	plumb
lamb	womb
limb	succumb

Dictation:
The plumber had a numb thumb.

-mn: test words *autumn, solemn*   8.4

autumn	damn
column	hymn
condemn	solemn

Dictation:
We sang a solemn hymn about autumn.

9   /**n**/ as in *not*

spelling alternatives: n, nn, kn-, gn, -en, -on, -an, ain, ern,

9.1   **n:** test words *in, no, on, no** "**key word**" see page 19

initial		final	
nag	no*	ban	in
Nan	nod	can	bin
nap	not	Dan	din
		fan	fin
Ned	nun	man	pin
net	nut	pan	sin
		ran	tin
nib		tan	win
nip		Ben	on
nit		den	
		hen	bun
		men	fun
		pen	pun
		ten	run
			sun

Dictation:
Dan and Ben ran in the sun.

9.2   **nn:**

For doubling rule (running) see Word Structure, page 224

funny	funnel
bunny	fennel
runny	tannin
granny	cannibal
dinner	cinnamon
kennel	

Dictation:
The funny bunny had dinner in the kennel.

Note: *single n following short vowel*

finish	manage
money	honest
honey	vanish
manor	punish
canon	diminish
tenor	replenish
banish	banister
benefit	

Dictation:
How did you manage to finish all the honey?

kn-: test words *knife, knit*   9.3

This spelling pattern is from Old English/German;
the k is pronounced in modern German words, e.g. knabe

know	knickers	knight
knew	knit	knapsack
knee	knock	knave
knob	knot	knead
knife	knowledge	knuckle
kneel		knoll
knelt		

Dictation:
The knight knocked on the door with his knuckles.
He knew he had a knot in his knickers.

gn-: test words *gnome, sign*   9.4

from Old English   *from French*

initial	final	
narl	sign	foreign
gnash	design	reign
gnat	resign	arraign
gnaw	assign	cologne
gnome	align	deign
	consign	ensign
	benign	impugn
	malign	sovereign
	campaign	feign

(contd)

Dictation:
The gnome gnashed his teeth at the sign of the gnat.

9.5   **-en:** test words *happen, rotten*

(See also Word Structure section, Verb endings, page 259)

taken	bitten	shaken
given	chosen	stolen
eaten	happen	wooden
golden	hidden	woollen
broken	rotten	chicken

Dictation:
The rotten chicken has hidden the golden egg.

9.6   **-on:** test words *dragon, lemon*

lemon	button
bacon	cotton
dragon	mutton
apron	

Dictation:
The dragon ate mutton, bacon and lemon.

9.7   **-an:** test words *organ, human*

human	sultan
organ	woman
orphan	

Dictation:
The woman played the organ to the sultan.

-ain: test words *bargain, curtain*   9.8

bargain	chieftain
Britain	curtain
captain	fountain
certain	mountain
chamberlain	porcelain
chaplain	villain

Dictation:
The villain was certain the curtain was a bargain.

-ern: test words *modern, cavern*   9.9

cavern	pattern
eastern	northern
govern	southern
modern	western
tavern	

Dictation:
They turned the cavern into a modern tavern.

/ŋ/ as in *ring*   10

**spelling alternatives: ng, ng (with g pronounced), ngue, n
(for nk, see page 191)**

-ng: test words *ring, long*   10.1

a	i	o	u
bang	sing	long	bung
sang	king	gong	dung
rang	ping	pong	hung
hang	ring	song	lung
pang	wing	thong	rung
tang	sting	strong	sung

(contd)

10.1 (contd)

	i	o	u
	fling	prong	stung
	thing	wrong	clung
	cling	along	flung
	sling	belong	
	swing		
	spring		
	string		

Dictation:
The young king sang a long song.

10.2 -n + g: test words (with g pronounced) *finger, anger*

anger	linger
angle	mangle
bangle	mingle
dangle	single
finger	strangle
hunger	tangle
jingle	tingle
jungle	

Dictation:
Do not linger a single moment longer in the jungle.

10.3 -ngue: test words *tongue, merinque*

harangue
meringue
tongue

10.4 -n: test word *anxiety*

anxiety
anxious

/f/ as in *fat*   11

---

spelling alternatives: f, ff, ph, gh,

f: test words *if**, *fat*, *fog*, *fox*   11.1

For "f" clusters see page 000

fan	fin	fog	if*	**"key word"** see page 19
fat	fit	fox		
fag	fig	fun		
fed				

Dictation:
He fed a fig to the dog.

-ff: test words *sniff*, *cliff*, *off** **"key word"** see page 19   11.2

---

staff	cliff	off	cuff	bluff
	stiff	huff	gruff	
	sniff	puff	snuff	
	fluff	stuff		

Dictation:
The gruff man fell off the cliff.
Blow the fluff off my cuff.

For double f + le (raffle), see page 174

effort	effect	coffee	toffee	suffer
differ	suffix	puffin	coffin	muffin
buffer	buffalo	daffodil	office	offend
affect	afflict	affirm	affair	giraffe
griffin	scaffold	buffet		

Dictation:
She had coffee and a toffee muffin in the office.

11.3   **ph:** test words *phone, photo*

This spelling pattern comes from Greek

initial	medial	final	
phantom	alphabet	hyphen	graph
pharmacy	amphibian	megaphone	nymph
phase	apostrophe	microphone	paragraph
pheasant	cacophony	nephew	telegraph
phenomenon	catastrophe	orphan	triumph
phial	decipher	orthography	
philately	diaphragm	pamphlet	
Philip	dolphin	sphere	
phlegm	elephant	sphincter	
phone	emphasis	sphinx	
phoneme	geography	symphony	
phoney	grapheme	trophy	
phonic	graphics		
phosphate	graphite		
photo	homophone		
phrase			
physical			
physics			

Dictation:
My nephew took a photograph of the elephant.
The opening phrase of the symphony was a triumph for the composer.

11.4   **-gh:** test words *cough, trough, laugh*

This is an Old English spelling pattern

cough	enough
rough	laugh
tough	draught
trough	

Dictation:
He got a rough cough from sitting in the draught.

/v/ as in *van*   12

spelling alternatives: v, vv, ve

V: test words *van, vet*   12.1

van	vent	vain	vote	ever
vat	vest	veal	vibe	never
vet	vamp	vow	vice	very
vim	verb	vile		
	vast	vine		
	volt			

Dictation:
The vet had a red van.

-ve: (final) test words *have, give*   12.2

give	move	dove
live	save	glove
have	grove	shove
rave	pave	shave
jive	grave	slave
hive	stove	Clive
five	love	arrive

Dictation:
Clive loves to jive at the rave.

13   /θ/ as in *thin*

13.1   **th:** (no spelling alternatives) test words *thin, think*

this is the voiceless "th" sound, which is often pronounced /f/ in some dialects and in the speech of many children; the letter "f" is therefore often substituted for "th"

initial	final
thin	both
thank	moth
think	path
three	month
thick	mouth
thorn	north
thirty	birth
thirteen	loath
	truth

Ordinal numbers

fourth	ninth
fifth	tenth
sixth	eleventh
seventh	twelfth
eighth	thirteenth

Dictation:
I think it is three-thirty.
It is his fifth birthday on the eighth of May.

/ð/ as in *that*   14

th: (no spelling alternatives) test words *they* this, the**   14.1

This is the voiced "th" sound, which is often confused with the letter "v"; because there is only one digraph (th) to represent both the voiceless and voiced sounds, we are less aware of this voicing distinction than the equivalent distinction between /f/ and /v/, which are represented by different letters. Teach **the** *and* **they** *as* **"key word"** *see page 19*

Initial		Final with -e	
the*	than	breathe	loathe
that	them	bathe	writhe
this	those	swathe	clothe
then	they*	wreathe	

Dictation:
This is the way they go home.
I loathe to bathe in cold water.
I could not breathe deeply when I ran out of breath.

/s/ as in *sad*   15

spelling alternatives: s, -ss, -se, c, st, sw, sc, ps

S: test words *sad, set*   15.1

Initial		Final	
sad		us	bogus
Sam		bus	bonus
sat		yes	chorus
sap		gas	citrus
set		this	focus
sip		plus	fungus
sin		pus	lotus
sit			minus
sob			status
sun			

(contd)

Dictation:
Sam sat on the bus with us.

15.2   -SS: test words *dress, press*

long a	short a	e	i	short o	long o	u
pass	ass	Bess	hiss	boss	gross	fuss
class	mass	mess	kiss	loss		
grass	lass	Tess	miss	moss		
brass	crass	dress	Swiss	toss		
		press	bliss	gloss		
		stress		cross		
				floss		

Dictation:
Tess was cross with her boss.
Pass a glass to Bess.

double s following a short vowel

gossip	mousse	classic	cassette
bassoon	casserole	embassy	masseur

15.3   -se: test words *house, mouse*

Vowel + se	2 Vowels + se	n + se	r + se
case	cease	rinse	horse
chase	goose	sense	gorse
base	loose	nonsense	hoarse
dose	noose	tense	course
use	mouse	dense	coarse
practise (verb)	house	immense	worse
	spouse	license (verb)	nurse
	douse		purse
	grouse		curse
	louse		hearse
	lease		
	release		

Dictation:
The mouse and the horse were loose in the house.
Of course I will release the goose.

-c + e/i/y: test words *nice, mice, cellar, cycle*   15.4

initial ce-	medial -ce-	final -ce	
cent	concert	ace	peace
cell	December	lace	fence
centre	parcel	pace	hence
cellar		price	pence
cease		twice	voice
cedar		advice	choice
cede		device	service
ceiling	race	piece	wince
celebrate	grace	niece	practice
celebrity	trace	farce	licence
cellophane	place	force	
cement	brace	pierce	
cemetery		fierce	
census	ice	dance	
centenary	lice	lance	
century	dice	enhance	
ceramic	mice	France	
cereal	rice	glance	
ceremony	nice	prance	
certain	vice	trance	
certificate	spice	stance	
certify	slice		
	splice	police	

initial ci-			medial -ci-
cider	circus		accident
cigar	cistern		decide
cinder	cite		decimal
cinema	citizen		excite
cinnamon	citric		pencil
circle	city		
circuit	civic		
circumference	civil		

(contd)

15.4 (contd)

initial cy-	final -cy		
cycle	cymbal	lacy	spicy
cyanide	Cyprus	racy	Lucy
cyclamen	cyberspace	icy	juicy
cyst	cylinder		
cyclone	cynic		
cygnet			

Dictation:
The mice ran the race at a quick pace.
I notice there is a nice concert on in December.
We decided to cycle to the circus in the centre of the city.

15.5 **-st-:** test words *listen, castle*

apostle	epistle	jostle	rustle
bristle	glisten	listen	thistle
bustle	gristle	mistletoe	trestle
castle	hasten	nestle	whistle
chestnut	hustle	pestle	wrestle

Dictation:
We joined the hustle and bustle on the way to the castle.

15.6 **SC:** test words *science, decent*

initial		medial		final
scene	science	abscess	discipline	omniscience
scenery	scintillate	ascend	fascinate	acquiesce
sceptre	scion	descend	florescence	convalescence
scent	scissors	descent	luminescence	
sciatica	scythe	crescent	iridescence	
		discern	muscle	

Dictation:
On the ascent we saw lovely scenery.

ps-: test words *psychic, psychology*   15.7

psalm	psyche
pseudonym	psoriasis
psychic	psychedelic
psychiatry	psychometric
psychology	psychotic

/z/ as in *zoo*   16

spelling alternatives: z, zz, s, ss, se, x

Z: test words *zoo, zip*   16.1

initial z-		medial -z-	final -z/ ze/zy	
zoo	zeal	razor	daze	prize
zip	zebra		maze	graze
Zen	zinc		gaze	seize
zoom	Zulu		craze	amaze
zone	zigzag		baptize	blaze
zero	zither			
zany	zodiac			

Dictation:
Tim is at the zoo.
I was amazed to see the crazy zebra in the maze.

ZZ: 16.2

double z following a short vowel

buzz	dizzy
fizz	blizzard
fuzz	buzzard
frizz	
jazz	
swizz	
whizz	

(contd)

Dictation:
He drank a fizzy drink at the jazz show.
The buzzard was lost in the blizzard.

---

single z following a short vowel

hazard	bizarre
lizard	bazaar
quiz	whiz
wizard	

16.3   S: test words *as**, *is**, *was**, *desert, miser, advise, chose*

---

as* is* his* hers* has* was* **"key words"** see page 00

---

medial -s-

busy	miser	bosom	present
desert	resin	cousin	reason
basil	misery	baptism	raisin
prison	closet	cosmetics	

---

final -se

hose	advise	cheese	surprise
rise	please	phase	disease
wise	choose	phrase	
revise	pause	arouse	
devise	raise	bruise	

Dictation:
The boys in the cars saw the dogs and pigs.
I advise you to get a surprise present for your cousin.

16.4   SS: test words *dessert, possess*

---

dessert
possess
dissolve
scissors

X: test word *anxiety*   16.5

anxiety xenophobia xylophone

/ʃ/ as in *shed*   17

spelling alternatives: sh, s/ss, ti, ci, ssi, si, ch, ce, sci, chs, xi

sh: test words *shed, dish*   17.1

initial		final	
she	shirt	cash	lush
ship	shoe	rash	blush
shed	shame	bash	stash
shop	shade	dash	smash
shin	shape	gash	slash
shot	share	hash	splash
shun	shave	lash	trash
sham	shoal	mash	brash
shut	shone	mesh	clash
shunt	shore	dish	crash
shy	shove	fish	flash
shack	show	wish	thrash
shock	shaft	gosh	slush
shall	shampoo	posh	thrush
shark	sheaf	wash	brush
shell	sherry	bush	crush
sheep	shear	rush	flush
sheet	shorn	gush	hush
shine	shook		
sheen			

Dictation:
She shut up the shop.
She had a gash on her shin.
I wish I had a shed.
A shark is a fish.

17.2   **s/ss:** test words *sure, sugar*

sure
sugar
assure
insure

17.3   **-ti-:** test words *operation, election*

This spelling pattern comes from French, and appears in modern French

two syllable -tion	three syllable -tion	four + syllables -tion	ti + al/a/ent
action	absorption	accommodation	circumstantial
faction	addition	communication	confidential
fraction	attention	competition	essential
function	collection	composition	influential
junction	commotion	corporation	initial
lotion	completion	decoration	partial
mention	connection	dictionary	torrential
motion	depletion	education	patient
nation	devotion	examination	inertia
notion	direction	information	
portion	edition	institution	
potion	elation	observation	
section	election	operation	
station	frustration	population	
	inscription	preposition	
	inspection	recognition	
	intention	repetition	
	invention		
	perfection		
	position		
	pollution		
	protection		
	reflection		
	selection		
	solution		

(contd)

Dictation:
We met our relations at the station.
I wrote a composition about the election for my examination.
The information about the patient was confidential.

-ci-: test words *ancient, special*   17.4

This is another French spelling pattern

ancient	social
crucial	special
delicious	species
especially	sufficient
gracious	suspicion
musician	vicious
official	vivacious
politician	

Dictation:
The ancient politician made a delicious meal for the gracious musician.

-ssi-: test words *mission, session*   17.5

– and another pattern from French

admission	permission
aggression	possession
compassion	profession
discussion	Russia
expression	session
impression	succession
mission	suppression
oppression	transmission
passion	

Dictation:
We had a discussion about the mission in Russia.

17.6 -si-: test words *pension, mansion*

– From French again

tension	aversion
pension	diversion
mansion	extension
version	comprehension

Dictation:
We followed the diversion to the mansion.

17.7 ch-: test words *brochure, parachute*

and yet again, from French – many of these words are actually French, and we have adopted them into English – some quite recently (brioche, quiche) and some a long time ago (machine, parachute)

chalet	chauffeur	brochure
cache	chef	chandelier
cachet	chivalry	chassis
crèche	machine	chauvinist
niche	nonchalant	moustache
panache	parachute	charade
champagne	ricochet	brioche
charlatan	sachet	crochet
chic	machete	cliché
chateau	avalanche	quiche

Dictation:
The chef washed his clothes in the machine.

17.8 -ce-: test word *ocean*

herbaceous
ocean

sci-: test words *conscious, unconscious*   17.9

conscious
luscious
fascia
fascism
fascist
conscience

x/xi   17.10

| luxury | anxious | noxious | obnoxious |

/ʒ/ sound as in *vision*   18

spelling alternatives: si, su, ge, z

si: test words *television, revision*   18.1

From French again

allusion	decision	fusion	occasion
collision	delusion	illusion	precision
collusion	erosion	inclusion	provision
conclusion	exclusion	intrusion	revision
confusion	explosion	invasion	television

Dictation:
There was confusion when we heard the explosion in the television.

su: test words *measure, casual*   18.2

casual	leisure	treasure
closure	measure	usual
enclosure	pleasure	visual

Dictation:
It was a pleasure to find treasure in the enclosure.

18.3   **ge:** test words *prestige, massage*

Yet another group of words adopted from French

beige
camouflage
deluge
massage
prestige
regime
espionage

18.4   **z:** test words *seizure, azure*

seizure
azure

19   **/h/** as in *heat*

spelling alternatives: h, wh,

19.1   **h:** test words *heat, hat, her**

initial h-			medial -h-
had	hog	hand	behave
hag	hop	hint	behind
ham	hot	help	behove
has	hug	held	behest
hat	hum	honk	inhale
hid	hut	hunk	exhale
him	huff	hunt	inherit
hip	have	hump	perhaps
his	head	hunch	rehearse
hit	hell	hulk	behold
hob	hill	hoof	
	her* **"key word"** see page 19		

Dictation:
The hen hid in a hot hut.
He hit him on the hip.

wh: test words *whole, who** 19.2

who* **"key word"** see page 19
whoever
whole
whom
wholly
whooping (cough)

Dictation:
Who ate the whole cake?

/tʃ/ as in *chip* 20

spelling alternatives: ch, tch, t, ti,

ch: test words *chip, much* 20.1

initial		final
chap	check	much
chat	char	such
chin	charm	rich
chip	chart	which
chit	church	touch
chop	churn	attach
chug	chain	ostrich
chum	chair	sandwich
chant	choke	
chest	chide	(and see cluster -nch on page 195)
chink	chive	
chunk	cheek	
chuck	child	
chow	cheer	
chore	cheap	
hick	cheese	
chill	cheat	
chew	change	
chess		

Dictation:
He is such a rich chap.
The child sat on a chair in the church.

20.2   -tch: test words *catch, fetch*

a	e	i	o	u
batch	etch	itch	scotch	hutch
catch	fetch	bitch	blotch	Dutch
hatch	ketch	ditch	notch	clutch
latch	sketch	hitch		
match	stretch	pitch		
patch		witch		
snatch		stitch		
scratch		switch		
thatch				
satchel				
ratchet				
watch				

Dictation:
Watch me catch the ball.
Shut the latch on the hutch.
Fetch the match from the shed.

20.3   t(u/ure): test words *tune, Tudor*

-ture is a French spelling pattern

tune	actual	capture	feature	lecture
tube	factual	picture	gesture	adventure
tuna	tulip	denture	nature	literature
tunic	tuition	culture	mixture	furniture
tuba	Tuesday	venture	fixture	manufacture
Tudor		stature	structure	legislature
		future	puncture	caricature
		creature		

Dictation:
I play a tune on the tuba.
He sees his tutor on Tuesdays.

ti(on): test words *question, suggestion*   20.4

question
suggestion
congestion
digestion

/dʒ/ as in *jump*   21

spelling alternatives: j, dge, ge/i/y, gg, d, dj

j: test words *jump, just*   21.1

initial j-				medial -j-
jam	jump	John	July	conjure
jet	junk	join	Japan	majesty
jig	jar	joke	junior	major
Jim	jaw	jolly		majority
job	jay	judge		perjury
jog	Jew	judo		prejudice
jot	just	jazz		
jug	jive	June		

Dictation:
Jim jogs to his job.
Jane and Jack got the jet to Japan.

21.2   -dge: test words *bridge, fridge*

-dge is used for the /j/ sound after these five short vowel sounds

a	e	i	o	u
badge	edge	ridge	dodge	budge
cadge	hedge	midge	lodge	fudge
badger	ledge	bridge		judge
gadget	sledge	fridge		grudge
	pledge	fidget		nudge
	wedge	cartridge		smudge
	dredge			trudge
				sludge
				budget

Dictation:
The badger sat on the edge of the bridge.
The judge ate fudge from the fridge.

21.3   g + e/i/y: test words *giant, gentle, sausage, courage*

The letter "j" never appears in word final position; in this position, the /dʒ/ sound is written "-ge".

initial ge-	medial/final -ge (see also Word Structure page 253)	gi	initial gy-	final/medial -gy
gel	age	gin	gymnastics	biology
gem	page	gist	gymnasium	energy
gin	rage	giant	gymkhana	geology
germ	gauge	ginger	gypsum	synergy
gentle	wage	giraffe	gypsy	Egypt
general	cabbage	agile	gyrate	
genius	cottage	fragile		
geography	damage	logic		
geology	average	magic		
George	courage	tragic		
German	luggage	rigid		

(contd)

21.3 (contd)

initial ge-	medial/final -ge (see also Word Structure page 253)	gi	initial gy-	final/medial -gy
legend tragedy sergeant pageant pigeon surgeon	manage sausage savage village language privilege			

Dictation:
The magic giant drank gin in the village.
George was in a rage when he lost his baggage in Germany.
It was a privilege to be taught gymnastics by such a genius.

-gg- test words **suggest, exaggerate** (sole items)   21.4

d (+ vowel): test word *duty, during*   21.5

due	dubious
duel	during
dual	endure
duet	soldier
duty	pendulum
dew	

Dictation:
The duke sang a duet with the soldier.

dj: test words *adjective, adjust*   21.6

(and see prefixes page 278)

adjacent	adjust
adjourn	adjunct
adjective	adjutant
adjoin	adjure
adjudicate	

22   /ks/ as in box

spelling alternatives: x, -xc, cc

22.1   -x (final and medial): test words *box, fox, expand, expect*

Final:

a + x	e + x	i + x exe n + x	o + x	u + x	y+x
					lynx
axe	vex	fix	ox	flux	
tax	flex	six	box		
lax	sex	mix	fox	influx	
wax	annex	pixie			
flax	perplex	affix	flummox		
climax		prefix			
relax		suffix			
		appendix			
		minx			
		sphinx			

Dictation:
The fox is in a box.

Medial:

axis	exit	extra
axiom	expand	extravagant
axle	expect	maxim
exchange	expense	maximum
exclaim	explain	Oxford
exclude	export	oxygen
excuse	express	taxonomy
exercise	extent	taxidermy
exhaust	extinct	uxorious
exhibit		

-XC-: test words *except, excite*   22.2

excel	excellent	excite
exceed	except	excerpt
excess	exception	excise

-CC-: test words *accident, success*   22.3

In these, a /k/ sound is followed by a /s/ sound; both are represented by c, hence cc; the rule is that c + a,o,u,l,r, or c is pronounced /k/, and c + e,i,y is pronounced /s/; when the two come together, the sound is /ks/

access	vaccinate
accent	eccentric
accident	occident
success	

Dictation:
They had to vaccinate the eccentric man after the accident.

/gz/ sound (*voiced x*)   23

x (no spelling alternatives): test words *exact, exam*   23.1

exact	exasperate
exist	exaggerate
exam	exile
example	exhaust

Dictation:
The teacher gave the exact example that they got in the exam.

24   /l/ as in *let*

spelling alternatives: l, ll, le, al/el/il(ol)

24.1   **initial and final l-:** test words *let, log, feel, girl*

initial l-				
lad	log	live	lend	lead
lap	lot	lobe	left	leaf
lab	lug	lope	lick	leap
lag	love	link	long	
leg	late	limp	low	
let	lame	lack	lock	
lid	lake	lash	lost	
lip	lace	land	loft	
lit	life	lamp	luck	
lob	line	last		

Dictation:
The lad hit his leg.
Let them look at the loft.

final -l			
ail	feel	tool	foal
pail	heel	wool	goal
sail	heal	spool	cowl
fail	keel	stool	foul
frail	meal	curl	fowl
hail	kneel	furl	howl
mail	peal	girl	jowl
nail	peel	hurl	boil
rail	reel	pearl	coil
tail	veal	whirl	foil
wail	steal	bowl	soil
snail	cool	coal	toil
trail	fool	dole	spoil
deal	pool		

-ll: test words *sell*, *well*   24.2

a "or" sound	a short	i	e	o short	o long	u *gull*	u *full*
all	shall	will	bell	doll	roll	dull	bull
ball		bill	fell		toll	gull	full
call		drill	dwell		poll	hull	pull
gall		fill	hell		droll	lull	
fall		frill	sell		troll	mull	
hall		grill	spell		scroll	skull	
pall		hill	swell		stroll	cull	
small		ill	tell		knoll		
stall		kill	well				
tall		mill	yell				
wall		pill					
		swill					
		skill					
		still					
		shrill					
		spill					
		thrill					
		till					

Dictation:
Will the ill man get well?
The ball is on the tall wall.
Shall we ring the bell?

Note: *double l following a short vowel*

silly	hollow	wallow	pillar	allow
balloon	lollipop	follow	allot	gallery
brilliant	ballerina	swallow	alligator	intelligent
parallel	pallid	mollify	allergy	allegory

Dictation:
A balloon is hollow.

Note: *single l following short vowel*

solid	salad	lily	polish	relish
talent	palace	squalid	balance	develop
embellish	stolid			

24.3   -le: test words *bottle, single*

double consonant + le (short vowel)
In these words, the "le" forms a syllable without a vowel sound (although there is a vowel letter in the spelling)

-bble	-pple	-ddle	-ttle	-ggle
dabble	apple	addle	battle	gaggle
rabble	dapple	paddle	rattle	haggle
pebble	nipple	saddle	wattle	straggle
nibble	ripple	meddle	kettle	waggle
quibble	tipple	peddle	fettle	giggle
bobble	cripple	fiddle	nettle	niggle
cobble	topple	middle	settle	wriggle
gobble	supple	riddle	little	boggle
hobble	grapple	toddle	bottle	goggle
wobble		cuddle	shuttle	toggle
bubble		huddle		snuggle
		muddle		struggle
		puddle		

-ffle	-zzle	-ssle	-ckle	-ngle
baffle	dazzle	hassle	cackle	angle
raffle	frazzle	tussle	tackle	bangle
waffle	frizzle		shackle	dangle
sniffle	drizzle		heckle	mangle
muffle	sizzle		fickle	wrangle
ruffle	nozzle		sickle	tangle
truffle	guzzle		tickle	wangle
snuffle	muzzle		buckle	mingle
shuffle	nuzzle		suckle	single
	puzzle		chuckle	tingle
				shingle

(contd)

24.3 (contd)

-mple	-mble	-ntle	-ndle	-nkle/cle
ample	amble	mantle	dandle	ankle
sample	ramble		handle	rankle
trample	bramble		candle	winkle
temple	shamble		dwindle	wrinkle
dimple	nimble		fondle	uncle
simple	thimble		bundle	
wimple	bumble			
crumple	fumble			
	grumble			
	humble			
	mumble			
	rumble			
	tumble			
	stumble			

single consonant + -le

-ble	-ple	-dle	-tle	-gle	-fle
able	maple	ladle	title	bugle	rifle
fable	staple	idle		eagle	trifle
cable	people	sidle		ogle	
sable	steeple	needle			
table	couple	poodle			
stable					
bible					
noble					

Dictation:
You will topple if you don't sit in the middle of the saddle.
The horse stumbled on the pebbles and hobbled to the stable.
Put a single candle in the middle of the table.

-al test word *animal* 24.4

animal	metal	critical
dismal	medal	
signal	mammal	

24.5 **el** test words *duel, fuel*

camel	easel	mackerel	satchel
cancel	fuel	minstrel	scalpel
channel	funnel	mussel	travel
chattel	hostel	navel	tunnel
chisel	jewel	panel	vessel
duel	kennel	rebel	

24.6 **il** test word *pencil*

anvil	pencil
April	peril
council	stencil
evil	weevil

Dictation:
The brutal animal killed its rival.
The dog dug a tunnel under the kennel.
I read a novel about travel.
I cannot control my pencil.

25   /ɹ/ as in *rug*

spelling alternatives: r, rr, wr, rh

25.1 **r:** test words **run, ran**

rag	rim	rash	road
rig	red	rush	rest
rug	rip	rich	read
rib	rod	rack	ripe
rob	rap	rock	rope
rub	rat	roll	
ran	rot		
run			
ram			

(contd)

Dictation:
The rat ran on the red rug.

rr 25.2

double r following a short vowel

carry	berry	marry	merry	worry
ferry	cherry	curry	horrid	flurry
quarry	marrow	burrow	corridor	terrapin
narrative	barrister			

Dictation:
Carry the curry to the merry men on the ferry.

Single r following a short vowel

very	bury	carol	forest	moral
orange	heron	coral	florist	peril
arid	baron	garage	cherish	beret

Dictation:
The orange coral was much cherished.

wr: test words *wrist, wrap* 25.3

This is an Old English/Germanic spelling pattern

wrangle	wreck	wriggle	write
wrap	wren	wring	writhe
wrath	wrench	wrinkle	wrote
wreak	wrestle	wrist	wrought
wreath	wretch	writ	wry

Dictation:
His wrist got sore when he wrote the letter.

25.4 **rh:** test words *rhinoceros, rhubarb*

This spelling pattern comes from Greek

rhinoceros	rhea
rhubarb	rhesus
rhapsody	rheumatism
rhyme	rhizome
rhythm	rhodium
Rhodes	rhododendron
rhetoric	diarrhoea

26   /w/ as in *want*

spelling alternatives: w, wh, o, u

26.1 **w:** test words *was*, want, way*

was*, we* **"key words"** see page 19

web	went	wine
wet	wash	won
wed	west	wood
wig	will	wool
wag	wax	word
win	way	work
wit	weep	wish
wigwam	well	away
	wide	

Dictation:
We lost the cat.
We had a wigwam.

wh: test words *where, which*   26.2

In some accents (e.g. Scottish, Northern Irish) ,the "wh" is aspirated (a slight blowing sound), distinguishing this spelling pattern from 26.1; in Received Pronunciation there is no such distinction

when	wham	whinny	whiting
why	wheat	whirl	whittle
where	wheel	wharf	whisk
which	wheeze	whelk	whisker
whether	whiff	whelp	whisky
while	whilst	whet	whisper
what	whine	whey	wheedle
where	white	whimper	whist
whip	whale	whinge	whistle
whim	whiz	whippet	overwhelm
whack			

Dictation:
Where is the white wheel?
He whistled while he whisked the eggs.

O: test words *one, once* (sole items)   26.3

one*, once* **"key words"** see page 19

U: *suede*   26.4

persuade
suede

27 /j/ sound as in *yes*

spelling alternatives y, i,

27.1 **y-:** test words *you, young*

you* **"key word"** see page 19

yes	yard	yodel	lawyer
yet	yarn	yoke	
yam	yawn	yolk	
yap	year	young	
yellow	yell	York	
yelp	your		
yew	youth		
	yo-yo		

Dictation:
Did you get a hat? Yes I did.
The young man with the yellow hat went to New York.

27.2 **i:** test words *opinion, million*

onion	million
union	brilliant
opinion	convenient
senior	dominion
billion	familiar

Dictation:
It is my opinion that my companion is brilliant.

CONSONANT CLUSTERS

(two or more consonant sounds occurring in sequence)

INITIAL CLUSTERS

Clusters with -*r*	Page
1. *tr* as in *tr*ap	183
2. *dr* as in *dr*ip	183
3. *pr* as in *pr*am	183
4. *br* as in *br*im	184
5. *cr* as in *cr*ab	184
6. *gr* as in *gr*ab	184
7. *fr* as in *fr*om	184

Clusters with -*l*

	Page
8. *pl* as in *pl*an	185
9. *bl* as in *bl*ot	185
10. *cl* as in *cl*ap	185
11. *gl* as in *gl*ad	185
12. *fl* as in *fl*ap	186

Clusters starting with *s*

	Page
13. *sl* as in *sl*ap	186
14. *sp* an in *sp*in	186
15. *st* as in *st*op	186
16. *sc* as in *sc*ab	187
17. *sk* as in *sk*id	187
18. *sm* as in *sm*og	187
19. *sn* as in *sn*ip	187

Clusters with *w*

	Page
20. *sw* as in *sw*im	188
21. *tw* as in *tw*in	188
22. *dw* as in *dw*ell	188

Three-sound clusters	Page
23. *spl* as in *spl*it	188
24. *spr* as in *spr*ing	189
25. *scr* as in *scr*ap	189
26. *str* as in *str*ap	189

Digraph clusters
(one consonant sound represented by 2 letters)

	Page
27. *shr* as in *shr*ub	189
28. *thr* as in *thr*ob	190
29. *thw* as in *thw*art	190

FINAL CLUSTERS

Page

1.	*-st* as in co*st*	190
2.	*-sp* as in wi*sp*	190
3.	*-sk/sc* as in ri*sk*	191
4.	*-nt* as in we*nt*	191
5.	*-nd* as in ha*nd*	191
6.	*-nk* as in ba*nk*	192
7.	*-mp* as in lu*mp*	192
8.	*-ft* as in li*ft*	192
9.	*-ct* as in a*ct*	193
10.	*-lk* as in si*lk*	193
11.	*-lp* as in he*lp*	193
12.	*-xt* as in ne*xt*	193
13.	*-ld* as in he*ld*	193
14.	*-pt* as in a*pt*	193
15.	*-lf* as in se*lf*	194
16.	*-sm* as in pri*sm*	194

Three-sound clusters

17.	*-nct* as in disti*nct*	194
18.	*-mpt* as in te*mpt*	194
19.	*-mpse* as in gli*mpse*	195

Digraph clusters
(one consonant sound represented by 2 letters)

20.	*-nch* as in bu*nch*	195
21.	*-nge* as in ra*nge*	195
22.	*-lth* as in hea*lth*	195
23.	*-mth* as in war*mth*	196
24.	*-nth* as in te*nth*	196
25.	*-pth* as in de*pth*	196
26.	*-lfth* as in twe*lfth*	196
27.	*-dth* as in wi*dth*	196
28.	*-thm* as in rhy*thm*	196

CONSONANT CLUSTER WORD LISTS

In each box, the first words listed represent the next step from the simple CVC form. The words listed below include other spelling patterns such as vowel digraphs, -ck, -ll, -ff, -er, final blends and silent -e.

The learner's vocabulary should be taken into account when using these lists for teaching, as many of the words with simple spelling patterns occur quite infrequently in both spoken and written English.

Initial Clusters

Clusters with "r"

tr: test words *trap, trim*   1

tram	track	tread
trap	trash	trench
trip	tramp	trick
trim	tract	trill

dr: test words *drip, drum*   2

drab	drop	draw	dress	drink
drag	drug	drain	drench	drive
dram	drum	drape	drill	dry
drip		dread	drift	

pr: test words *pram, prop*   3

pram	pray
prim	press
prop	present
	prick

4   br

brag	brass	branch
bran	brave	bread
brat	brain	break
brim	brand	breast
	brash	

5   cr

crab	crass	crane	cross
crag	crash	crest	cry
cram	crank	crew	crush
crop	cramp	crisp	crown
crib	craft	crock	crowd

6   gr

grab	grid	grass	grill
gram	grim	grain	grind
Gran	grip	grant	groan
Greg	grit	graft	grow
grin	grub	greed	grunt
		green	gruff

7   fr

Fred	frame	fresh	frill
from	frank	French	fry
	free	frisk	frump

Dictation:
Greg will grab the drum from Fred.
Do not drop the crab in the crib.
He went on a trip and had a crash.

Clusters with "l"

pl: test words *plum, plot*   8

plan	plug	plank	play
plot	plum	plant	plump
plop	plus	place	plush
		planet	

bl   9

blob	black	blade
blot	blast	blame
	blank	bless
	bland	

cl: test words *clap, clip*   10

clam	class	clay	cliff
clap	claw	clench	clink
clip	clasp	cleft	cloth
club	clamp	clean	clock
	clash	click	close

gl   11

glad	glade	gleam	globe
glen	gland	glean	gloom
glib	glare	glint	glory
glum	glass	glow	glue

12   **fl**: test words *flag*, *flat*

flab	flip	flake	fleck	flock
flag	flit	flame	flesh	floss
flan	flog	flask	flick	flow
flap	flop	flank	fling	flush
flat		flash	flinch	fly

Dictation:
I am glad the flat is in the club.
That is a plum flan.

Clusters with "s"

13   **sl**: test words *slip*, *slam*

slab	slid	slack	slash
slam	slim	slay	slosh
slap	slip	slick	slush
slat	slit		
sled	slob		

14   **sp**: test words *spin*, *spit*

spam	speck	space
spat	spark	spade
spin	spoon	Spain
spit		

15   **st**: test words *stem*, *stop*

stab	stop	stack	stink	star
stag	stub	stick	stock	stuff
stem	stud	stiff	stuck	stunt
step	stun	still	stand	stash

sc   16

scab	scar	scold
scam	scull	scamp
scan	scarf	scalp
Scot	scoot	
Scum		

sk   17

skid	skill	ski
skip	sketch	skirt
skim	sky	skull
skin		

sm   18

smog	smack	smile
smut	small	smoke
	smell	smash

sn: test words *snap, snip*   19

snag	snack
snap	snake
snip	snow
snob	
snub	

Dictation:

Tom spun on the step and slid.
The sled slips in the snow.

Clusters with "w"

20   **SW:** test words *swim, swam*

swam	swab
swim	swan
swig	swap

21   **tw**

twin	twist
twit	twenty
twig	twice
	twelve

Dictation:
The twins swam to the twig.

22   **dw**

dwarf
dwell
dwindle

Three-sound Clusters

23   **spl:** test words *split, splash*

split	splash	splint	splodge
	splay	splinter	splendid
	splatter	splice	splutter
	spleen		

spr   24

sprat	sprang	spread	sprung
sprig	sprain	spree	spruce
	sprawl	spring	spry
	spray		

scr   25

scrap	scrape	screech
scrub	scratch	screen
scrum	scrawl	screw
	scream	script

str: test words *strap, strip*   26

strap	strong	stray	stretch	stripe
strip	strain	streak	strict	strive
strum	strand	stream	strife	stroke
	strange	street	strike	stroll
	straw	stress	string	

Dictation:
His strap split in the scrum.
Was that a straw in the stream?

Digraph Clusters

(one of the consonant sounds is represented by two letters)

shr: test word *shrub*   27

shred	shrew	shrink
shrub	shriek	shrank
shrug	shrill	shrimp
	shrine	shroud

Dictation:
The snake shed its skin under the shrub.

28   thr: test word *three*

throb	thrash	thrift	through
	three	throat	throw
	thread	throne	thrush
	threat	throng	thrust
	threw		

Dictation:
The thrush did not snap up the shrimp.

29   thw

thwart	thwack

Final Clusters

Words are, where possible, listed by rime rather than alphabetical order
(e.g. cast, fast, last, best etc.).

1   -st: test words *lost, rest, just*

cast	list	just	trust
fast	mist	must	breast
last	cost		frost
mast	lost		least
past	post		roast
rest			

2   -sp

gasp	clasp
rasp	grasp
wisp	crisp
lisp	
cusp	

Dictation:
He must have just lost his best vest.
The bread went crisp in the sun.

-sk/sc: 3

ask	flask	task	whisk	dust
bask	mask	risk	disc	

-nt   4

rant	rent	dint	font	slant	glint
want	sent	hint	hunt	scant	flint
bent	tent	tint	punt	plant	stunt
dent	vent	lint	runt	spent	blunt
lent	went	mint		stint	

-nd test words *send, pond*   5

and	wand	send	rind	stand	spend
end	bend	tend	wind	strand	trend
band	fend	wend	bond	bland	blend
hand	lend	hind	fond	gland	blind
land	mend	kind	pond	grand	grind
sand		mind	fund		

blonde *(from French)*

Dictation:
We went hand in hand in the sand to the end of the pond.
I bent the end of the wand that you sent.
Do you mind that I lent him the tent?

-nk: test words *bank, tank*   6

bank	link	bunk	stank	thank	blink
rank	pink	dunk	spank	stink	think
sank	rink	hunk	drank	slink	plonk
tank	sink	junk	plank	shrink	trunk
ink	wink	sunk	blank	drink	drunk
kink	monk		crank	brink	chunk
			flank		

Dictation:
I think it is bad to drink pink ink, but the man at the bank drank it.

7   **-mp:** test word *jump*

camp	dump	stamp	stump
damp	hump	swamp	slump
lamp	jump	scamp	trump
ramp	lump	tramp	plump
imp	pump	clamp	clump
limp	rump	skimp	frump
wimp		stomp	thump

Dictation:
It was damp at the camp.
The imp lit the lamp for the tramp.
If I jump, I land with a thump.

8   **-ft:** test words *gift, loft*

daft	lift	craft
raft	rift	cleft
waft	sift	swift
left	loft	shift
deft	soft	drift
gift	tuft	croft

Dictation:
He left the gift in the loft.

9   **-ct**

act	compact
fact	respect
pact	expect
tact	

-lk   10

milk	bulk
silk	hulk

-lp   11

help	scalp
yelp	whelp

-xt   12

next
text
betwixt

-ld   13

bald	wild	gold	scald
held	bold	hold	scold
weld	cold	sold	
mild	fold	told	

Dictation:
The bald man sold the gold to a man with a cold.

-pt   14

apt
rapt
corrupt

15   -lf

elf	shelf
self	
golf	
wolf	
gulf	

Dictation:
The elf sat on the shelf.

16   -sm

prism (see also -ism in Noun Endings section, page 247)
spasm
sarcasm

Dictation:
We will camp in the pink tent in the damp sand by the pond.
He sent me junk in the last post.
The elf will hold the gold lamp.

Three-sound Clusters

17   -nct

distinct
precinct
succinct

18   -mpt

tempt
attempt
contempt
exempt

-pse/ -mpse   19

lapse
corpse
collapse
relapse
glimpse

Digraph Clusters

(one of the consonant sounds is represented by two letters)

-nch   20

ranch	pinch	branch
bench	lunch	drench
inch	munch	clench
winch	punch	stench
	flinch	

Dictation:
We sat on the bench to drink the punch.
Do not pinch my lunch.

-nge   21

mange	binge	strange	cringe
range	singe	orange	plunge
grange	lunge	fringe	

-lth   22

health
wealth
stealth

23   -mth

| warmth |

24   -nth

| -tenth |
| month |

25   -pth

| depth |

26   -lfth

| twelfth |

27   -dth

| breadth |
| width |

28   -thm

| rhythm |
| algorithm |

Homophones and Silent Letters

Section 4

Homophones

Words that sound the same, but are spelled differently,
and have different meanings

Vowel Homophones

In which the difference between the words lies in the spelling of the vowel sound

1

/ε/	
berry	bury
led	lead
red	read

Dictation:
He read the red book.
She led the way to the lead pipe.
The mouse will bury the berry.

2

/ɪ/	
hymn	him

Dictation:
She told him to sing the hymn.

3

/ʌ/	
none	nun
one	won
some	sum
sun	son

Dictation:
The nun said there were none left.
My son sat in the sun.
Do some sums.
He won one prize.

4

/ɛɪ/				
ate	eight	rain	rein	reign
bail	bale	raise	raze	
break	brake	sail	sale	
faint	feint	slay	sleigh	
gate	gait	straight	strait	
great	grate	steak	stake	
lain	lane	Sunday	sundae	
maid	made	tail	tale	
mail	male	vein	vane	vain
main	mane	veil	vale	
maze	maize	waist	waste	
pail	pale	wait	weight	
pain	pane	wave	waive	
plaice	place	way	weigh	whey
pray	prey			

Dictation:

There was a great big fire in the grate.
The maid made the bed.
He ate eight buns.
He was up to his waist in waste.
She had an ice cream sundae on Sunday.
Try not to break the brake on the car.

5

/ĭ/			
be	bee	meat	meet
beach	beech	peace	piece
bean	been	peak	peek
ceiling	sealing	peal	peel
cheap	cheep	read	reed
creak	creek	scene	seen
discrete	discreet	sea	see
feat	feet	seam	seem
flea	flee	steal	steel
freeze	frieze	story	storey
heal	heel	sweet	suite

(contd)

/i/ (contd)			
key	quay	tea	tee
knead	need	we	wee
leak	leek	weak	week
mean	mien		

Dictation:

Meet me at the meat shop.
Can you see the sea?
The beech tree was near the beach.
Have you been growing a bean plant?
The cut on your heel will heal.
You need to knead the bread.
He will steal the steel bar.
She felt weak all week.
He ate his piece of cake in peace.
He was sealing the gap in the ceiling.

6

/aɪ/		
bye	by	buy
dye	die	
I	eye	
isle	aisle	
might	mite	
pie	pi	
right	rite	write
sight	site	
slight	sleight	
time	thyme	

Dictation:

You will not die if you dye your hair.
Write with your right hand.
I have cut my eye.

7

/əʊ/				
dough	doe	row	roe	
grown	groan	sew	sow	so
know	no	soul	sole	
lone	loan	thrown	throne	
poll	pole	toe	tow	
rode	road	wrote	rote	
Rome	roam	yoke	yolk	
brooch	broach			

Dictation:
He rode his bike on the road.
No, I don't know him.
It is fun to roam around Rome.

8

/u/		
blew	blue	
cue	queue	
loot	lute	
new	knew	
root	route	
shoe	shoo	
threw	through	
to	too	two
you	ewe	

Dictation:
I am going to give you two sweets too.
He threw the ball through the net.
He knew I had a new car.
She blew out the blue candle.

9

/ɔː/					
ball	bawl		more	moor	
board	bored		oar	or	ore
bore	boar	[paw	pore	pour	poor
caught	court		roar	raw	
course	coarse		sore	saw	soar
for	fore	four]	sort	sought	
fought	fort		sure	shore	
fourth	forth		taut	taught	
hall	haul		tour	tore	
lord	laud		wore	war	

Dictation:
They fought near the fort.
Four children came for tea.
He saw she had a sore foot.
There were more horses on the moor.

10

/ɛː/	
birth	berth
colonel	kernel
earn	urn
heard	herd
pearl	purl
surf	serf

Dictation:
She heard the herd of cows in the barn.
She had a pearl necklace.
He took his surf board to the beach.
How much money will you earn?
What is your date of birth?
The colonel left the army.

11

/aʊ/	
bough	bow
foul	fowl

Dictation:
The bough of the tree bent in the wind.
They took a bow at the end of the play.
There was a foul smell from the dustbin.
Chickens are a type of fowl.

12

/iə/	
deer	dear
eyrie	eerie
hear	here
pier	peer
shear	sheer
tier	tear

Dictation:
Come here and hear the bells.
We saw deer in the woods.
There was an eerie silence in the room.

13

/ɛə/	
air	heir
bare	bear
fare	fair
hare	hair
mare	mayor

(contd)

/ɛə/ (contd)

pare	pair	pear
stare	stair	
there	their	

Dictation:
Here is the bus fare to the fun fair.
They left their books over there.

14

/aɪə/

lyre	liar
tire	tyre

15

/au/

flower	flour
our	hour

Dictation:
Our train leaves in one hour.

16

/ʊ/
would	wood

Dictation:
Would you chop some wood?

17

/ɔɪ/	
boy	buoy
groin	groyne

18

/juə/	
duel	dual

19

/ə/	
complement	compliment
current	currant

Consonant Homophones

In which the difference lies in the spelling of the consonant sound

1

/f/	
phase	faze
prophet	profit

2

/g/	
guild	gild
guilt	gilt

3

/h/	
whole	hole

4

/k/	
arc	ark
cheque	check
colonel	kernel
conquer	conker
kerb	curb
racket	racquet
scull	skull

Dictation:
Can you check that the cheque has been posted?

5

/l/	
bridal	bridle
gamble	gambol
idle	idol
pedal	peddle

6

/n/	
finish	Finnish
nave	knave
no	know
not	knot
heroin	heroine

Dictation:
The Finnish man did not finish his meal.
I did not know if I should say yes or no.
That is not the best knot to tie up the mast.

7

/r/	
wrap	rap
wreak	reek
wring	ring
write	right
wrote	rote
wrung	rung
wry	rye

Dictation:
Write the right name on the form.

8

/s/		
canvas	canvass	
ceiling	sealing	
cellar	seller	
cygnet	signet	
muscle	mussel	
seen	scene	
sell	cell	
sent	scent	cent
serial	cereal	
counsellor	councillor	

Dictation:
He spent so much time at his law practice he had no time to practise the piano.
Have you seen him acting in the next scene?
She sent her mother a new scent.

9

/t/	
mat	matt
what	watt

10

/ʃ/	
shoot	chute

11

/w/	
witch	which
wine	whine
weather	whether

Dictation:

Which witch has the biggest hat?
I don't know whether the weather will get better.

12

/ks/	
accept	except

13

/z/	
desert	dessert

Dictation:

He was stranded in the desert.
He chose ice cream for dessert.

Word Structure/Grammar-related Homophones

Noun	Verb	Adjective
effect	affect	
licence	license	
practice	practise	
principle		principal*
stationery		stationary
	altar	alter
lumber	lumbar	

Dictation:

He spent so much time at his law practice he had no time to practise the piano.

What was his principal reason for leaving?

This is a very important principle.

* The principal (head teacher) is used as a noun but stems from the phrase "principal teacher" in which principal is an adjective (see adjectives, see page 264)

Silent Letters

The following "silent" letter patterns that appear in a relatively large number of words can be found in the Consonant Word Lists and Vowel Word Lists:

		Page
silent h as in	**Th**omas	134
	ghost	141
	r**h**ino	178
silent p as in	**p**sychic	157
silent b as in	lam**b**	143
silent t as in	lis**t**en	150
silent n as in	autum**n**	143
silent k as in	**k**nee	145
silent g as in	**g**nome	145
silent w as in	**w**hole	165
	wrap	177

There are, however, other words that contain silent letters with only a few examples of each spelling pattern. The most common spelling errors in these words are the omission of the silent letters. These are listed here in alphabetical order.

1

---

silent b: test words *debt, doubt*

de**b**t
dou**b**t
su**b**tle

Dictation:
I doubt if he can pay his debt.

2

> **silent c:** test word ***indict***
>
> indict

Dictation:
Indict means accuse.

3

> **silent d:** test word ***Wednesday***
>
> Wednesday
> handkerchief

Dictation:
He forgot his handkerchief on Wednesday.

4

> **silent f:** test word ***twelfth***
>
> twelfth

Dictation:
His birthday is on the twelfth of June.

5

> **silent g:** test words ***diaphragm, paradigm***
>
> diaphragm
> paradigm
> phlegm

Dictation
The singer used her diaphragm to take deep breaths.

6

> **silent h:** test words *exhaust, exhibit, silhouette*
>
> exhaust   honest
> exhibit   honour
> exhilarate   silhouette
> hour   yoghurt
> vehicle   vehement
> khaki   diarrhoea

Dictation:
She was exhilarated to see the silhouette as a new exhibit.
He was vehement in his argument against petrol driven vehicles.
He ate one yoghurt an hour.

7

> **silent i:** test words *miniature, parliament*
>
> miniature
> parliament

Dictation:
She had a miniature model of the Houses of Parliament.

8

> **silent l:** test word *salmon*
>
> salmon

Dictation:
The salmon leapt over the waterfall.

9

> **silent m:** test word ***mnemonic***
>
> **m**nemonic

Dictation:
He had a mnemonic to remember the spelling.

10

> **silent p:** test words ***pneumonia, pneumatic, receipt***
>
> **p**neumonia
> **p**neumatic
> recei**p**t
> **p**tarmigan
> **p**terodactyl
> sa**pp**hire

Dictation:
She kept the receipt for the sapphire ring.

11

> **silent r:** test words ***February, library***
>
> Feb**r**uary
> lib**r**ary

Dictation:
The new library opened in February.

12

> **silent t:** test word ***mortgage***
>
> mor**t**gage
> rappor**t**
> depo**t**
> debu**t**
> ches**t**nut

Dictation:
He took out a mortgage to pay for the depot.
She had a rapport with the chestnut pony.

13

---

silent th: test word *asthma*
asthma

Dictation:
He had suffered from asthma since he was a baby.

14

---

silent u: test word *gauge*
gauge

Dictation:
Can you gauge the distance between the posts?

15

---

silent w: test words *answer, sword*
answer sword

Dictation:
Answer my question or I will pull out my sword.

16

---

silent s: test word *island*
island

Word Structure and Grammar

Section 5

Section Index

                                            Page

1.	**General Rules Applying to Suffixes**		224
1.1	**Doubling a final consonant**		224
1.1.1	Doubling with CVC words	*swimming*	224
1.1.2	No doubling with consonant suffixes	*sadly*	225
1.1.3	No doubling after CC	*stamped*	225
1.1.4	No doubling after VVC	*bleeding*	226
1.1.5	No doubling of certain letters	*mixing*	227
1.1.6	Doubling when stress is on final syllable	*beginning*	227
1.1.7	No doubling if stress is on first syllable	*galloped*	227
1.1.8	Double after "clear" vowel in unstressed second syllable	*kidnapped*	228
1.1.9	Double -l	*traveller*	228
1.1.10	-ic words	*panicky*	229
1.2	**Suffixes and final -e**		230
1.2.1	Drop -e before vowel suffix	*taking*	230
1.2.2	Do not drop -e before consonant suffix	*hopeless*	231
1.2.3	Keep -ge/-ce before -a /-o	*noticeable*	231
1.2.4	keep -e in -nge words	*singeing*	232
1.2.5	-ie changes to -y + -ing	*dying*	232
1.2.6	keep -ee + -ing	*seeing*	232
1.3	**Suffixes and words ending in -y**		233
1.3.1	Change -y to i + suffix	*hurried*	233
1.3.2	Keep -y before -ing, -ish	*carrying*	234
1.3.3	Keep -y when preceded by a vowel	*played*	234
2.	**Grammar-related Rules for Suffixes and Endings**		234
Nouns			236
2.1	**Forming the plural (nouns)**		236
2.1.1	Add -s	*cats*	237
2.1.2	Add -es	*boxes*	238
2.1.3	-f, fe words (-ves)	*wolves*	238
2.1.4	Change -y to i + -es	*berries*	238
2.1.5	-o + s/o + es	*potatoes*	239
2.1.6	-is becomes -es	*crises*	240
2.1.7	-ix /-ex becomes -ices	*matrices*	240
2.1.8	- on becomes -a	*criteria*	240
2.1.9	-um becomes -a	*media*	241

Pages

2.2	**Noun endings**		241
2.2.1	-age	*courage*	243
2.2.2	-ance	*hindrance*	243
2.2.3	-ar	*cellar*	244
2.2.4	-ary	*dictionary*	244
2.2.5	-cy	*bankruptcy*	244
2.2.6	-cide	*homicide*	244
2.2.7	-ee	*employee*	245
2.2.8	-dom	*kingdom*	245
2.2.9	-eer	*engineer*	245
2.2.10	-ence	*independence*	245
2.2.11	-er	*baker*	246
2.2.12	-ery	*nursery*	246
2.2.13	-ese	*journalese*	246
2.2.14	-esse/-ette	*largesse*	246
2.2.15	-eum	*museum*	246
2.2.16	-eur	*amateur*	247
2.2.17	-hood	*childhood*	247
2.2.18	-ice	*service*	247
2.2.19	-iom	*idiom*	247
2.2.20	-ism	*communism*	247
2.2.21	-ist	*optimist*	248
2.2.22	-ity	*activity*	248
2.2.23	-ium	*tedium*	248
2.2.24	-let	*leaflet*	249
2.2.25	-ling	*duckling*	249
2.2.26	-ment	*enjoyment*	249
2.2.27	-ness	*kindness*	250
2.2.28	-ology	*biology*	250
2.2.29	-or	*factor*	250
2.2.30	-ory	*factory*	250
2.2.31	-our	*harbour*	251
2.2.32	-ship	*friendship*	251
2.2.33	-sion	*tension*	251
2.2.34	-ssion	*admission*	251
2.2.35	-tion	*operation*	252
2.2.36	-ture	*picture*	252
2.2.37	-ty	*certainty*	252
Verbs			253
2.3	**Verb suffixes**		253
2.3.1	Adding -ing	*looking*	253
2.3.2	Past tense + ed	*acted*	254

			Pages
2.3.3	Past tense with -t	*slept*	257
2.3.4	-s/es third person singular	*washes*	258
2.3.5	-en past participles	*eaten*	258
2.4	**Verb endings**		259
2.4.1	-ate	*decorate*	260
2.4.2	-efy	*liquefy*	260
2.4.3	-en	*widen*	260
2.4.4	-end	*offend*	260
2.4.5	-ify	*clarify*	261
2.4.6	-ise	*realise*	261
2.4.7	-ish	*furnish*	261
2.5	**Adjective endings**		262
2.5.1	-able	*capable*	264
2.5.2	-al	*final*	264
2.5.3	-an	*pagan*	265
2.5.4	-ant	*instant*	265
2.5.5	-ar	*solar*	266
2.5.6	-ary	*voluntary*	266
2.5.7	-ate	*accurate*	266
2.5.8	-en	*golden*	257
2.5.9	-ent	*confident*	257
2.5.10	-eous	*hideous*	258
2.5.11	-er	*cleaner*	258
2.5.12	-est	*cleanest*	259
2.5.13	-ern	*modern*	270
2.5.14	-ful	*hopeful*	270
2.5.15	-ible	*horrible*	270
2.5.16	-ic	*athletic*	271
2.5.17	-id	*horrid*	272
2.5.18	-ious	*previous*	272
2.5.19	-ish	*stylish*	272
2.5.20	-ive	*active*	273
2.5.21	-less	*hopeless*	273
2.5.22	-ous	*ridiculous*	273
2.5.23	-some	*handsome*	274
2.5.24	-y	*noisy*	274
2.6	**Forming adverbs from adjectives**		275
2.6.1	Add -ly	*quickly*	275
2.6.2	Change -i to -y + ly	*happily*	276
2.6.3	Keep final -e + ly	*safely*	276

Pages

| 2.6.4 | Drop -le + ly | | *simply* | 277 |
| 2.6.5 | Add -ally | | *historically* | 277 |

3	**Prefixes**			278
3.1	**Prefixes with negative meaning**			278
3.1.1	in-		*inaccurate*	278
3.1.2	im-	+b, p, m	*imbalance*	279
3.1.3	ir-	+r	*irregular*	279
3.1.4	il-	+l	*illegal*	280
3.1.5	un-		*unaware*	280
3.1.6	dis-		*disability*	281
3.1.7	mis-		*misbehave*	281
3.1.8	anti-		*anticlimax*	282
3.1.9	contra-		*contradict*	282

3.2	**Prefixes derived from Latin com- (with)**			282
3.2.1	com- +p, b, m		*combine*	282
3.2.2	col- (before -l)		*collaborate*	282
3.2.3	cor- (before -r)		*correlate*	283
3.2.4	con-		*concert*	283

3.3	**Prefixes derived from Latin ad-**			283
3.3.1	ad-		*adapt*	283
3.3.2	ac-	+ c, +qu	*accident*	284
3.3.3	af-	+f	*affable*	284
3.3.4	an-	+ n, t, d	*annex*	284
3.3.5	ap-	+p	*appear*	284
3.3.6	ar-	+r	*arrange*	285
3.3.7	as-	+s	*assail*	285
3.3.8	at-	+t	*attach*	285
3.3.9	ag-	+g	*aggravate*	285

3.4	**Prefixes meaning "before"**			286
3.4.1	pre-		*precaution*	286
3.4.2	fore-		*forecast*	286
3.4.3	ante-		*antenatal*	286

3.5	**Other prefixes**			286
3.5.1	al-	all > al	*although*	286
3.5.2	ambi-	both	*ambiguity*	287
3.5.3	bi-/tri-	two and three	*bicycle*	287
3.5.4	circum-	around	*circumference*	287
3.5.5	de-	down/away	*descend*	288

Pages

3.5.6	ex-	out of	*exit*	288
3.5.7	extra-	beyond	*extraordinary*	288
3.5.8	for-	away/prohibit	*forgive*	289
3.5.9	ful-	full > ful	*fulfil*	289
3.5.10	hetero-	different	*heterodox*	289
3.5.11	homo-	same	*homograph*	289
3.5.12	inter-	between	*interact*	289
3.5.13	post-	after	*postscript*	290
3.5.14	pro-	for/forth	*proceed*	290
3.5.15	re-	again/back	*repeat*	290
3.5.16	sub-	under	*subway*	290
3.5.17	super-	over/above	*supernatural*	291
3.5.18	sym-	together	*sympathy*	291
3.5.19	syn-	together	*synopsis*	291
3.5.20	trans-	across	*transfer*	291

4	**Use of Apostrophe**		292
4.1	**Apostrophe for abbreviation**		292
4.1.1	Abbreviations with "not"	*didn't*	292
4.1.2	Abbreviations with "will"	*they'll*	293
4.1.3	Abbreviations with "have"	*I've*	293
4.1.4	Abbreviations with "be"	*isn't*	293

4.2	**Apostrophe to denote "possession"**	294
5	**Use and spelling of possessive pronouns**	295

1 General Rules Applying to Suffixes and Endings

Suffixes are units of sound or letter strings which, when added to words, have an effect on their grammatical function. Suffixes can affect tense: *trust + ed* = past tense *trusted*; they can denote plurality: *cat + s* = plural *cats*, or they can change the syntactic category in various different ways, for example, from an adjective to an adverb : *bad + ly* = *badly*, or from a verb to an adjective: *differ + ent* = *different*. Some suffixes can also affect meaning: *home + less* = *homeless*.

Sometimes it makes more sense to refer to *endings* instead of *suffixes*, because the letter string is not added to a root word. For example *-able* is a suffix in words such as *acceptable* (*accept + able*), but is used as an ending in words such as *inevitable*. The same would apply to *perilous* (*peril + ous*) and *jealous*.

Spelling rules differ according to whether the suffix begins with a vowel or with a consonant. The most common "vowel suffixes" are **-ed, -ing, -er, -est, -y**. The most common "consonant suffixes" *are* **-ly, -ness, -ful**.

1.1	Doubling rules
1.2	Final -e rules
1.3	Final -y rules

1.1 Doubling a Final Consonant

1.1.1   When adding a suffix beginning with a vowel to one-syllable words, with one vowel letter followed by one consonant letter, double the final consonant.

test words: ***bigger, fatter, clapping, swimming, hopped, stopped***

big	+	er, est	=	bigger etc.
clap	+	ed, er, ing	=	clapped etc.
fat	+	en, er, est, ish, y	=	fatten etc.
hop	+	ed, er, ing	=	hopped etc.
jam	+	ed, ing, y	=	jammy etc.

mat	+	ed, ing	=	matted etc.
net	+	ed, ing	=	netted etc.
pat	+	ed, ing	=	patted etc.
run	+	er, ing, y	=	running etc.
skip	+	ed, er, ing	=	skipped etc.
stop	+	ed, er, ing	=	stopped etc.
thin	+	ed, er, est, ing, ish	=	thinner etc.
wet	+	ed, er, est, ing	=	wettest etc.

Other examples:

bat	grip	prop	spin
beg	hem	rip	spit
blot	hug	rob	stop
brim	hum	sad	swim
clip	mop	shot	tan
dip	nip	skim	trap
drip	nod	slip	trip
drop	pat	snap	trot
flip	pop	snip	wag
flop	prod	sob	wet

1.1.2 Do not double when adding a suffix beginning with a consonant.
(see list of endings beginning with a consonant)

test words: ***sadly, badly***

bad	+	ly	=	badly
man	+	hood	=	manhood
rim	+	less	=	rimless
sad	+	ly, ness	=	sadly etc
thin	+	ly	=	thinly

1.1.3 Do not double after two or more consonant letters.

test words: ***stamped, trusted***

act	+	ed, or, ing	=	acted etc.
bind	+	er, ing	=	binding etc.
frown	+	ed, ing	=	frowning etc.
hold	+	er, ing	=	holder etc.

(contd)

1.1.3 (contd)

limp	+	ed, er, ing	=	limped etc.
match	+	ed, ing	=	matched etc.
stamp	+	ed, ing	=	stamped etc.
trust	+	ed, ing, y	=	trusted etc.
want	+	ed, ing	=	wanting etc.

Other examples:

band	hand	mend	send
bang	hint	pant	sift
bend	land	rant	sing
camp	lend	rest	test
damp	lift	ring	think
fend	limp	risk	tint

1.1.4 Do not double when there are two vowel letters together.

test words: ***bleeding, needing***

aid	+	ed, ing	=	aided etc.
aim	+	ed, ing	=	aimed etc.
bleed	+	ing	=	bleeding etc.
cheat	+	ed, ing	=	cheated etc.
dread	+	ing, ed	=	dreaded etc.
feed	+	er, ing	=	feeding etc.
float	+	er, ed, ing	=	floated etc.
groan	+	ed, ing	=	groaning etc.
leak	+	ed, ing, y	=	leaking etc.
need	+	ed, ing, y	=	needed etc.
read	+	able, ing, er	=	readable etc.
speak	+	er, ing	=	speaker etc.

Other examples:

aim	greet	oil	stain
break	groan	peep	stoop
clean	haul	raid	strain
drain	heed	rain	tour
eat	join	read	train
fail	lean	rein	wait
float	load	sail	weed
gain	look	seem	
gloat	need	shout	

1.1.5 Do not double the following final consonant letters:

test words: ***mixing, rowing***

w:	row	+	ing	=	rowing	
x:	mix	+	ing	=	mixing	
y:	say	+	ing	=	saying	

Doubling and stress

1.1.6 When adding a suffix beginning with a vowel to words with more than one syllable, ending in 1 vowel letter + 1 consonant letter, double the final consonant if the stress is on the final syllable.

test words: ***beginning, admitted***

ad**mit**	+	ing, ance, ed	=	admitting etc.
be**gin**	+	ing, er,	=	beginning etc.
com**mit**	+	al, ed	=	committal etc.
de**bar**	+	ed, ing	=	debarred etc.
equip	+	ed, ing	=	equipped etc.
for**bid**	+	en, ing	=	forbidden etc.
in**ter**	+	ed, ing	=	interred etc.
out**bid**	+	en, ing	=	outbidden etc.
out**wit**	+	ed, ing	=	outwitted etc.
per**mit**	+	ed, ing	=	permitted etc.
pre**fer**	+	ed, ing	=	preferred etc.
re**cur**	+	ed, ing	=	recurred etc.
re**fer**	+	al, ing, ed	=	referral etc.
re**gret**	+	ed, ing	=	regretted etc.

1.1.7 When adding a suffix beginning with a vowel to words with more than one syllable ending in 1 vowel letter + 1 consonant letter, do not double the final consonant if the stress is on the first (or penultimate) syllable.

test words: ***galloped, happened***

alter	+	ing, ation	=	altered etc.
ballot	+	ed, ing	=	balloted etc.
budget	+	ed, ing	=	budgeted etc.
enter	+	ed, ing	=	entered etc.
fasten	+	ed, ing	=	fastened etc.
gallop	+	ed, ing	=	galloped etc.

(contd)

1.1.6 (contd)

hamper	+	ed, ing	=	hampered etc.	
happen	+	ed, ing	=	happened etc.	
hasten	+	ed, ing	=	hastened etc.	
hinder	+	ed, ing	=	hindered etc.	
limit	+	ation, ed, ing	=	limitation etc.	
market	+	ed, ing	=	marketed etc.	
number	+	ed, ing	=	numbered etc.	
offer	+	ed, ing	=	offered etc.	
orbit	+	ed, ing	=	orbited etc.	
pocket	+	ed, ing	=	pocketed etc.	
pivot	+	al, ed, ing	=	pivotal etc.	
profit	+	ed, ing	=	profited etc.	

Other examples:

banquet	**diff**er
beckon	**gos**sip
buffet	**orph**an
carpet	**vis**it
debit	**vom**it
de**pos**it	

exception:

worship	+	ed, ing	=	worshi**pp**ed, worshi**pp**ing

1.1.8 If the stress in the word is more evenly placed, the final consonant should be doubled.

kidnap	+	ed, er	=	kidna**pp**ed etc.
format	+	ed, er	=	forma**tt**ed etc.

1.1.9 Double final -l irrespective of stress.

(in American English spelling this does not apply; the stress rule is followed, giving traveler, rebelled)

test words: ***traveller, pedalling***

bevel	+	ed	=	bevelled etc.
cancel	+	ed, ing, ation	=	cancelled etc.
label	+	ed, ing	=	labelling etc.
pedal	+	ed, ing	=	pedalled etc.
quarrel	+	ed, ing	=	quarrelled etc.
signal	+	ed, ing	=	signalled etc.
travel	+	ed, er, ing	=	travelled etc.
con**rol**	+	ed, er, ing	=	controlled etc.
pat**rol**	+	ed, ing	=	patrolled etc.
ap**pal**	+	ed, ing	=	appalled etc.
re**pel**	+	ed, ing, ent	=	repelled etc.
re**bel**	+	ed, ing, ion, ious	=	rebelled etc.

exceptions:				
formal	+	ity, ise	=	formality, formalise
legal	+	ity, ise	=	legality, legalise

1.1.10 When adding a suffix beginning with e/i or y to words ending in -ic, add k (-ick + suffix). This preserves the /k/ sound, which would otherwise become /s/.

test words: ***panicky, picnicking***

col**ic**	+	y	>	col**icky** etc.
frol**ic**	+	ing, ed	>	frol**icked** etc.
mim**ic**	+	ing, ed	>	mim**icking** etc.
pan**ic**	+	ing, ed, y	>	pan**icky** etc.
picn**ic**	+	ing, ed	>	picn**icking** etc.
traff**ic**	+	ing, ed	>	traff**icking** etc.

1.2   Suffixes and Final "e"

1.2.1 When adding a suffix beginning with a vowel to words ending in Consonant + e (silent "e"), drop the "e".

test words: ***taking, making, saved, loved***

believe	+	ed, er, ing	=	believ**ed** etc.
choose	+	ing, y	=	choos**y** etc.
come	+	ing	=	com**ing** etc.
drive	+	ing, er, able	=	driv**ing** etc.
fade	+	ed, ing	=	fad**ing** etc.
fame	+	ed, ous	=	fam**ous** etc.
give	+	er, ing	=	giv**ing** etc.
hope	+	ed, ing	=	hop**ed** etc.
leave	+	er, ing	=	leav**ing** etc.
move	+	able, ed, er, ing	=	mov**able** etc.
poke	+	er, ing, ed	=	pok**er** etc.
style	+	ed, ing, ish	=	styl**ish** etc.
wade	+	ed, er, ing	=	wad**ing** etc.

Other examples:

bake	flake	save
bite	give	shave
blame	glide	skate
choke	have	slide
compete	hide	snooze
complete	joke	take
cope	leave	trace
dine	live	trade
dive	love	use
fake	make	wake
	note	

Note: Although it might see illogical, it is better to learn the rule initially as "drop e and add -ed/er", rather than simply "add d or r". This preserves the integrity of the suffix as a meaningful element, and minimises the risk of errors such as peerd*/ paird*.

1.2.2 When adding a suffix beginning with a consonant to words ending in "silent e", do not drop the "e".

test words: ***hopeless, safety***

bale	+	ful	=	baleful
blame	+	less	=	blameless
bore	+	dom	=	boredom
brave	+	ly	=	bravely
come	+	ly	=	comely
fate	+	ful	=	fateful
grace	+	ful, less	=	graceful etc.
hope	+	ful, less	=	hopeful etc.
hope	+	less	=	hopeless
late	+	ly, ness	=	lately etc.
love	+	ly	=	lovely
nice	+	ly, ty	=	nicely etc.
note	+	let	=	notelet
pave	+	ment	=	pavement
pure	+	ly	=	purely
rude	+	ness, ly	=	rudeness etc.
safe	+	ly, ty	=	safely etc.
severe	+	ly	=	severely
shame	+	ful	=	shameful
spine	+	less	=	spineless
taste	+	less	=	tasteless
time	+	ly	=	timely
tire	+	less	=	tireless
tone	+	less	=	toneless

1.2.3 When adding a suffix beginning with a or o (e.g. able, -ous,) to words ending in "ce" or "ge", do not drop the final "e".
The "soft" /s/, and /j/ sound in the root words is thus maintained.

test words: ***noticeable, traceable***

notice	+	able	=	noticeable
pronounce	+	able	=	pronounceable
service	+	able	=	serviceable
trace	+	able	=	traceable

(contd)

1.2.2 (contd)

advantage	+	ous	=	advantageous
change	+	able	=	changeable
courage	+	ous	=	courageous
knowledge	+	able	=	knowledgeable
manage	+	able	=	manageable
outrage	+	ous	=	outrageous

1.2.4 When adding -ing to words ending in -nge, do not drop the final "e". This maintains the /j/ sound.

test word: ***singeing***

binge	+	ing	=	bingeing
fringe	+	ing	=	fringeing
singe	+	ing	=	singeing
whinge	+	ing	=	whingeing

1.2.5 When adding -ing to words ending in "ie", change "ie" to "y".

test words: ***dying, lying***

die	+	ing	=	dying
lie	+	ing	=	lying
tie	+	ing	=	tying
vie	+	ing	=	vying

1.2.6 When adding –ing to words ending in "ee", keep "ee".

test words: ***seeing, fleeing***

see	+	ing	=	seeing
flee	+	ing	=	fleeing
free	+	ing	=	freeing
agree	+	ing	=	agreeing

exceptional words ending in -i, keep the -i:

ski	+	ing	=	skiing
taxi	+	ing	=	taxiing

Suffixes and Words Ending in "y"   1.3

1.3.1 When adding a suffix to a word ending in Consonant + y, change "y" to "i" (unless the suffix starts with "i"). This rule applies whether the suffix begins with a vowel or a consonant.

test words: ***hurried, married***

apply	+	ed, es, cation	=	applied, applies etc.
army	+	es	=	armies
baby	+	es	=	babies
beauty	+	ful, fy, es	=	beautiful, beautify etc.
berry	+	es	=	berries
body	+	ly, es	=	bodily, bodies
bury	+	al, ed, es	=	burial, buried etc.
busy	+	er, est	=	busier, busiest
carry	+	age, er, ed, es	=	carriage, carrier etc.
city	+	es	=	cities
clumsy	+	ly, er, est	=	clumsily, clumsier etc.
copy	+	ed, es, er	=	copied, copies etc.
copy	+	er, ed, es	=	copier, copies etc.
cry	+	ed, es	=	cried, cries
deny	+	al, ed, es	=	denial, denied etc.
dirty	+	er, est, ed, es	=	dirtier, dirtiest etc.
easy	+	ly, er, est	=	easily, easier etc.
empty	+	er, est, ed, es	=	emptier, emptiest etc.
forty	+	eth	=	fortieth
fry	+	ed, es, er	=	fried, fries etc.
happy	+	ly, er, est	=	happily, happier etc.
hurry	+	ed, es	=	hurried, hurries
simply	+	ed, es, cation	=	simplied, simplies etc.
lucky	+	ly, er, est	=	luckily, luckier etc.
marry	+	age, ed, es	=	marriage, married etc.
ninety	+	eth	=	ninetieth
noisy	+	er, est, ly	=	noisier, noisily etc.
occupy	+	ed, es	=	occupies, occupied etc.
pity	+	ful, ed, es	=	pitiful, pitied etc.
qualify	+	es, ed, cation	=	qualifies, qualified etc.
rely	+	able, es, ed	=	reliable, relies etc.
reply	+	ed, es, cation	=	replied, replies etc.
satisfy	+	ed, es	=	satisfied, satisfies
scurry	+	ed, es	=	scurried scurries
spy	+	es, ed	=	spies, spied
study	+	ed, es, ous	=	studious, studies etc.
supply	+	es, ed, er	=	supplies, supplied etc.
try	+	al, ed, es	=	trial, tried etc.
twenty	+	eth	=	twentieth
worry	+	er, es, ed	=	worrier, worries etc.

1.3.2 Do not change "y" to "i" when adding -ing, -ish (a suffix beginning with "i")

test words: ***carrying, flying***

apply	+	*t*ing	=	applying
baby	+	*is*h	=	babyish
carry	+	ing	=	carrying
copy	+	ing	=	copying
fly	+	ing	=	flying
hurry	+	ing	=	hurrying
marry	+	ing	=	marrying
study	+	ing	=	studying
try	+	ing	=	trying
worry	+	ing	=	worrying

1.3.3 Do not change "y" to "i" if there is a vowel before the "y"

test words: ***played, stayed***

ann**oy**	+	ed, ance	=	ann**oy**ance etc.
del**ay**	+	ed	=	delayed
destr**oy**	+	ed	=	destr**oy**ed
j**oy**	+	ful	=	j**oy**ful
ob**ey**	+	ed, ance	=	ob**ey**ed etc.
pl**ay**	+	ed, ful	=	pl**ay**ed etc.
pr**ay**	+	ed	=	pr**ay**ed
st**ay**	+	ed	=	st**ay**ed
sw**ay**	+	ed	=	sw**ay**ed etc.

2 Grammar Related Rules for Suffixes and Endings

Nouns

A noun is a word that can be used in phrases such as "*the **house**", "*my **mother***". All nouns except the names of people or places can form a phrase with "*my*" or "*the*". Phrases such as "*my mother*", or "*the large house*" are known as noun phrases, because they fit into the "noun slot" in a sentence:

Noun	Verb	Noun
(noun phrase)	Verb	(noun phrase)
James	saw	**Emma**
The **boy**	saw	the **girl**
The small **boy**	met	the tall **girl**
Speed	causes	**accidents**
Happiness	is	a great **feeling**

The following nouns are written with capital letters:
Names of people and places (*Richard, Bob, London, New York, France, Meridian Hotel, Bond Street*)

The days of the week (*Monday, Tuesday* etc.) *

The months of the year (*January, February.*) *

* that these are usually used as nouns can be demonstrated by putting them into noun phrases:

the first January *of the century*;   **the worst Monday** *of my life.*

as in:

the first house *in the street*;   **the worst coffee** *I have ever tasted*

It is often impossible to assign a word to grammatical categories without knowing its context in a sentence. Words may fulfil different roles depending on context. Take the word **round** as an example:

*   *the **round** table*   Adjective as part of a noun phrase
*   ***the excellent round*** *of golf*   Noun as part of a noun phrase
*   ***I round*** *up the sheep*   Verb (was round**ing**, round**ed** up)
*   *he walks **round** the building*   Preposition (behind, over, under)

Nouns can be either singular, referring to one "item", or plural, referring to more than one: ***one animal***; ***two or more animals***.

2.1   Changing singular nouns to plural nouns

2.1.1	add –s	cubs
2.1.2	add –es	bushes
2.1.3	–ves	wolves
2.1.4	y > i + es	babies
2.1.5	-o +s /es	radios/potatoes
2.1.6	-is > es	crises
2.1.7	-ix / ex > ices	indices
2.1.8	-on > a	criteria
2.1.9	-um > a	data

2.1.1 add -s

-s is the most common plural ending in English, used with most nouns that do not end in "s", "sh", "ch", "x", "fe", "lf" or "consonant + y".

test words: ***cats, hands***

cub	+s	= cubs	test	+s	= tests
trick	+s	= tricks	crisp	+s	= crisps
topic	+s	= topics	mint	+s	= mints
bed	+s	= beds	hand	+s	= hands
cliff	+s	= cliffs	bank	+s	= banks
log	+s	= logs	lump	+s	= lumps
doll	+s	= dolls	raft	+s	= rafts
room	+s	= rooms	act	+s	= acts
gun	+s	= guns	scalp	+s	= scalps
trap	+s	= traps	cave	+s	= caves
car	+s	= cars	key	+s	= keys
cat	+s	= cats	cloth	+s	= cloths
paw	+s	= paws	ring	+s	= rings
boy	+s	= boys	wage	+s	= wages
egg	+s	= eggs	river	+s	= rivers

When the last sound is a word is "voiced" (see page 256), the s has a /z/ sound e.g. rooms = /uːmz/. If the last sound in a word is voiceless, "s" has a /s/ sound, e.g. /klɪfs/.

This can lead to spelling errors (e.g. boyz). It is important to stress that –s is a unit of meaning (more than one) in these words, and that it does not matter whether "S" sounds like /z/ or /s/.

2.1.2 add -es

-es is the plural ending for words ending in s, ss, sh, ch and x.

test words: ***boxes, foxes***

bus	+ es	= buses	box	+ es	= boxes
gas	+ es	= gases	fox	+ es	= foxes
ass	+ es	= asses	tax	+ es	= taxes
kiss	+ es	= kisses	annex	+ es	= annexes
dress	+ es	= dresses			
glass	+ es	= glasses			
cross	+ es	= crosses			

test words: ***branches, churches***

bush	+ es	= bushes	rich	+ es	= riches
brush	+ es	= brushes	batch	+ es	= batches
dish	+ es	= dishes	latch	+ es	= latches
wish	+ es	= wishes	match	+ es	= matches
rash	+ es	= rashes	sketch	+ es	= sketches
gash	+ es	= gashes	ditch	+ es	= ditches
bush	+ es	= bushes	witch	+ es	= witches
splash	+ es	= splashes	stitch	+ es	= stitches
crash	+ es	= crashes	watch	+ es	= watches
thrush	+ es	= thrushes	arch	+ es	= arches
branch	+es	= branches	church	+ es	= churches

-es *rather than* **-s** *is used in these words, because it would not be possible to pronounce e.g.* foxs, wishs.

The **-es** *ending sounds like* /**iz**/ – *but as for the* **-s** *ending, the link with meaning (more than one) should be stressed. If the endings* **-s** *and* **-es** *are associated with plurality, spelling errors such as* bushiz *or* bushis *are less likely to be made.*

2.1.3 -ves

To form the plural of words ending in -**f** and -**fe**, change **f** or **fe** to **v**, and add **es**.

test words: ***wolves, shelves***

elf:	f > v	+ es	=	el**ves**
self:	f > v	+ es	=	sel**ves**
shelf:	f > v	+ es	=	shel**ves**
calf:	f > v	+ es	=	cal**ves**
half:	f > v	+ es	=	hal**ves**
wolf:	f > v	+ es	=	wol**ves**
leaf:	f > v	+ es	=	lea**ves**
loaf:	f > v	+ es	=	loa**ves**
scarf:	f > v	+ es	=	scar**ves**
sheaf:	f > v	+ es	=	shea**ves**
thief:	f > v	+ es	=	thie**ves**

wife:	fe > v	+ es	=	wi**ves**
knife:	fe > v	+ es	=	kni**ves**
life:	fe > v	+ es	=	li**ves**

The plural of **dwarf, hoof, roof** *and* **wharf** *can be formed as above:*
dwar**ves**, hoo**ves**, roo**ves**, whar**ves**

or by adding -***s***
dwarf**s**, hoof**s**, roof**s**, wharf**s**

To form the plural of **chief, handkerchief, gulf, waif** *and* **oaf***, add* -*s:*

chief**s**, handkerchief**s**, gulf**s**, waif**s** and oaf**s**

2.1.4 -y > i + es

To form the plural of nouns ending in consonant + y, change "y" to "i" and add -**es**.
(See also 1.3.1, page 233 for the general rule)

test words: ***berries, babies***

army:	y > i	+	es	=	armies
baby:	y > i	+	es	=	babies
berry:	y > i	+	es	=	berries
body:	y > i	+	es	=	bodies
city:	y > i	+	es	=	cities
copy:	y > i	+	es	=	copies
dairy:	y > i	+	es	=	dairies
daisy:	y > i	+	es	=	daisies
duty:	y > i	+	es	=	duties
fairy:	y > i	+	es	=	fairies
jelly:	y > i	+	es	=	jellies
lady:	y > i	+	es	=	ladies
party:	y > i	+	es	=	parties

2.1.5 -o + s/es

To form the plural of some nouns ending in **-o** , add **-es**

test words: ***potatoes, tomatoes***

domino	+	es	=	dominoes
echo	+	es	=	echoes
hero	+	es	=	heroes
mosquito	+	es	=	mosquitoes
potato	+	es	=	potatoes
tomato	+	es	=	tomatoes
torpedo	+	es	=	torpedoes

In these words, both **-os** and **-oes** spellings are considered correct

buffalo	+ s	=	buffalos	or	+ es	=	buffaloes
cargo	+ s	=	cargos	or	+ es	=	cargoes
commando	+ s	=	commandos	or	+ es	=	commandoes
halo	+ s	=	halos	or	+ es	=	haloes
innuendo	+ s	=	innuendos	or	+ es	=	innuendoes
motto	+ s	=	mottos	or	+ es	=	mottoes
tornado	+ s	=	tornados	or	+ es	=	tornadoes
volcano	+ s	=	volcanos	or	+ es	=	volcanoes

To form the plural of words from Italian (many associated with music), words with a vowel before the **"o"** and words imported from other languages, add **-s**.

test words: ***pianos, radios***

Many of these words, especially those associated with music, come from Italian

banjo	+ s	=	banjos
cello	+ s	=	cellos
concerto	+ s	=	concertos
contralto	+ s	=	contraltos
curio	+ s	=	curios
dynamo	+ s	=	dynamos
piano	+ s	=	pianos
radio	+ s	=	radios
solo	+ s	=	solos
soprano	+ s	=	sopranos

2.1.6 -is > -es
These words come from Greek

amanuensis	>	amanuenses
analysis	>	analyses
apotheosis	>	apotheoses
basis	>	bases
crisis	>	crises
emphasis	>	emphases
hypothesis	>	hypotheses
metamorphosis	>	metamorphoses
oasis	>	oases
synopsis	>	synopses
synthesis	>	syntheses
thesis	>	theses

2.1.7 -i/ex > ices

appendix	>	appendices
index	>	indices
matrix	>	matrices

2.1.8 -on > -a
from Greek

criterion	>	criteria

2.1.9 -um > a

from Latin

bacter**ium**	>	bacter**ia**
compend**ium**	>	compend**ia**
continu**um**	>	continu**a**
curricul**um**	>	curricul**a**
dat**um**	>	dat**a**
gymnas**ium**	>	gymnas**ia**
med**ium**	>	med**ia**
referend**um**	>	referend**a**

Noun Endings   2.2

Some word endings are associated with nouns, and these are listed below with examples. Phrases are given to demonstrate the use of nouns, alongside simple alternatives to illustrate the idea that nouns occupy a particular slot in a phrase or sentence:

2.2.1	-age	damage	*we inspected the **damage*** *we inspected the **drain***
2.2.2	-ance	elegance	*her impressive **elegance*** *her impressive **hat***
2.2.3	-ar	vicar	*I visited the **vicar*** *I visited the **teacher***
2.2.4	-ary	anniversary	*the first **anniversary*** *the first **night***
2.2.5	-cy/-ency	bankruptcy	*his **bankruptcy** was a disaster* *his **haircut** was a disaster*
2.2.6	-cide	suicide	*his **suicide** was very sad* *his **story** was very sad*
2.2.7	-ee	employee	*she was an **employee** of the company* *she was a **friend** of the family*
2.2.8	-dom	freedom	*he had the **freedom** to decide* *he has the **bricks** to build*
2.2.9	-eer	engineer	*the **engineer** was ill* *the **boy** was ill*
2.2.10	-ence	confidence	*she had great **confidence*** *she had great **clothes***

(contd)

2.2 (contd)

2.2.11	-er	baker	the **baker** was successful
			the **boy** was successful
2.2.12	-ery	brewery	the famous **brewery**
			the famous **man**
2.2.13	-ese	legalese	**legalese** is hard to understand
			the **lesson** is hard to under-stand
2.2.14	-esse/ette	finesse	he has no **finesse**
			he has no **socks**
2.2.15	-eum	petroleum	**petroleum** comes from oil
			sugar comes from the Caribbean
2.2.16	-eur	masseur	she went to the **masseur**
			she went to the **school**
2.2.17	-hood	childhood	he forgot his **childhood**
			he forgot his **teddy**
2.2.18	-ice	cowardice	they noticed his **cowardice**
			they noticed his **coat**
2.2.19	-iom	idiom	he used a good **idiom**
			he used a good **knife**
2.2.20	-ism	fascism	**fascism** inspires fear
			music inspires people
2.2.21	-ist	communist	he was a **communist**
			he was a **schoolboy**
2.2.22	-ity	university	we saw the **university**
			we saw the **horse**
2.2.23	-ium	tedium	the **tedium** was unbearable
			the **heat** was unbearable
2.2.24	-let	piglet	my tiny **piglet**
			my tiny **flat**
2.2.25	-ling	duckling	the fluffy **duckling**
			the fluffy **toy**
2.2.26	-ment	enjoyment	her **enjoyment** was obvious
			her **limp** was obvious
2.2.27	-ness	kindness	we appreciate your **kindness**
			we appreciate your **letter**
2.2.28	-ology	geology	she likes **geology**
			she likes **bats**
2.2.29	-or	actor	the **actor** read the play
			the **girl** read the play
2.2.30	-ory	factory	the prosperous **factory**
			the prosperous **landowner**

(contd)

2.2 (contd)

2.2.31	-our	harbour	*the yacht sailed into the* **harbour** *the yacht sailed on to the* **beach**
2.2.32	-ship	friendship	*her* **friendship** *was valuable* *her* **necklace** *was valuable*
2.2.33	-sion	tension	*we could feel the* **tension** *we could feel the* **sand**
2.2.34	-ssion	possession	*my favourite* **possession** *my favourite* **doll**
2.2.35	-tion	invention	*her clever* **invention** *her clever* **sister**
2.2.36	-ture	structure	*the* **structure** *of the building was sound* *the* **roof** *of the building was sound*
2.2.37	-ty	certainty	*it's an absolute* **certainty** *it's an absolute* **nightmare**

All the words in these lists can be put into sentence structures like those shown above.

2.2.1 -age; pronounced /ɪdʒ/

test words: ***courage, sausage***

average	dosage	luggage	plumage
garage	orphanage	sausage	courage
garbage	package	spillage	coverage
homage	peerage	village	breakage
damage	image	pilgrimage	wreckage

2.2.2 -ance

test words: ***hindrance, elegance***

This ending is from French – and appears in many modern French words

abundance	countenance	fragrance	maintenance
ambulance	defiance	hindrance	petulance
arrogance	elegance	ignorance	reluctance
assistance	extravagance	instance	significance
brilliance			

2.2.3 -ar

test words: ***cellar, collar***

altar	collar	pillar	vinegar
beggar	cougar	popular	
burglar	grammar	singular	
cellar	hangar	vicar	

2.2.4 -ary

test words: ***dictionary, salary***

adversary	constabulary	itinerary	secretary
anniversary	dictionary	January	seminary
boundary	dignitary	library	summary
burglary	dispensary	luminary	tributary
capillary	dromedary	ovary	
centenary	February	quandary	
commentary	granary	salary	

2.2.5 -cy/-ency

bankruptcy	dependency	latency	tendency
baronetcy	despondency	leniency	
bureaucracy	Excellency	persistency	
clemency	fluency	solvency	
competency			

2.2.6 -cide

Meaning "killing of". The first parts of the words come from Latin, and mean (in order) brother, fungus, people, man, mother, father, pests and oneself.

fratricide	matricide
fungicide	patricide
genocide	pesticide
homicide	suicide

2.2.7 -ee

formed from verbs (shown in brackets) and representing the person "at the receiving end" of the action of the verb

addressee	(address)	examinee	(examine)	nominee	(nominate)
deportee	(deport)	internee	(intern)	payee	(pay)
divorcee	(divorce)	interviewee	(interview)	referee	(refer)
employee	(employ)	lessee	(lease)	trainee	(train)
devotee	(devote)	licensee	(license)	trustee	(trust)

2.2.8 -dom

test words: ***freedom, wisdom***

-dom is an Old English ending

dukedom	kingdom
earldom	martyrdom
fiefdom	wisdom
freedom	

2.2.9 -eer

test words: ***engineer, mountaineer***

auctioneer	mutineer
buccaneer	pioneer
engineer	profiteer
mountaineer	

2.2.10 -ence

test words: ***independence, evidence***

(nouns formed from -ent adjectives)

absence	corpulence	fraudulence	opulence
abstinence	correspondence	imminence	persistence
affluence	decadence	impudence	presence
belligerence	dependence	independence	prominence
beneficence	difference	indolence	reverence
benevolence	eloquence	insolence	silence
coherence	eminence	intelligence	turbulence
competence	evidence	magnificence	violence
confidence	excellence	negligence	virulence
convenience	flatulence	obedience	

2.2.11 -er (see also verb endings)

baker	cleaner	mother	silver
brother	father	plumber	sister
builder	gardener	robber	teacher
carpenter	letter	shopper	worker

2.2.12 -ery

test words: **brewery, nursery**

bravery	embroidery	monastery
brewery	forgery	nursery
cemetery	grocery	prudery
confectionery	jewellery	refinery
crockery	joinery	stationery
discovery	machinery	

2.2.13 -ese

-ese is used to refer to different registers of language – as in newspapers, the law etc. The ending is that used for some languages as shown below

Chinese	legalese
Portuguese	journalese
Japanese	motherese

2.2.14 -esse/-ette

These are French endings

finesse	cigarette	pirouette	silhouette
largesse	etiquette	rosette	statuette
brunette	launderette	roulette	suffragette
cassette	pipette	serviette	usherette

2.2.15 -eum

This ending is from Latin

linoleum
mausoleum
museum
petroleum

2.2.16 -eur

These are French words, adopted into English

amateur	restaurateur
entrepreneur	saboteur
masseur	voyeur

2.2.17 -hood

This ending comes from Old English

adulthood	knighthood	sisterhood
boyhood	likelihood	widowhood
brotherhood	manhood	womanhood
childhood	motherhood	
falsehood	sainthood	

2.2.18 -ice

test words: ***service, prejudice***

An ending from French

apprentice	chalice	justice	office
armistice	cowardice	liquorice	practice
artifice	crevice	malice	prejudice
avarice	edifice	notice	service
bodice	jaundice	novice	solstice

2.2.19 -iom

axiom
idiom

2.2.20 -ism

(referring to a movement or concept)

communism	nihilism
fascism	optimism
Judaism	pessimism

2.2.21 -ist

(referring to a person's affiliation, outlook or occupation)

test words: **optimist, pessimist**

communist	pessimist
bigamist	therapist
fascist	rapist
optimist	

2.2.22 -ity

test words: **activity, celebrity**

This ending is from French; most of the words below have an equivalent French form, ending in -ité

ability	curiosity	modality	rigidity
acceptability	educability	morbidity	sanctity
acidity	enormity	musicality	sensitivity
activity	eternity	necessity	solidity
alacrity	fatality	negativity	stupidity
amenity	festivity	opportunity	timidity
animosity	finality	passivity	tonality
audacity	generosity	possibility	university
brutality	impunity	prosperity	quantity
capability	infirmity	publicity	quality
capacity	iniquity	punctuality	visibility
charity	inscrutability	rapidity	
compatibility	intelligibility	regularity	
celebrity	legibility	reliability	
credibility	mediocrity	responsibility	

2.2.23 -ium/(-uum)

This ending comes from Latin

bacterium	gymnasium	continuum
calcium	helium	potassium
compendium	medium	premium
delirium	opium	radium
delphinium	opprobrium	stadium
geranium	podium	tedium

2.2.24 -let

test words: **leaflet, bracelet**

This is a diminutive ending (meaning "small")

booklet	hamlet
bracelet	leaflet
cygnet	notelet
eyelet	platelet
gimlet	starlet
goblet	

2.2.25 -ling

This is another diminutive ending (meaning "small"); it is from German where it is also used in terms of endearment (Liebling = darling)

darling	inkling
duckling	sapling
gelding	sibling
gosling	starling
hireling	

2.2.26 -ment

test words: **enjoyment, ornament**

This is another French ending; several of the words below are written the same way in modern French

advancement	enjoyment	monument
amazement	environment	movement
appeasement	excitement	ornament
commitment	firmament	parliament
compliment	fragment	pronouncement
development	government	recruitment
document	implement	retirement
elopement	increment	statement
employment	inducement	supplement
enactment	infringement	
encouragement	investment	
engagement	management	

2.2.27 -ness

(adjectives expressing abstract qualities)
–ness is added to the basic adjective with a more "concrete" meaning.

This is an Old English ending

abruptness	fitness	meanness	softness
attractiveness	friendliness	neatness	sordidness
business	happiness	readiness	steadiness
candidness	harmlessness	sadness	strangeness
clumsiness	kindness	loudness	ugliness
completeness	laziness	silliness	vagueness
darkness	loveliness	sloppiness	weariness

2.2.28 -ology

test words: ***biology, geology***

This ending means "the study of"; it comes from the French – logie

anthropology	pathology
archaeology	psychology
astrology	sociology
biology	tautology
geology	zoology

2.2.29 -or

test words: ***factor, actor***

actor	conjuror	factor	radiator
ambassador	contractor	instructor	solicitor
ancestor	doctor	monitor	successor
calculator	director	motor	tractor
chancellor	elector	mirror	visitor
collector	emperor	professor	

2.2.30 -ory

test words: ***factory, history***

accessory	history
advisory	laboratory
category	observatory
dormitory	refectory
factory	territory

2.2.31 -our

test words: **harbour, armour**

Equivalent to the French -eur (honeur, humeur)

ardour	fervour	humour	rumour
armour	flavour	labour	saviour
behaviour	glamour	neighbour	valour
colour	harbour	odour	vapour
favour	honour	parlour	vigour

2.2.32 -ship

This is an Old English ending; it often translates into modern German -schaft, e.g. Freundschaft (friendship)

authorship	lordship
brinkmanship	receivership
craftsmanship	scholarship
friendship	sportsmanship
guardianship	workmanship
judgeship	hardship

2.2.33 -sion

(also listed in consonants 17.6, page 162)

aversion	mansion
comprehension	pension
diversion	tension
extension	version

2.2.34 -ssion

(also listed in consonants, page 161)

test words: **admission, discussion**

A French ending; many of the words below have exactly the same written from in modern French

admission	expression	passion	session
aggression	impression	permission	succession
compassion	mission	possession	suppression
discussion	oppression	profession	transmission

2.2.35 -tion

(For more examples see consonants, page 160)

test words: **operation, election**

Another French ending; many of the words below have exactly the same written from in modern French

two syllable -tion	three syllable -tion	four syllable -tion
action	absorption	competition
fraction	addition	composition
function	attention	corporation
junction	collection	decoration
lotion	commotion	dictionary
mention	completion	education
motion	connection	examination
nation	depletion	information
notion	devotion	institution

2.2.36 -ture

(see also Consonants, page 166)

Another French ending; some of the words below have exactly the same written from in modern French

adventure	departure	lecture	posture
agriculture	feature	legislature	puncture
capture	fixture	literature	stature
caricature	furniture	manufacture	stricture
creature	future	mixture	structure
culture	gesture	nature	tincture
denture	investiture	picture	venture

2.2.37 -ty/-ety

test words: **notoriety, certainty**

Another French ending; modern French form is usually -té

anxiety	notoriety	sobriety
certainty	piety	sovereignty
frailty	propriety	specialty
loyalty	royalty	variety

Verbs

1. The child **kicks** the ball
2. A man **is coming** up the drive
3. I **wanted** to go out
4. They **have bought** a car
5. We **slept** well
6. She **is** only four years old

In simple English "statement" sentences, as above, the verb comes after the subject (either a noun: man, child, or pronoun: I, they, we). Verbs are commonly thought of as "doing" words because they often relate to some sort of "action". Very often though, they seem to describe a "state" rather that an action (sentence 6).

Verb Suffixes   2.3

added to the "stem" or basic form of the verb to denote tense or person

2.3.1	-ing	present continuous
2.3.2	-ed	past tense
2.3.3	-t	past tense
2.3.4	-s/-es	third person singular
2.3.5	-en	past participle

2.3.1 Present Continuous + ing

All main verbs in English have the -ing form. It is added to the infinitive, or "root form", e.g. being, going, having etc. It is often used with the verb "to be".

I **am** look**ing**
He **was** cook**ing**
She **has been** sing**ing**
They **will be/might be** coming

or as a noun

I like **shopping** (as in *I like* **tomatoes**)
He hates **singing** (as in *He hates* **books**)

or as an adjective

The **boiling** rice (as in *the* **hot** *rice*)
His **bleeding** heart (as in *his* **kind** *heart*)

Spelling rules for adding suffixes beginning with a vowel apply. The following are examples with references to the general rules part of this section.

aim**ing** bleed**ing** boil**ing**	**1.1.5** *add to root*	cla**pp**ing ho**pp**ing ski**pp**ing	**1.1.1** *doubling rule*
limp**ing** mend**ing** stand**ing**	**1.1.4** *add to root*	gallop**ing** orbit**ing** limit**ing**	**1.1.7** *add to root* *(stress rule)*
begi**nn**ing forbi**dd**ing admi**tt**ing	**1.1.8** *doubling* *stress rule*	driv**ing** skat**ing** hop**ing**	**1.2.1** *drop "e"*
trave**ll**ing binge**ing** see**ing**	**1.1.10** *double "l"* **1.2.4** *keep "e"* **1.2.6** *keep "ee"*	kidna**pp**ing dy**ing** marry**ing**	**1.1.9** *double* **1.2.5** *"ie" > "y"* **1.3.2** *keep "y"*

2.3.2 Past Tense + ed

The **-ed** ending is the most common past tense form. It is added to the infinitive, or root form of the verb, but as for **-ing**, the spelling rules for adding suffixes beginning with a vowel apply. The following are examples with references to the general rules part of this section.

aim**ed** need**ed** boil**ed**	**1.1.5** *add to root*	cla**pp**ed ho**pp**ed ski**pp**ed	**1.1.1** *doubling rule*
limp**ed** mend**ed** land**ing**	**1.1.4** *add to root*	gallop**ed** orbit**ed** limit**ed**	**1.1.7** *add to root* *(stress rule)*
  admi**tt**ed	**1.1.8** *doubling* *stress rule*	divid**ed** skat**ed** hop**ed**	**1.2.1** *drop "e"*
trave**ll**ed marr**ied**	**1.1.10** *double "l"* **1.3.1.** *change "y" to "i"*	kidna**pp**ed	**1.1.9** *double*

The **-ed** past tense ending is pronounced in three different ways, /ɪd/, /d/ or /t/, depending on the last sound in the infinitive (or root) of the verb.

(a) If the last sound is /t/ or /d/, the ed sounds like /ɪd/.

As **id** is an adjective ending of relatively high frequency (see 2.4.4), and as "**id**" more closely reflects the sound of these verbs, misspellings such as "*huntid*" may occur. An awareness of the function of the **-ed** ending (to change from present to past tense) will minimise this confusion.

test words: ***waited, hunted***

act	+	ed	=	acted	/ɪd/
aid	+	ed	=	aided	/ɪd/
bond	+	ed	=	bonded	/ɪd/
delight	+	ed	=	delighted	/ɪd/
distract	+	ed	=	distracted	/ɪd/
end	+	ed	=	ended	/ɪd/
hand	+	ed	=	handed	/ɪd/
hound	+	ed	=	hounded	/ɪd/
hunt	+	ed	=	hunted	/ɪd/
land	+	ed	=	landed	/ɪd/
mend	+	ed	=	mended	/ɪd/
need	+	ed	=	needed	/ɪd/
plead	+	ed	=	pleaded	/ɪd/
raid	+	ed	=	raided	/ɪd/
wait	+	ed	=	waited	/ɪd/
want	+	ed	=	wanted	/ɪd/

This also applies to words ending in **-de,** and **-te** (see rule, 1.2.1)

shad**ed** fad**ed** trad**ed** wad**ed** hat**ed** stat**ed** grat**ed** glid**ed**   /ɪd/.

(b) If the last sound of the verb is "voiced", the -ed sounds like /d/

allow	+	ed	=	allowed	/d/
annoy	+	ed	=	annoyed	/d/
appear	+	ed	=	appeared	/d/
claim	+	ed	=	claimed	/d/
clean	+	ed	=	cleaned	/d/
complain	+	ed	=	complained	/d/
cover	+	ed	=	covered	/d/
cream	+	ed	=	creamed	/d/
delay	+	ed	=	delayed	/d/
destroy	+	ed	=	destroyed	/d/
fail	+	ed	=	failed	/d/
fear	+	ed	=	feared	/d/
fill	+	ed	=	filled	/d/
form	+	ed	=	formed	/d/
lower	+	ed	=	lowered	/d/
wander	+	ed	=	wandered	/d/

And in words with silent -e (see rule, 1.2.1)

named shaved dined scaled timed toned scared ignored closed /d/

When **-ed** sounds like **/d/**, errors such as *faild, scard, allowd* arise. It is therefore important to teach **-ed** as a complete unit which has a meaning (changing from the present to the past tense)

(c) If the last sound of the verb is "voiceless", the -ed sounds like /t/

test words: ***helped, thanked***

brush	+	ed	=	brushed	/t/
hatch	+	ed	=	hatched	/t/
help	+	ed	=	helped	/t/
kiss	+	ed	=	kissed	/t/
laugh	+	ed	=	laughed	/t/
miss	+	ed	=	missed	/t/
peep	+	ed	=	peeped	/t/
reach	+	ed	=	reached	/t/
rush	+	ed	=	rushed	/t/
sniff	+	ed	=	sniffed	/t/
thank	+	ed	=	thanked	/t/
walk	+	ed	=	walked	/t/
wish	+	ed	=	wished	/t/

And with words ending in unvoiced consonant + e (see rule, 1.2.1).

> bak**ed** rak**ed** hik**ed** pok**ed** pac**ed** rac**ed** lik**ed** spic**ed** swip**ed** hop**ed**

When **-ed** sounds like /**t**/, errors such as *snift, peept* may arise. It is therefore important to teach **-ed** as a complete unit which has a meaning (changing from the present to the past tense).

2.3.3 Past Tense with -t

There is a small group of verbs whose past tense form ends in -t

To form the past tense of the following verbs with **-ee-**, change **ee** to **e** (reflecting the change in vowel sound from /**i**/ to /ɛ/), and add **-t**

test words: ***slept, crept***

creep	>	cr**ept**
feel	>	f**elt**
keep	>	k**ept**
kneel	>	kn**elt**
sleep	>	sl**ept**
sweep	>	sw**ept**
weep	>	w**ept**

The following verbs with **-ea-**, just add **t** to form the past tense (the vowel sound changes from **i**/ to /ɛ/

deal	>	dealt			
mean	>	meant			
dream	>	dreamt	or	+ed	dream**ed**
lean	>	leant	or	+ed	lean**ed**
leap	>	leapt	or	+ed	leap**ed**

The following verbs ending in **-ll** have both **-t** and **-ed** endings (drop the final **-l** when adding **-t**)

sme**ll**	>	sme**lt**	or	smell**ed**
spe**ll**	>	spe**lt**	or	spell**ed**
spi**ll**	>	spi**lt**	or	spill**ed**

> Note:
> **spilled** is usually used for the past tense: *she **spilled** her drink*
> and **spilt** as an adjective: *the **spilt** milk* / as in *the **fresh** milk*
> or past participle: *he **has spilt** the tea*

2.3.4 -s/-es Third Person Singular

The he/she/it "person" of the verb has the ending –s or –es in the present tense. The rule is as for adding -s/-es to form the plural of nouns (see 2.1.1 and 2.1.2).

Verbs ending in **sh, ch, ss** and **x**, add **-es**:

test words: washes, catches

I wash	he /she/ it wash**es**
you catch	he /she / it catch**es**
we guess	he / she guess**es**
they fix	he / she fix**es**

To all other verbs, just add -s

I love	he / she / it love**s**
you aim	he / she / it aim**s**
we win	he / she / it win**s**
they lick	he / she / it lick**s**

2.3.5 Past Participle -en

The past participle is the part of the verb used with **have** in phrases like I have **waited**; you have **arrived**; he has **worked**; I have **sung**; they have **come**; we have **done**; it has **been**; she has **gone**.

The past participle of regular verbs is the same as the past tense form (-ed); the vowel sound of some verbs changes for the past tense and for the past participle (I sing, I sang, I have **sung**); some are irregular, such as **come** which does not change at all, and **done** and **gone** which do not follow a particular pattern.

A very common past participle form is -en

In the following verbs the vowel sound does not change:

beat	we beat	you have beat**en**	
eat	I eat	I have eat**en**	
fall	you fall	you have fall**en**	
forbid	I forbid	he has forbidd**en**	(doubling 1.1.7)
forgive	I forgive	you have forgiv**en**	(silent –e rule 1.2.1)
give	we give	they have giv**en**	(silent –e rule 1.2.1)
shake	we shake	you have shak**en**	(silent –e rule 1.2.1)
take	they take	I have tak**en**	(silent –e rule 1.2.1)

The vowel sound in the following verbs changes from /aɪ/ to /ɪ/ but this does not affect the spelling:

drive	I drive	I have driv**en**
rise	you rise	she has ris**en**
strive	we strive	they have striv**en**

The vowel sound in the following verbs also changes from /aɪ/ to /ɪ/ and the consonant is doubled (see 1.1.1):

bite	we bite	they have bitt**en**
hide	you hide	she has hidd**en**
ride	they ride	we have ridd**en**
write	I write	I have writt**en**

The vowel sound in the following verbs changes completely, and the spelling reflects the change; doubling and silent e rules apply (1.1.1 and 1.2.1):

break	I break	I have brok**en**
choose	they choose	I have chos**en**
forget	I forget	I have forgott**en**
freeze	you freeze	he has froz**en**
speak	you speak	he has spok**en**
tread	they tread	we have trodd**en**
wake	you wake	I have wok**en**
weave	you weave	I have wov**en**

2.4 Verb Endings

These endings are an integral part of the verbs below; all form the past tense
and past participle with -ed (observing the general rules for suffixes).

2.4.1 -ate

*this ending comes from French; the modern French equivalent is the
infinitive in -er (calculer, démonstrer, simuler).*

abdicate	create	indicate	satiate
administrate	decorate	inflate	sedate
agitate	deflate	initiate	simulate
appreciate	demonstrate	ingratiate	substantiate
assimilate	educate	insulate	
calculate	equate	negotiate	
commentate	generate		

2.4.2 -efy

-efy is much more unusual – but has the same meaning as -ify

liquefy	rarefy	stupefy	putrefy

2.4.3 -en

*-en is not always a verb ending – there are many other words that end
with these letters (ten, siren etc.). When used as a suffix to an adjective, as
in the words below, it forms verbs which have a sense of changing the
physical property of something.*

batten	harden	moisten	strengthen
dampen	lengthen	neaten	thicken
darken	lessen	sadden	tighten
deaden	lighten	shorten	toughen
deafen	liven	slacken	weaken
fasten	madden	soften	widen

2.4.4 -end

The -end verb ending is always stressed

amend	commend	offend
append	defend	portend
apprehend	descend	pretend
ascend	intend	transcend

2.4.5 -ify

-ify is always a verb ending; it has a sense of "process" in a more abstract sense than -en above – e.g. to make beautiful = to beautify; to make holy = to sanctify; to make clear = to clarify.

test words: ***clarify, qualify***

This ending comes from French; the modern French equivalent is the infinitive form –ifier (glorifier, quantifier, vérifier).

amplify	falsify	pacify	stultify
beautify	glorify	purify	terrify
calcify	gratify	qualify	verify
certify	horrify	quantify	vilify
clarify	identify	ramify	
classify	magnify	ratify	
deify	modify	rectify	
dignify	mollify	sanctify	
edify	notify	signify	
electrify	nullify	specify	

2.4.6 -ise

The -ise form has become almost standard in British English, whereas -ize is the accepted spelling in American English. This is always a verb ending.

test words: ***realise, organise***

This ending comes from French; the modern French equivalent is the infinitive form -iser (compromiser, organiser).

advertise	dramatise	realise
authorise	humanise	standardise
capitalise	improvise	supervise
circumcise	naturalise	
compromise	organise	

2.4.7 -ish

test words: ***vanish, finish***

This ending is originally from Middle English, Germanic, but is related to the French –ir verb ending (finir, punir, garnir).

abolish	embellish	nourish	vanish
admonish	establish	perish	vanquish
astonish	famish	polish	
banish	finish	publish	
burnish	flourish	punish	
cherish	furnish	ravish	
demolish	garnish	relish	
diminish	lavish	replenish	

the verbs below have the same spelling as their related adjectives (see page 267) but are distinguished by pronunciation; the verb ending is stressed and is pronounced /ɛɪt/ while the adjective ending is unstressed and is pronounced /ət/.

advocate	associate	duplicate	moderate
articulate	certificate	elaborate	predicate
animate	coordinate	estimate	separate
aggregate	correlate	expatriate	subordinate
appropriate	delegate	graduate	syndicate
approximate	deliberate	intimate	

2.5   Adjective Endings

The final letter strings, or endings, in this section are commonly associated with the class of words known as adjectives.

Simple adjectives, without particular endings, include:

- all the colours: *red, white, blue, pink* etc.
- all numbers: *six, twenty, eighth, fourteenth*
- words related to age: *old, young, antique*
- words relating to nationality: *English, Welsh, Chinese*
- words to describe size: *thin, tiny, large, huge*
- words to describe sounds: *loud, quiet*
- words to describe materials: *golden, wooden*
- words to describe character traits: *kind, mean*

Adjectives generally fit into sentences in either of two ways:

a. before the noun to which they relate, e.g.

the **red** car   (the + Adjective + Noun)
loud noises   (Adjective + Noun)
a **large** garden   (a + Adjective + Noun)

Phrases such as these can be combined with a verb (*make* in this example) to make a whole sentence: *The **red** car made **loud** noises in the **large** garden.*

When more than one adjective is used, they should be separated by commas: *The two, fine, old, English, antique tables …*

b. after the noun to which they relate, e.g.

> the car is **red**
> the noises were **loud**
> the garden is **large**

When more than one adjective is used in this position, they should be separated by commas, and the last two should be conjoined by "and": The garden was **large, neat** and **colourful.**

If a word can be used in the way described above, it is almost certain to be an adjective.

Adjectives for languages or nationality are written with a capital letter: The French education system; the German language.

Adjective endings are listed below, with examples.
Phrases are given to demonstrate the use of adjectives, alongside simple alternatives.

2.5.1	-able	acceptable:	*the **acceptable** meal/ the **good** meal*
2.5.2	-al	final:	*the **final** call/ the **loud** call*
2.5.3	-an, -ian	Georgian:	*the **Georgian** house/ the **huge** house*
2.5.4	-ant	elegant:	*the **elegant** model / the **tall** model*
2.5.5	-ar	solar:	*the **solar** system / the **simple** system*
2.5.6	-ary	necessary:	*the **necessary** plans/ the **poor** plans*
2.5.7	-ate	delicate:	*the **delicate** flower/ the **purple** flower*
2.5.8	-en	golden:	*the **golden** crown/ the **big** crown*
2.5.9	-ent	evident:	*the **evident** truth / the **sad** truth*
2.5.10	-eous	hideous:	*the **hideous** monster/the **ugly** monster*
2.5.11	-er	colder:	*the **colder** water/ the **cold** water*
2.5.12	-ern	northern:	*the **northern** light/ the **bright** light*
2.5.13	-est	hottest:	*the **hottest** weather / the **fine** weather*
2.5.14	-ful	careful:	*the **careful** driver/ the **good** driver*
2.5.15	-ible	horrible:	*the **horrible** music/ the **sweet** music*
2.5.16	-ic	athletic:	*the **athletic** boy / the **small** boy*

(contd)

2.5 (contd)

2.5.17	-id	horrid:	the **horrid** film / the **long** film
2.5.18	-ious	hilarious:	the **hilarious** joke/the **funny** joke
2.5.19	-ish	reddish:	the **reddish** glow / the **red** glow
2.5.20	-ive	active:	the **active** mouse / the **brown** mouse
2.5.21	-less	careless:	the **careless** mistake/ the **silly** mistake
2.5.22	-ous	famous:	the **famous** man / the **thin** man
2.5.23	-some	handsome:	the **handsome** boy /the **kind** boy
2.5.24	-y	funny:	the **funny** joke/ the **bad** joke

2.5.1 -able

(-able added to verbs, shown in brackets)

test words: ***capable, lovable***

This ending comes from French

acceptable	(accept)	enjoyable	(enjoy)
comfortable	(comfort)	lovable	(love)
believable	(believe)	noticeable	(notice)
changeable	(change)	reliable	(rely)
enforceable	(enforce)		

(not directly formed from verbs)

abominable	explicable
capable	impeccable
educable	inscrutable
inevitable	

2.5.2 -al

(formed directly from nouns, shown in brackets)

test words: ***final, brutal***

This ending comes from French

accidental	(accident)	magical	(magic)
basal	(base)	modal	(mode)
bridal	(bride)	musical	(music)
brutal	(brute)	oriental	(orient)
clinical	(clinic)	tidal	(tide)
conical	(cone)	tonal	(tone)

(contd)

2.5.2 (contd)

digital	(digit)	topical	(topic)
fanatical	(fanatic)	tribal	(tribe)
fatal	(fate)	tropical	(tropic)
logical	(logic)	universal	(universe)

(-al ending – not directly formed from a noun)

actual	fungal	marital	practical	vital
annual	glottal	mental	principal	vocal
comical	individual	municipal	regal	
conjugal	legal	natal	renal	
dental	lethal	papal	royal	
equal	local	penal	skeletal	
final	loyal	plural	usual	
frugal	manual	potential	venal	

2.5.3 -an, -ian

agrarian	Christian	mammalian	sectarian
African	Georgian	Norman	urban
American	German	pagan	utilitarian
Asian	Gregorian	reptilian	vegan
avian	human	Roman	Victorian

2.5.4 -ant

(these adjectives are generally formed from -ance nouns. See 2.5.3)

test words: ***instant, vacant
informant, ignorant***

This ending comes from French

abundant	flamboyant	redundant
assistant	fragrant	reluctant
blatant	ignorant	significant
brilliant	informant	vacant
defiant	instant	vagrant
elegant	mutant	vibrant
extravagant	petulant	

2.5.5 -ar

columnar	regular
liar	similar
lumbar	singular
lunar	solar
particular	titular
polar	velar
popular	

2.5.6 -ary

This ending comes from French; the modern French equivalent is -aire (binaire, nécessaire)

binary	sanctuary
exemplary	solitary
honorary	stationary
military	temporary
necessary	unitary
ordinary	voluntary

2.5.7 -ate

Unstressed and pronounced /ət/

accurate	fortunate
adequate	incarnate
affectionate	intricate
corporate	obdurate
delicate	temperate
desperate	

NOTE:
definite *– this word is often misspelled as definate, however; the root is "finite"(see Teaching Word Structure, page 28)*

The adjectives below have the same spelling as their related verbs but are distinguished by pronunciation; the adjective ending is unstressed and is pronounced /ət/, while the verb ending is stressed and is pronounced

/ɛɪt/.

advocate	associate	duplicate	moderate
articulate	certificate	elaborate	predicate
animate	coordinate	estimate	separate
aggregate	correlate	expatriate	subordinate
appropriate	delegate	graduate	syndicate
approximate	deliberate	intimate	

2.5.8 -en

This ending comes from Old English

flaxen
golden
leaden
wooden

2.5.9 -ent

(these adjectives are generally formed from -ence nouns. See 2.5.4)

test words: ***confident, different***

This ending comes from French

absent	corpulent	imminent	persistent
abstinent	decadent	impudent	present
affluent	deficient	insolent	prominent
apparent	dependent	intelligent	reverent
belligerent	despondent	intermittent	silent
beneficent	different	iridescent	solvent
benevolent	eloquent	latent	strident
clement	eminent	lenient	sufficient
coherent	excellent	magnificent	turbulent
competent	fervent	negligent	urgent
confident	fluent	obedient	violent
convenient	fraudulent	opulent	virulent

2.5.10 -eous

This ending comes from French

advantageous	gaseous	miscellaneous
aqueous	gorgeous	nauseous
beauteous	herbaceous	outrageous
bounteous	heterogeneous	piteous
contemporaneous	hideous	righteous
courteous	homogeneous	simultaneous
erroneous	igneous	spontaneous
extraneous	instantaneous	subterraneous

2.5.11 -er

This is the "comparative adjective ending" for one-syllable words, and two-syllable words ending in Consonant + y (easy > easier).

It is used to make comparisons between two items:
The **older** boy (of two)
This house is **bigger** than that one
My **younger** brother (of two)

And to express the concept "more" / "less" of something:
I want to do **better**, grow **older**, feel **younger**, become **fitter;** The world's getting **smaller.** Here the comparison is with the "status quo".

Use **"more"** with longer adjectives:
more interesting; more exciting, more impressive

bigg**er**	fast**er**	loud**er**	slimm**er**
brav**er**	fatt**er**	luck**ier**	small**er**
clean**er**	funn**ier**	mean**er**	smart**er**
cold**er**	fuss**ier**	nast**ier**	sweet**er**
cool**er**	grand**er**	old**er**	tall**er**
dark**er**	happ**ier**	pal**er**	tid**ier**
deep**er**	hard**er**	quiet**er**	weak**er**
dirt**ier**	hott**er**	rud**er**	wett**er**
eas**ier**	lat**er**	sharp**er**	young**er**
empt**ier**	light**er**	short**er**	

2.5.12 -est

This is the "superlative" adjective ending" for one-syllable words, and two-syllable words ending in consonant + y (easy > easiest).

It is used to make comparisons between more than two items:

The **oldest** boy (of three or more)
This house is the **biggest** of all
My **youngest** child (of three or more)
And to express the concept "most" / "least" of something.

Use **"most"** with longer adjectives:
most interesting, most exciting, most impressive

biggest	fastest	loudest	slimmest
bravest	fattest	luckiest	smallest
cleanest	funniest	meanest	smartest
coldest	fussiest	nastiest	sweetest
coolest	grandest	oldest	tallest
darkest	happiest	palest	tidiest
deepest	hardest	quietest	weakest
dirtiest	hottest	rudest	wettest
easiest	latest	sharpest	youngest
emptiest	lightest	shortest	

For both -er and -est, spelling rules for adding suffixes beginning with a vowel apply. The following are examples with references to the general rules part of this section.

neater/est	**1.1.5**	bigger/est	**1.1.1**
cooler/est	*add to stem*	sadder/est	*doubling rule*
fainter/est	**1.1.4**	whiter/est	**1.2.1**
grander/est	*add to root*	paler/est	*drop e*
easier/est			
fussier/est	**1.3.1**		
	-y rule		

2.5.13 -ern

| eastern |
| modern |
| northern |
| southern |
| western |

2.5.14 -ful

(add -ful to nouns, shown in brackets)

test words: ***hopeful, careful***

beautiful	(beauty)	joyful	(joy)
careful	(care)	masterful	(master)
fateful	(fate)	mouthful	(mouth)
forceful	(force)	peaceful	(peace)
graceful	(grace)	wonderful	(wonder)
hopeful	(hope)		

(others)

| bashful |
| forgetful |
| grateful |
| mournful |

2.5.15 -ible

(-ible added to verbs, shown in brackets)

test words: ***horrible, terrible***

This ending comes from French

comprehensible	(comprehend)
corruptible	(corrupt)
divisible	(divide)
permissible	(permit)

(not directly formed from verbs)

compatible	legible
credible	possible
edible	responsible
horrible	terrible
intelligible	visible
invincible	

2.5.16 -ic

Formed from nouns (shown in brackets).

test words: ***artistic, domestic***

This ending comes from French; the modern French equivalent is -ique (artistique, athlétique)

anaemic	(anaemia)	idiotic	(idiot)
artistic	(artist)	magnetic	(magnet)
athletic	(athlete)	manic	(mania)
basic	(base/basis)	myopic	(myopia)
cubic	(cube)	neurotic	(neurosis)
diabetic	(diabetes)	operatic	(opera)
domestic	(domesticity)	organic	(organ)
dramatic	(drama)	patriotic	(patriotism/patriot)
electric	(electricity)	sadistic	(sadism/sadist)
energetic	(energy)	scientific	(science)
erotic	(eroticism)	strategic	(strategy)
euphoric	(euphoria)	sympathetic	(sympathy)
fantastic	(fantasy)	synthetic	(synthesis)
heroic	(hero)	telescopic	(telescope)
historic	(history)	terrific	(terror)
horrific	(horror)		

(not directly formed from nouns)

acoustic	frenetic
Atlantic	optic
chronic	pathetic
comic	rheumatic
exotic	static
frantic	

2.5.17 -id

(almost all words ending in -id are adjectives)

test words: ***timid, solid***

This ending comes from French; the modern French equivalent is -ide (candide, placide, rapide, timide)

arid	languid	rigid
avid	livid	solid
candid	lurid	sordid
fetid	morbid	stolid
flaccid	pallid	stupid
florid	placid	tepid
frigid	putrid	timid
horrid	rabid	torrid
intrepid	rapid	vapid

2.5.18 -ious

This ending comes from French; the modern French equivalent is -ieux (mystérieux, réligieux)

acrimonious	harmonious	propitious
cautious	hilarious	religious
ceremonious	ingenious	sacrilegious
conscious	insidious	sanctimonious
contagious	laborious	sententious
contentious	litigious	serious
copious	mysterious	spacious
curious	obvious	spurious
delicious	parsimonious	tedious
devious	precarious	tendentious
dubious	pretentious	various
fastidious	previous	victorious

2.5.19 -ish

babyish	reddish
bluish	sluggish
fattish	snobbish
hellish	stylish

2.5.20 -ive

Formed from verbs (shown in brackets).

test words: ***active, massive***

active	(act)	extensive	(extend)
adhesive	(adhere)	responsive	(respond)
comparative	(compare)	sensitive	(sense)
consultative	(consult)		

(not directly formed from verbs)

aggressive	fugitive	negative	positive
festive	massive	passive	vindictive

2.5.21 -less

(add -less to nouns, shown in brackets)

airless	(air)	noiseless	(noise)
blameless	(blame)	peerless	(peer)
careless	(care)	sleepless	(sleep)
clueless	(clue)	spineless	(spine)
homeless	(home)	stateless	(state)
hopeless	(hope)	timeless	(time)
loveless	(love)	tuneless	(tune)
luckless	(luck)		

(others)

gormless	hapless	ruthless

2.5.22 -ous

Formed from nouns (shown in brackets).

test words: ***ridiculous, tremendous, instantaneous, heterogeneous precarious, curious***

courageous	(courage)	perilous	(peril)
humorous	(humour)	ridiculous	(ridicule)
jealous	(jealousy)	vacuous	(vacuum)
marvellous	(marvel)	zealous	(zeal)
outrageous	(outrage)		

(not directly formed from nouns)

callous	parlous
fatuous	populous
gorgeous	presumptuous
heinous	scurrilous
impetuous	specious
meticulous	tremendous

2.5.23 -some

bothersome	irksome
gruesome	lonesome
handsome	winsome

2.5.24 -y/ly

(Formed from nouns or verbs: fun, bog, smell, laze etc.).

test words: **noisy, lucky**

angry	creepy	hazy	noisy
boggy	easy	hearty	scary
brawny	faulty	hungry	smelly
buttery	funny	lazy	spooky
crazy	greedy	lucky	sugary

(-y ending – not directly formed from another word)

clumsy	silly
happy	steady
merry	ugly
pretty	weary
ready	

(Formed from nouns/verbs ending in -le. Replace -le with -ly).

bubbly	(bubble)	giggly	(giggle)
cuddly	(cuddle)	prickly	(prickle)
dimply	(dimple)	straggly	(straggle)
drizzly	(drizzle)	tickly	(tickle)
fiddly	(fiddle)	wobbly	(wobble)
freckly	(freckle)		

Forming Adverbs from Adjectives   2.6

Just as adjectives relate to nouns, adverbs relate to verbs.

The **graceful** dancer / The **tall** dancer (the + adjective + noun)

She dances **gracefully** / He sits **quietly** (he/she + verb + adverb)

Very often, adverbs give more information about the way in which something is done (for example, **carefully, clumsily, badly**). Most adverbs are formed from their corresponding adjectives and the most common suffix for adverbs of this kind is **-ly**.

2.6.1 Forming Adverbs by simply adding – ly

to adjectives ending in a consonant letter other than -y or -c – including adjectives ending in **-ant, -ent, -al, -id, -ous, -ive, -ar, less** and **some**: for more examples see adjective endings, page 262.

test words: **quickly, silently, fatally, mentally**
badly, sadly

---

bad**ly** bright**ly** cheap**ly** crisp**ly** fair**ly** kind**ly** light**ly** loud**ly** mild**ly**

month**ly** odd**ly** poor**ly** proud**ly** quick**ly** quiet**ly** sweet**ly** tight**ly**

blat**antly** brilli**antly** eleg**antly** inst**antly** vac**antly** vibr**antly**

flu**ently** intellig**ently** obedi**ently** pres**ently** sil**ently** urg**ently** viol**ently**

cand**idly** morb**idly** plac**idly** rap**idly** rig**idly** stup**idly** tim**idly**

call**ously** jeal**ously** meticul**ously** peril**ously** ridicul**ously** zeal**ously**

act**ively** aggress**ively** extens**ively** fest**ively** pass**ively** posit**ively**

popul**arly** regul**arly**

blame**lessly** care**lessly** pain**lessly** ruth**lessly** spine**lessly**

hand**somely** win**somely**

> **Note: adjectives ending in -l will have double l when -ly is added**
>
> brut**ally** digit**ally** equ**ally** fat**ally** fin**ally** tid**ally** trib**ally** usu**ally**
>
> beauti**fully** care**fully** force**fully** grace**fully** ment**ally** peace**fully** power**fully**

2.6.2 Forming Adverbs from Adjectives ending in –y
(see general suffix rule, 1.3.1, page 233)

test words: ***lazily, happily***

angry	+	ly	>	angr**ily**
crazy	+	ly	>	craz**ily**
easy	+	ly	>	eas**ily**
greedy	+	ly	>	greed**ily**
happy	+	ly	>	happ**ily**
hearty	+	ly	>	heart**ily**
lucky	+	ly	>	luck**ily**
lucky	+	ly	>	luck**ily**
merry	+	ly	>	merr**ily**
necessary	+	ly	>	necessar**ily**
noisy	+	ly	>	nois**ily**
ready	+	ly	>	read**ily**
scary	+	ly	>	scar**ily**
shabby	+	ly	>	shabb**ily**
steady	+	ly	>	stead**ily**
temporary	+	ly	>	temporar**ily**
voluntary	+	ly	>	voluntar**ily**
weary	+	ly	>	wear**ily**

2.6.3 Forming Adverbs from Adjectives ending in silent -e
(see general suffix rule, 1.2.2, page 231)

test words: ***safely, lately***

brav**e**	+	ly	=	brav**ely**
fin**e**	+	ly	=	fin**ely**
lat**e**	+	ly	=	lat**ely**
nic**e**	+	ly	=	nic**ely**
pur**e**	+	ly	=	pur**ely**

(contd)

2.6.3 (contd)

rude	+	ly	=	rude**ly**
safe	+	ly	=	safe**ly**
sane	+	ly	=	sane**ly**
severe	+	ly	=	severe**ly**
sole	+	ly	=	sole**ly**
sore	+	ly	=	sore**ly**
sure	+	ly	=	sure**ly**
wide	+	ly	=	wide**ly**
wise	+	ly	=	wise**ly**

2.6.4 Forming Adverbs from Adjectives ending in -le
Change -le to -ly
The integrity of the -ly adverb ending should be maintained, so it is better not to teach the replacement of "e" with "y".

test words: ***simply, gently***

ample	+	ly	>	amp**ly**
comfortab**le**	+	ly	>	comfortab**ly**
feeb**le**	+	ly	>	feeb**ly**
gent**le**	+	ly	>	gent**ly**
horrib**le**	+	ly	>	horrib**ly**
humb**le**	+	ly	>	humb**ly**
nimb**le**	+	ly	>	nimb**ly**
nob**le**	+	ly	>	nob**ly**
possib**le**	+	ly	>	possib**ly**
probab**le**	+	ly	>	probab**ly**
sensib**le**	+	ly	>	sensib**ly**
simp**le**	+	ly	>	simp**ly**
sing**le**	+	ly	>	sing**ly**
suitab**le**	+	ly	>	suitab**ly**
terrib**le**	+	ly	>	terrib**ly**

2.6.5 Forming Adverbs from Adjectives ending in -ic
Add -ally

For more examples, see Adjectives, 2.5.16, page 271.

test words: ***historically, artistically***

artis**tic**	>	artistic**ally**
bas**ic**	>	basic**ally**
com**ic**	>	comic**ally**
domes**tic**	>	domestic**ally**
elect**ric**	>	electric**ally**
energe**tic**	>	energetic**ally**
fantas**tic**	>	fantastic**ally**
fran**tic**	>	frantic**ally**
horri**fic**	>	horrific**ally**
terri**fic**	>	terrific**ally**

Exception: public + ly = ***publicly***

3   Prefixes

Prefixes are units of sound or letters which are added to the beginning of
words. Those that were the earliest imports from Latin have become part
of the stem, and cannot be removed. For example *forlorn, irrigation*.
Prefixes do not change the grammatical function of words, but alter or
modify their meaning. For example, **unkind** has the opposite sense to
kind, and **disregard** has the opposite sense to **regard**.

Most prefixes have been absorbed into English though Latin. They were
Latin prepositions (words that refer to the position of something – *in, out*
etc). Gradually, many Latin preposition prefixes have become modified to
assimilate with the first sound of the root word, and this is reflected in the
spelling. For example, the preposition **ad**, when prefixed to **count,** **front**,
and claim results in **account, affront** and **acclaim**.

3.1   Negative Prefixes

3.1.1 in- (Latin)

These words are all adjectives;
they can be changed to adverbs by adding -ly (see page 275).
the prefix means **not**

inaccessible	indirect	infallible
inaccurate	indiscreet	innocuous
inactive	indispensable	innumerable

(contd)

3.1.1 (contd)

inadequate	indomitable	inoperable
inappropriate	inedible	inordinate
inarticulate	ineffable	inorganic
incapable	ineligible	insane
incomprehensible	inept	insecure
inconsistent	inestimable	insincere
incorrect	inexpensive	insomnia
independent	inexplicable	insupportable
indifferent	inextricable	invisible

when in- is prefixed to a word beginning with "n", there will be double "n": innumerable.

3.1.2 im-

test words: ***immoral, immature***

*From Latin **in**, assimilated to initial **m, p** and initial **b**, the prefix means **not***

imbalance	impassable	impolite
immaterial	impatient	impolitic
immature	impeccable	imponderable
immobile	impecunious	impossible
immoral	impenitent	impotent
immortal	impermeable	impractical
immune	impersonal	impregnable
immutable	impervious	improper
impartial	impious	impure

when im- is prefixed to a word beginning with, there will be double "m": immature

3.1.3 ir- (from Latin in-)

test words: ***irregular, irrational***

*from Latin **in**, assimilated to initial **r***

irrational	irrelevant	irrespective
irreconcilable	irreparable	irresponsible
irrecoverable	irreplaceable	irretrievable
irredeemable	irrepressible	irreverent
irreducible	irreproachable	irreversible
irrefutable	irresistible	irrevocable
irregular	irresolute	

as ir- is prefixed to a word beginning with "r", there will be double "r": irregular.

3.1.4 il (from Latin in-)

test words: ***illegal, illegible***

*From Latin **in**, assimilated to initial **l***

illegal	illimitable
illegible	illiterate
illiberal	illogical
illicit	

3.1.5 un-

*This prefix also means **not** when prefixed to adjectives*

unaccountable	unconscionable	unimpeachable	unsavoury
unaffected	undoubted	unjust	unsightly
unassailable	uneasy	unkempt	unspeakable
unattached	unemployed	unkind	unsung
unavailing	unexceptional	unmitigated	unsteady
unaware	unfriendly	unnatural	untrue
unbidden	unfortunate	unnecessary	unwell
uncommon	unfounded	unpopular	unwieldy
uncompromising	unguarded	unreliable	unwilling
unconscious	unhappy	unruly	unwitting

when un- is prefixed to a word beginning with "n", there will be double "n": unnatural.

*When prefixed to verbs it means **to reverse** an action*

uncover	unpick
undo	unravel
unhinge	untie
unpack	

3.1.6 dis-

test words: **discomfort, dislike, dissolve, dissuade**

This prefix is also originally from Latin; it usually has a more active meaning than **not**, more like **stop**

disability	disconsolate	disgrace	disorder
disaccord	discontent	disgruntle	dispel
disadvantage	discontinue	disgust	displace
disaffect	discord	disharmony	displease
disagree	discount	dishonest	disown
disallow	discourage	disillusion	disquiet
disappear	discover	disingenuous	dissimilar
disappoint	discredit	disintegrate	dissidence
disapprove	discrepant	disinterest	dissipate
disarray	disease	dislike	dissolve
disbelieve	disenchant	dislocate	dissuade
discard	disenfranchise	disloyal	distraction
disclaim	disengage	dismiss	distress
disclose	disentangle	dismantle	distrust
discolour	disfavour	dismember	disturb
discomfort	disfigure	dismount	disused
disconnect	disgorge	disobedient	

when dis- is prefixed to a word beginning with "s", there will be a double "s": dissimilar

3.1.7 mis-

This prefix is from Middle English; it means **wrongly**, **improperly** or **badly**.

misadventure	misdeed	mismatch
misadvise	misdemeanour	misnomer
misalign	misfire	mispronounce
misapply	misfit	misread
misbelieve	misfortune	misshapen
miscarry	misgiving	misspell
mischief	mishap	misspend
misconception	misinform	mistake
misconduct	misjudge	mistrust
miscreant	mislay	misunderstand
miscue	mislead	misuse

When mis- is prefixed to a word beginning with "s", there will be a double "s": misspell.

3.1.8 anti

this prefix is from Greek; it means **opposed to, against.**

antibiotic	antipathy
antibody	antiseptic
anticlimax	antisocial
antidote	

3.1.9 contra-

*this prefix, from Latin, means **against**, **opposite**.*

contraband	contraindicate	contrary
contraceptive	contraposition	contravene
contradict	contraption	contravention
contradistinction		

3.2   Prefixes Derived from Latin cum- (with)

*These prefixes have a sense of **together**, **community** or **grouping**.*

3.2.1 com- (before p, b and m)

combine	compartment
command	compassion
commemorate	compatible
commiserate	compatriot
communicate	compendium
community	compete
companion	compound
compare	compromise

com-, used before "m", gives double "m" (commemorate).

3.2.2 col- (before l)
                                        test word: ***colleague***

collaborate	college
collage	collide
collate	collocate
collateral	colloquial
colleague	collusion

3.2.3 cor- (before r)

correlate
correspond
corroborate

3.2.4 con-

concert	conform
conclave	confraternity
concoct	conglomerate
concord	congregate
concur	congress
condolence	congruence
confederacy	conjoin
conference	conjugal
confide	conjugate
confluence	consonant

Prefixes Derived from Latin ad-   3.3

*These prefixes have the sense of **movement towards** or **change in state**.*

3.3.1 ad-

test words: ***adjective, adjust, address, addition***

adapt	adjoin	adopt
addition	adjunct	advance
addict	adjust	advantage
address	adjudge	advent
adduce	adjure	adventure
adduct	administer	adverb
adequate	admire	adverse
adjacent	admit	admonish
adjective	admonish	advocate

When ad- is prefixed to stems beginning with "d", there will be a double "d": addition.

The assimilation of ad- to the following consonant results in doubling of the consonant. Omitting to double the consonant is a common spelling error:

3.3.2 ac- (before c, k and qu)

test words: ***accident, success, acquire, acquit***

accelerate	acclimatise	account	acquaint
accent	accommodate	accredit	acquiesce
accept	accompany	accrue	acquire
access	accomplice	accumulate	acquit
accessory	accomplish	accurate	
accident	accord	accuse	
acclaim	accost	accustom	

3.3.3 af- (before f)

affable	affix
affair	afflict
affect	affluent
affection	afford
affiliate	affray
affinity	affront
affirm	

3.3.4 an- (before n)

annex	announce
annihilate	annoy
annotate	annul

3.3.5 ap- (before p)

test words: ***appear, appeal***

appal	appendage	appraise
apparatus	appendix	appreciate
apparel	appertain	apprehend
apparent	appetite	apprentice
apparition	applaud	approach
appeal	apply	appropriate
appear	appoint	approve
appease	apposition	approximate

3.3.6 ar- (before r)

arraign
arrange
array
arrest
arrive

3.3.7 as- (before s)

assail	assist
assault	assize
assemble	associate
assent	assonance
assess	assort
asset	assuage
assiduous	assume
assign	assure
assimilate	

3.3.8 at- (before t)

attach	attest
attack	attire
attain	attorney
attempt	attract
attend	attribute
attention	attune

3.3.9 ag- (before g)

agglomerate	aggregate
aggrandise	aggression
aggravate	aggrieve

3.4   Prefixes Meaning "Before"

3.4.1 pre-

preamble	predecease	prefix	prerogative
prearrange	predilection	prejudge	presage
precaution	predisposition	prejudice	prescience
precede	predominant	premature	presuppose
preclude	pre-eminent	premise	prevent
precognition	pre-empt	premonition	previous
preconception	preface	preoccupation	
precursor	prefect	prepare	
predate	preference	preposition	

3.4.2 fore-

test words: ***forehead, forecast***

forearm	forehead	foresight
foreboding	forelock	forestall
forecast	foreman	foretaste
forefather	forename	forethought
forego	foremost	forewarn
foreground	foreshorten	foreword

3.4.3 ante-

antecedent	antenatal
ante-date	ante-room
antediluvian	

3.5   Other Prefixes

3.5.1 al -

*This prefix means **all***
When "all" is used as a prefix, one "l" is dropped.

albeit	also
almighty	although
almost	altogether
already	

3.5.2 ambi-

*This prefix means **on both sides** or **two-sided***

ambidextrous	ambiguity
ambient	ambivalent

3.5.3 bi- and tri-

*These prefixes from Latin mean **two** and **three***
(quad- = 4, quin- = 5, sex- = 6, sept- = 7, oct- = 8, non- = 9 and dec- = 10)

biceps	bilateral
bicycle	binary
bipolar	binocular
biennial	binomial
bifurcate	biped
bigamy	bisect

triangle	trilogy
tribunal	trimester
trice	trinity
tricolour	trinomial
tricycle	triple
trident	triplet
triennial	triplicate
trifoliate	tripod
trigonometry	trireme
trilateral	triptych

3.5.4 circum-

*This prefix, from Latin, means **around/about***

circumambulate	circumference	circumscribe
circumcise	circumflex	circumspect
circumnavigate	circumstance	circumlocution

3.5.5 de-

*This prefix, from Latin, means **down/away/removal***

debar	decompose	deject	describe
debase	decompress	demoralise	
debilitate	deduct	denounce	
debrief	defame	depart	
decalcify	default	depend	
decapitate	defend	deploy	
deceive	deflate	deport	
declare	deform	deride	
decline	degrade	descend	
decode	dehydrate	deviate	

3.5.6 ex-

*This prefix, from Latin, means **out of***

exasperate	exotic
exclude	expatriate
excruciate	expel
excuse	expire
exhume	explode
exile	express
exit	external
exodus	extol
exonerate	exude
exorcise	

3.5.7 extra-

*This prefix, from Latin, means **beyond***

extraction	extraneous	extrasensory
extracurricular	extraordinary	extrapolate
extraterrestrial	extramarital	extravagant

3.5.8 for-

test words: ***forgive, forget***

this prefix, from Old English, has a range of meanings expressing **rejection**, **warding off** *or* **exclusion**

forbear	forfeit
forbid	forlorn
forget	forgive
forswear	

3.5.9 ful-

When ful- is used as a prefix, one "l" is dropped.

fulfil
fulsome

3.5.10 hetero-

This prefix, from Greek, means **different.**

heterodox
heterogeneous
heterosexual

3.5.11 homo-

This prefix, from Greek, means **same**

homogeneous
homograph
homonym
homophone
homosexual

3.5.12 inter-

This prefix, from Latin means **among/between**

interact	interconnect	international
interbreed	interface	interpret
intercede	interfere	interrogate
intercept	interlace	intersection
interchange	intermediate	intervene
intercom	intermittent	interview
interrupt	internal	

3.5.13 post-

*This prefix, from Latin, means **after**, **behind***

posterior	post-mortem
postgraduate	postpone
posthumous	postscript

3.5.14 pro-

*This prefix, from Latin, means **for**, **forth***

proceed	procreate	progress
process	produce	promote
procession	product	provide

3.5.15 re-

*This prefix, from Latin, means **back**, **again***

readjust	recompose	reopen
reapply	recur	repeat
rearrange	redress	retrieve
rebuild	reduce	revise
recall	regain	revive
receive	regress	rewind
recommence	relax	

3.5.16 sub-

*This prefix, from Latin, means **under***

sub-aquatic	sublime	subsoil
subconscious	submarine	substance
subcontinent	submerge	substitute
subcontract	submit	subsume
subdivide	subordinate	subterranean
subdue	subscribe	sub-terrestrial
sub-editor	subservient	subtract
subject	subsidence	suburb
subjective	subsidy	subversive
subjugate	subsist	subway

3.5.17 super-

*this prefix, from Latin, means **over***

superb	superlative	superpower
superficial	supermarket	superstition
superhuman	supernatural	supervise
superintendent	supernova	

3.5.18 sym- (assimilated form of syn-)

*this prefix, from Greek, means **together** it is the assimilated form of syn, which becomes sym before **m**, **p** or **b***

symbiosis	symphonic
symbol	symphony
symmetry	symposium
sympathetic	symptom

When sym- is prefixed to stems beginning with "m", there will be a double "m": symmetry

3.5.19 syn-

*this prefix, from Greek, means **together***

synapse	synod
synchromesh	synonym
synchronise	synonymous
syndicate	synopsis
syndrome	synthetic

3.5.20 trans-

*this prefix, from Latin, means **across***

transaction	transform	transmit
transatlantic	transgress	transparent
transcendental	transient	transplant
transcribe	transit	transport
transfer	translate	transverse

4   Use of Apostrophe

4.1   Apostrophe for Abbreviation

test words: ***can't, don't***

It is very common in speech, and in informal written English, to contract certain phrases.

cannot > ***can't***
did not > ***didn't***

The process for written English is twofold:

1.   The phrase is written as **one word**
2.   An apostrophe (') is used in place of the omitted letter(s).

4.1.1 Abbreviation with not

the "o" of not is omitted

are not	>	aren't (***no*** is omitted)
cannot	>	can't
could not	>	couldn't
did not	>	didn't
do not	>	don't
had not	>	hadn't
has not	>	hasn't
have not	>	haven't
is not	>	isn't
might not	>	mightn't
must not	>	mustn't
should not	>	shouldn't
was not	>	wasn't
were not	>	weren't
would not	>	wouldn't
will not	>	won't (irregular)

4.1.2 Abbreviation with will

The "wi" of will is omitted

I will	>	I'll
you will	>	you'll
he will	>	he'll
she will	>	she'll
it will	>	it'll
we will	>	we'll
they will	>	they'll
who will	>	who'll

4.1.3 Abbreviation with the verb to have

The "ha" of have/has is omitted

I have	>	I've
you have	>	you've
he has	>	he's
she has	>	she's
it has	>	it's
we have	>	we've
they have	>	they've
who has	>	who's
could have	>	could've
would have	>	would've
should have	>	should've

4.1.4 Abbreviation with the verb to be

I am	>	I'm
you are	>	you're
he is	>	he's
she is	>	she's
it is	>	it's
we are	>	we're
they are	>	they're
who is	>	who's

Notes:

1.   The abbreviated forms of *he/she/it who **is**,* and *he/she/it/ who **has*** are the same (***he's, she's, it's, who's***)

2.   It is important to distinguish ***who's*** *(who is/who has)* from whose (***whose*** *is that pen?) (see possessive pronouns no. 5 in this section)*

3.   It is important to distinguish ***they're*** (***they are***) from ***their*** (***their car***) and ***there*** (***She went there***) *(see possessive pronouns)*

4.   It is important to distinguish ***it's*** (the abbreviated form of ***it has*** and ***it is***) from its (it hurt ***its paw***) *(see possessive pronouns)*

5.   It is important to distinguish ***you're*** (***you are***) from ***your*** (***your house***) *(see possessive pronouns)*

6.   The abbreviated forms ***could have, would have*** and ***should have*** (***could've, would've*** and ***should've***) are frequently (and wrongly) thought to be ***could of, would of*** and ***should of**.* This error is also evident in spoken English if the "o" in ***of*** is given its stressed sound.

4.2   Apostrophe to Denote "Possession"

test words: ***boy's, girl's, dogs', cats'***

The use of apostrophe for "possession" causes much confusion, the greatest of which seems to relate to the plural suffix -s (*"Should the apostrophe go before the -s or after it?"*)

In fact the -s is a complete "red herring" – there is no need to pay any attention to it.

The "rule", as demonstrated below, is that you put the apostrophe at the end of the word you are focusing on. And if you can hear **-/s/** you add that on afterwards. For example:

If you are writing

•	about a **boy**:	the **boy's** football
•	about a **girl**:	the **girl's** bike
•	about **dogs**:	the **dogs'** leads
•	about **cats**:	the **cats'** tails
•	about the **teacher**:	the **teacher's** pen
•	about a **child**:	the **child's** health
•	about the **teachers**:	the **teachers'** pens
•	about **children**:	the **children's** health
•	about **a man**:	the **man's** hat
•	about **men**:	the **men's** umbrellas
•	about a **city**:	the **city's** cathedral
•	about **cities**:	the **cities'** cathedrals
•	about **James**:	**James's** brother
•	about the **Jones** family:	keeping up with the **Jones's**

Note:

- the apostrophe is never used before the plural suffix -s potatoes, tomatoes (not potatoe's, tomatoe's)
- it should not be used with acronyms: GCSEs (rather than GCSE's) or with dates: the 1970s (rather than the 1970's)

Use and Spelling of Possessive Pronouns   4.3

There is much confusion about the spelling of some of the possessive pronouns – see notes 2, 3, 4 and 5 – Apostrophe for Abbreviation, page 294.

Possessive pronouns fall into the same "sentence slot" as "Determiners" – words such as **the**, **this**, **that**, **those**, **these**, etc. They are always used with a noun (see Nouns on page 234), forming a Noun Phrase

my house
your mother
his work
her car
its kennel
our cat
their clothes

Apostrophes are never used with possessive pronouns. Confusion is caused because apostrophes are associated with possession (see 4.2, page 294).

Their is frequently confused with ***there***. An understanding that ***their*** must be used in a noun phrase should help to clarify this:

Noun Phrase	Verb Phrase (the rest of the sentence)
The cat	sleeps on the bed.
That cat	sleeps on the bed.
My cat	sleeps on the bed.
His black cat	sleeps on the bed.
Their cat	sleeps on the bed.
Their fluffy black cat	sleeps on the bed.

The concept "possession" is not always helpful, especially when more abstract nouns are used: *They lost **their way*** (they didn't really "possess" it) – but ***their*** is correct here, as in *They lost **their cat.***

The use of possessive pronouns can be practised by creating noun phrases for use in sentences:

Possessive Pronoun	Adjective	Noun
my	new	house
your	red	hat
his	hard	work
her	only	son
its	sore	paw
our	summer	holiday
their	kind	invitation

The word **whose** can be used in a similar way, but as a "question" or "interrogative" pronoun:

Whose red hat is this?

(like which, what etc.)

It can also be used to link clauses:
The small boy, **whose** mother I knew at school … etc.

The word lists in the adjective and noun sections can be used to practise creating more abstract noun phrases, for example:

Possessive Pronoun	Adjective(s)	Noun
his	creative	ambition
their	tragic	relationship
her	imminent	arrival
your	loyal	friendship

References

ADAMS, M.J. (1990). *Beginning to Read: Learning and Thinking about Print*. Cambridge, MA: MIT Press.

BRADLEY, L. (1981). The organisation of Motor Patterns for Spelling: an effective remedial-strategy for backward readers. *Developmental Medicine and Child Neurology*, **23**, 83–91.

BRADLEY, L. and BRYANT, P.E. (1983). Categorising Sounds and Learning to Read: A causal connexion. *Nature* **301**, 419–21.

BROOKS, P. (1995). A Comparison of the Effectiveness of Different Teaching Strategies in Teaching Spelling to a Student with Severe Specific Learning Difficulties. *Educational and Child Psychology*, **12**.

BROWN, G.D.A and WATSON, F. (1991). Reading Development in Dyslexia: A Connectionist Approach. In: SNOWLING, M.J. and THOMSON, M. (Eds) *Dyslexia: Integrating Theory and Practice*. London: Whurr. pp. 165–82.

BRUCK, M. (1992). Persistence of Dyslexics' Phonological Awareness Deficits. *Developmental Psychology*, **28** (5), 874–86.

BRYANT, P.E. and BRADLEY, L. (1980). Why Children Sometimes Write Words which they do not Read. In: FRITH U. (Ed.) *Cognitive Processes in Spelling*. London: Academic Press. pp. 355–70.

CARAVOLAS, M., HULME, C. and SNOWLING, M. (2001). The Foundations of Spelling Ability: Evidence from a 3-year Longitudinal Study. *Journal of Memory and Language*, **45**, 751–74.

EHRI, L.C. (1991). The Development of Reading and Spelling in Children: An Overview. In: SNOWLING, M. and THOMSON, M. (Eds) *Dyslexia: Integrating Theory and Practice*. London: Whurr. pp. 63–79.

EHRI, L.C. (1992). Review and Commentary: Stages of spelling development. In: TEMPLETON, S. and BEAR D. (Eds) *Development of Orthographic Knowledge and Foundations of Literacy: A memorial festschrift for Edmund H. Henderson*, pp. 307–32.

EHRI, L., NUNES, S.R., WILLOWS, D.M., SCHUSTER, B.V., YAGHOUB-ZADEH, Z. and SHANAHAN, T. (2001). Phonemic Awareness Instruction Helps Children Learn to Read: Evidence from the National Reading Panel's meta-analysis. *Reading Research Quarterly*, **36**, (3), pp. 250–87.

FRITH, U. (1985). Beneath the Surface of Developmental Dyslexia. In: PATTERSON, K.E., MARSHALL, J.C. and COLTHEART, ?.?. (Eds) *Surface Dyslexia: Neuropsychological and Cognitive Studies of Phonological Reading*. London: Lawrence Erlbaum Associates.

GILLINGHAM, A.M. and STILLMAN, B.U. (1956). *Reading, Spelling and Penmanship*. (5th Edition. New York: Sackett and Wilhelms.

GOSWAMI, U. and BRYANT, P.E. (1990). *Phonological Skills and Learning to Read*. Hove: Lawrence Erlbaum.

HATCHER, P.J., HULME, C. and ELLIS, A.W. (1994). Ameliorating Early Reading Failure by Integrating the Teaching of Reading and Phonological Skills: The Phonological Linkage Hypothesis. *Child Development*, **65**, 41–57.

HULME, C., SNOWLING, M.J. and QUINLAN, P. (1991). Connectionism and Learning to Read: Steps towards a psychologically plausible model. *Reading and Writing*, **3**, 159–68.

MASTERSON, J.J. and APEL, K. (2000). Spelling Assessment: Charting a Path to Optimal Intervention. *Topics in Language Disorders*, **20** (3), 50–65.

MOATS, L. (1994). Assessment of Spelling in Learning Disabilities Research. In: LYON, G.R. (Ed.) *Frames of Reference for Assessment of Learning Disabilities*. Baltimore: York Press. pp. 333–50.

MORRISON, C.M., CHAPPELL, T.D. and ELLIS, A.W. (1997). Age of Acquisition Norms for a Large Set of Object Names and Their Relation to Adult Estimates and Other Variables. *Quarterly Journal of Experimantal Psychology*, **50A** (3), 528–59.

NUNES, T., BRYANT, P. and BINDMAN, M. (1997). Morphological Spelling Strategies: Developmental Stages and Processes. Developmental Psychology, **33**, 637–49.

RACK, J and HATCHER, J. (August 2002). SPELLIT Summary Report. The Dyslexia Institute. www.dyslexia-inst.org.uk/spellitsum.htm

RITTLE-JOHNSON, B. and SIEGLER, R.S. (1999). Learning to Spell: Variability, Choice and Change in Children's Strategy Use. *Child Development*, **70**, 332–48.

SCOTT, C. M., (2000). Principals and Methods of Spelling Instruction: Application for Poor Spellers. *Topics in Language Disorders*, **20** (3), 66–82.

SNOWLING, M.J. (2000). Dyslexia. 2nd Edition. Oxford: Blackwell.

STANOVICH, K.E. and SIEGEL, L.S. (1994). The Phenotypic Performance Profile of Reading-Disabled Children: A regression-based test of the phonological-core variable-difference model. *Journal of Educational Psychology*, **86**, 24–53.

WAGNER, R.K. and TORGESEN, J.K. (1987). The Nature of Phonological Processing and its Causal Role in the Acquisition of Reading Skills. *Psychological Bulletin*, **101**, 191–212.

Bibliograpy

BROOMFIELD, H. and COMBLEY, M. (1997). *Overcoming Dyslexia. A Practical Handbook for the Classroom*. London: Whurr.

CARNEY, E. (1994). *A Survey of English Spelling*. London and New York: Routledge.

COOTES, C. and SIMPSON, S. (1996). Teaching Spelling. In: SNOWLING, M. and STACKHOUSE, J. (Eds) *Dyslexia, Speech and Language*. London: Whurr.

CRYSTAL, D. (1996). *Rediscover Grammar* Revised edition. London: Longman.

Including All Children in the Daily Literacy Hour and Daily Mathematics Lesson. (2002). London: Department for Education and Skills.

NATIONAL LITERACY STRATEGY (1998). *Framework for Teaching*. London: Department for Education and Skills.

POLLOCK, J. and WALLER, E. (1994). *Day-to-Day Dyslexia in the Classroom*. London: Routledge.

REASON, R. and BOOTE, R. (1994). *Helping Children with Reading and Spelling. A Special Needs Manual*. London: Routledge.

Shorter Oxford English Dictionary (2002). Oxford: Oxford University Press.

STEERE, A., PECK C.Z. and KAHN, L. (1988). *Solving Language Difficulties*. Revised Edition. Educators Publishing Service, Inc.

WALTON, M. (1998). *Teaching Reading and Spelling to Dyslexic Children*. London: David Fulton.

Word Index

a 112
abattoir 118
abbey 84, 132
abdicate 260
ability 248
able 175
abolish 262
abominable 264
about 108
above 75
abruptness 250
abscess 156
abseil 80
absence 245
absent 267
absorption 160, 252
abstinence 245
abstinent 267
abundance 243
abundant 265
abuse 94
abyss 70
accelerate 284
accent 171, 284
accept 209, 284
acceptability 248
acceptable 264
access 171, 284
accessory 250, 284
accident 155, 171,
  284
accidental 264
acclaim 284
acclimatise 284
accommodate 284
accommodation
  160
accompany 284
accomplice 284
accomplish 284
accord 284
accost 284
account 284
accredit 284
accrue 284
accrue 97
accumulate 284
accurate 266, 284
accuse 94, 284

accustom 284
ace 155
ache 138
achieve 84
acidity 248
acne 82
acoustic 271
acquaint 284
acquaintance 142
acquiesce 142, 156,
  284
acquire 142, 284
acquit 142, 284
acre 111
acrimonious 272
act 192
acted 225, 255
action 160, 252
active 273
actively 275
activity 248
actor 250
actual 166, 265
adapt 283
add 135
adder 135
addict 283
addition 160, 252,
  283
addle 174
address 283
addressee 245
adduce 283
adduct 283
adequate 266, 283
adhesive 273
adjacent 169, 283
adjective 169, 283
adjoin 169, 283
adjourn 169
adjudge 283
adjudicate 169
adjunct 169, 283
adjure 169, 283
adjust 169, 283
adjutant 169
administer 283
administrate 260
admire 283

admission 161, 251
admit 283
admitted 227
admonish 262, 283
adopt 283
adult 136
adulthood 247
advance 101, 283
advancement 249
advantage 283
advantageous 232,
  268
advent 283
adventure 166, 252,
  283
adverb 283
adversary 244
adverse 283
advertise 261
advice 155
advise 158
advisory 250
advocate 262, 267,
  283
aegis 86
aeon 86
aerate 116
aerial 116
aeroplane 116
aerosol 116
aesthete 85, 86
affable 284
affair 115, 149, 284
affect 149, 210, 284
affection 284
affectionate 266
affiliate 284
affinity 284
affirm 149, 284
affix 170, 284, 284
afflict 149
affluence 245
affluent 267, 284
afford 284
affray 284
affront 284
Afghan 141
African 265
aft 101

after 101, 110
again 78
age 78, 168
agenda 112
agglomerate 285
aggrandise 285
aggravate 262, 267,
  285
aggregate 262, 267,
  285
aggression 161, 251,
  285
aggressive 273
aggressively 275
aggrieve 285
aghast 141
agile 168
agitate 260
agrarian 265
agreeing 232
agriculture 252
aided 226, 255
ail 78, 172
aim 78
aimed 226
air 115, 204
airless 273
aisle 201
alacrity 248
albeit 286
ale 77
algorithm 196
alibi 89
align 145
all 103, 173
allegory 173
allergy 173
alley 84
alligator 173
allot 173
allow 173
allowed 256
allusion 163
almighty 286
almond 101
almost 286
alms 101
alphabet 150
already 286

also 286
altar 111, 210, 244
alter 210
altered 227
although 93, 276
altitude 94
altogether 286
am 66
amanuenses 240
amanuensis 240
amateur 247
amaze 157
amazement 249
ambassador 250
ambidextrous 287
ambient 287
ambiguity 287
ambivalent 287
amble 175
ambulance 243
amend 260
amenity 248
American 265
amoeba 86
amok 76
among 75
amongst 76
amphibian 150
ample 175
amplify 261
amply 277
amuse 94
anaemia 86, 271
anaemic 271
anaemic 86
anaesthetist 86
analyses 240
analysis 240
ancestor 250
anchor 138
ancient 161
and 76, 191
anemone 82
anger 148
angle 148, 174
angrily 276
angry 274
animal 175
animate 262, 267
animosity 248
ankle 175
annex 284
annexe 170

annexes 237
annihilate 284
anniversary 244
annotate 284
announce 284
annoy 109, 284
annoyed 234, 256
annual 265
annul 284
another 75
answer 215
ant 66
antecedent 286
antedate 286
antediluvian 286
antenatal 286
anteroom 286
anthropology 250
antibiotic 282
antibody 282
anticlimax 282
antidote 282
antipathy 282
antique 138
antiseptic 282
antisocial 282
antonym 70
anvil 176
anxiety 148, 159,
    252
anxious 148
any 68, 83
apostle 156
apostrophe 82, 150
apotheoses 240
apotheosis240
appal 103, 284
appalled 229
apparatus 284
apparel 284
apparent 267, 284
apparition 284
appeal 284
appear 113, 284
appeared 256
appease 284
appeasement 249
append 260
appendage 284
appendices 240
appendix 170, 240,
    284
appertain 284

appetite 87, 284
applaud 284
apple 174
apply 284
applying 234
appoint 284
apposition 284
appraise 284
appreciate 260, 284
apprehend 260, 284
apprentice 247, 284
approach 284
appropriate 262,
    267, 284
approve 284
approximate 262,
    267, 284
April 176
apron 146
apt 193
aqueous 268
arabesque 138
arc 207
arch 101
archaeology 86, 138,
    250
arches 237
architect 138
archive 138
ardour 112, 251
are 100
arid 177, 272
ark 100, 207
arm 101
armies 239
armistice 247
armour 112, 251
army 83
arouse 158
arraign 145, 285
arrange 285
array 285
arrest 285
arrive 151, 285
arrogance 243
arrow 92
art 100
Arthur 112
articulate 262, 267
artifice 247
artistic 136, 271
artistically 278
as 158

ascend 156, 260
ascent 285
ash 66
Asian 265
ask 101, 136, 191
askew 94
ass 154
assail 285
assault 285
assemble 285
asses 237
assess 285
asset 285
assiduous 285
assign 145, 285
assimilate 260, 285
assist 285
assistance 243
assistant 265
assize 285
associate 262, 267,
    285
assonance 285
assort 285
assuage 285
assume 285
assure 160, 285
asthma 215
astonish 262
astrology 250
astronaut 105
asylum 88
ate 77, 200
athlete 85
athletic 136, 271
Atlantic 136, 271
attach 165, 285
attack 285
attain 285
attempt 194, 285
attend 285
attention 160, 252,
    285
attest 285
attic 136
attire 285
attitude 94
attorney 84, 285
attract 285
attractiveness 250
attribute 285
attune 285
auction 105

auctioneer 245
audacity 248
augur 112
August 105
aunt 102
Australia 74
Austria 74
author 105, 111
authorise 261
authorship 251
autumn 105, 143
avalanche 162
avarice 247
average 168, 243
aversion 162, 251
avian 265
avid 272
avoid 110
away 79, 178
awful 104
awkward 104
axe 170
axel 170
axiom 170, 247
axis 170
azure 164
babies 239
baboon 132
baby 83
babies 239
babyish 234, 272
back 137
bacon 146
bacteria 241
bacterium 241, 248
bad 66, 131, 134
bade 78
badge 168
badger 168
badly 225, 275
baffle 174
bag 66, 131, 139
bail 78, 200
bait 78
bake 77, 136
baked 257
baker 246
balance 174
bald 103, 193
bale 77, 200
baleful 231
ball 103, 173, 203
ballerina 173

ballet 81
balloon 173
balloted 227
balm 101
ban 66, 131, 144
band 66, 191
bang 66, 147
bangle 148, 174
banish 145, 262
banister 145
banjos 240
bank 66, 136, 191
bankruptcy 244
bap 131
baptism 158
baptize 157
bar 100
barb 101
bard 100
bare 116, 204
bargain 147
bark 100
barley 84
barn 100
baron 177
baronetcy 244
baroque 138
barrister 177
basal 264
base 154
bases 240
bash 75, 159
bashful 270
basic 271
basically 278
basil 158
basis 240
bask 101, 191
basket 101
baste 78
bat 66, 131, 132
batch 166
batches 237
bath 101
bathe 153
baton 133
batten 260
batter 133
batting 225
battle 174
bauble 105
bawl 104, 203
bay 79

bazaar 158
be 81, 200
beach 83, 200
bead 83
beak 83
beam 83
bean 83, 200
bear 116, 204
beat 83
beaten 259
beauteous 268
beautiful 270
beautifully 276
beautify 261
beauty 95
because 74
bed 67, 131, 134
bee 82, 200
beech 82, 200
been 82, 200
beer 113
before 103
beg 67, 131, 139
beggar 244
begging 225
beginning 227
behave 164
behaviour 112, 251
behest 164
behind 89, 164
behold 164
behove 164
beige 80, 164
believable 264
believed 230
bell 173
belligerence 245
belligerent 267
belong 148
Ben 67, 131, 144
bench 195
bend 67, 191
beneficence 245
beneficent 267
benefit 145
benevolent 245, 267
benign 145
bent 67, 191
beret 81, 177
Berkshire 102
berries 239
berry 177, 199
berth 106, 203

Bess 154
best 67
bet 66, 131, 133
betwixt 193
bevelled 229
bias 118
bib 69, 131
bible 175
biceps 287
bicycle 70 287
bid 69, 134
bide 86
biennial 287
bifurcate 287
big 69, 131, 139
bigamist 248
bigamy 287
bigger 224
biggest 224
bike 87, 136
bilateral 287
bile 87
bill 173
billion 180
bin 69, 144
binary 266, 287
bind 89
binding 225
binge 195
bingeing 232
binocular 287
binomial 287
biology 168
biped 287
bipolar 287
bird 106
birth 106, 152, 203
biscuit 71
bisect 287
bit 69, 131, 132
bitch 166
bite 86
bitten 146, 259
bizarre 158
black 137, 185
blade 185
blame 77, 185
blameless 231, 273
blamelessly 275
bland 185, 191
blank 136, 185, 191
blare 116
blast 101, 185

blatant 265
blatantly 275
blaze 78, 157
bleach 83
bleak 83
bleat 83
bled 67
bleeding 226
bleep 82
blend 191
bless 185
blew 197, 202
blind 89, 191
blink 191
bliss 154
blizzard 157
blob 72, 85
block 137
bloke 91
blonde 191
blood 76
bloom 96
blot 82, 185
blotch 166
blotting 225
blow 92
blue 97, 202
bluff 149
bluish 272
blunt 191
blush 159
boar 203
board 105, 203
boast 92
boat 92
Bob 72, 131
bobbin 132
bobble 174
bode 91
bodice 135, 247
bodies 239
body 83, 135
bog 72, 131, 139
boggle 174
boggy 274
bogus 153
boil 110, 172
bold 90, 193
bomb 143
bond 72, 191
bonded 255
bone 91
bonus 153

book 99, 136
booklet 249
boom 96
boon 96
boot 96
booze 97
bop 131
bore 103, 203
bored 203
boredom 231
born 102
bosom 158
boss 154
both 152
bothersome 274
bottle 174
bough 109, 204
bought 106
boulder 93
bound 109
boundary 244
bounteous 268
bouquet 81
bout 109
boutique 138
bow 92, 108, 204
bower 119
bowl 92, 172
box 72, 131, 170
boxes 237
boy 109, 206
boyhood 247
brace 155
bracelet 249
brag 66, 184
braid 79
brain 184
brake 77, 200
bramble 175
bran 66, 184
branch 184, 195, 237
brand 184
brash 159, 184
brass 154, 184
brat 66, 184
brave 78, 184
bravely 231, 276
bravery 246
brawny 274
bread 68, 184
breadth 196
break 79, 184, 200
breakage 243

bream 83
breast 68, 184, 190
breath 68
breathe 153
breech 82
breed 82
brewery 246
briar 118
brick 137
bridal 207, 264
bride 87
bridge 168
bridle 207
brief 84
brigadier 114
bright 88
brightly 275
brilliance 243
brilliant 173, 180, 265
brilliantly 275
brim 69, 184
brine 87
brink 191
brinkmanship 251
brioche 162
bristle 156
Britain 147
British 133
broach 202
broccoli 138
brochure 162
broke 91
broken 146, 259
brooch 202
brood 96
brook 99
broom 96
brother 75, 110, 246
brotherhood 247
brought 106
bruise 98, 158
brunette 246
brush 159
brushed 256
brushes 237
brusque 138
brutal 264
brutality 248
brutally 276
brute 99
bubble 174
bubbly 274

buccaneer 138, 245
buck 137
buckle 174
bud 74, 131, 134
budge 168
budget 168
budgeted 227
buffalo 149
buffaloes 239
buffalos 239
buffer 149
buffet 81, 149
bug 74, 131, 139
buggy 140
bugle 175
build 71
builder 71, 246
building 71
built 71
bulk 193
bull 100, 173
bum 74, 131, 142
bumble 175
bump 75
bun 74, 131, 144
bundle 175
bung 75, 147
bunk 75, 137, 191
bunny 144
buoy 206
burden 107
bureau 93
bureaucracy 74, 244
burglar 107, 111, 244
burglary 244
burlesque 138
burn 107
burnish 262
burp 107
burr 107
burrow 177
burst 107
bury 68, 177, 199
bus 74, 131, 153,
buses 237
bush 159
bushes 237
busiest 233
business 71, 250
busk 75
bust 75
bustle 156

busy 71, 158
but 74, 131, 132, 139
butt 133
butter 133
buttery 274
button 146
buy 90, 201
buzz 157
buzzard 157
by 87, 201
bye 201
byre 118
cab 66, 131, 135
cabaret 81
cabbage 132, 168
cabin 132
cable 175
cache 162
cachet 81, 162
cackle 174
cacophony 150
cadge 168
Caesar 86
caffeine 84
cage 78
cake 136
calcify 261
calcium 248
calculate 260
calculator 250
calendar 111
calf 101
calibre 111
call 173
callous 274
callously 275
calm 101
calves 238
camel 143, 176
camouflage 164
camp 66, 182
campaign 145
can 66, 135, 144
cancel 176
cancelled 229
candid 272
candidly 275
candidness 250
candle 175
cane 77
cannibal 144
canoe 98
canon 145

canvas 208
canvass 208
cap 66, 130, 135
capability 248
capable 264
capacity 248
capillary 244
capitalise 261
captain 147
capture 166, 252
car 100
card 100
care 116
careful 270
carefully 276
careless 273
carelessly 275
cargo 239
cargoes 239
cargos 239
caricature 166, 252
carol 177
carp 101
carpenter 246
carry 83, 177
carrying 234
cart 100
cartridge 168
case 154
cash 66, 159
cashier 114
cask 101
cassette 246
cast 101, 190
castle 101, 156
castor 111
casual 163
cat 66, 132, 135
catalogue 140
catastrophe 82, 150
catch 166
catches 258
category 250
caught 105, 203
cauliflower 74
caution 105
cautious 272
cave 78
cavern 147
cease 154, 155
cedar 155
cede 155
ceiling 84, 200, 208,

255
celebrate 155
celebrity 155, 248
cell 155, 208
cellar 111, 155, 208,
    244
cellophane 155
cellos 240
cement 155
cemetery155, 246
census 155
cent 155, 208
centenary 155, 244
centre 111, 155
ceramic 155
cereal 114, 155, 208
ceremonious 272
ceremony 155
certain 106, 147, 155
certainty 252
certificate 155, 262,
    267
certify 155, 261
chafe 78
chain 165
chair 115, 165
chalet 81, 162
chalice 247
chalk 104
chamberlain 147
champagne 162
chance 101
chancellor 250
chandelier 114, 162
change 165
changeable 232, 264
channel 176
chant 165
chaos 138
chap 165
chapel 131
chaplain 147
char 165
character 138
charade 162
charity 248
charlatan 162
charm 165
chart 165
chase 154
chassis 162
chaste 78
chat 165

chateau 93 162
chattel 176
chauffeur 162
chauvinist 162
cheap 165, 200
cheaply 275
cheat 165
cheated 226
check 137, 165, 207
cheek 165
cheep 200
cheer 165
cheese 158, 165
cheetah 113
chef 162
chemist 138, 143
cheque 138, 207
cherish 177, 262
cherry 177
chess 165
chest 165
chestnut 156, 214
chew 97, 165
chic 162
chick 137, 165
chicken 146
chide 87, 165
chief 84
chiefs 238
chieftain 147
child 89, 165
childhood 247
chill 165
chimney 84
chin 69, 165
Chinese 246
chink 165
chip 165
chisel 176
chit 165
chivalry 162
chive 165
choice 110, 155
choir 118, 138, 141
choke 91, 165
choose 97, 158
choosing 230
chop 165
chore 103, 165
chorus 138, 153
chosen 146, 259
chow 165
Christian 265

Christine 138
Christmas 138
Christopher 138
chronic 271
chronicle 138
chuck 137
chuckle 174
chug 165
chum 165
chunk 165, 191
church 107, 165
churches 237
churn 107, 165
chute 209
chutney 84
cider 155
cigar 155
cigarette 246
cinder 155
cinema 112, 155
cinnamon 144, 155
circle 106, 155
circuit 71, 155
circumambulate 287
circumcise 261, 287
circumference 155, 287
circumflex 287
circumlocution 287
circumnavigate 287
circumscribe 287
circumspect 287
circumstance 287
circumstantial 160
circus 106, 155
cistern 155
cite 155
cities 239
citizen 155
citric 155
citrus 153
city 83, 133, 155
civic 155
civil 155
claimed 256
clam 66, 185
clamp 185, 192
clan 66
clap 66, 185
clapped 224
clapper 224
clapping 224
clarify 261

clash 159, 185
clasp 185, 190
class 154, 185
classify 261
clause 105
claw 104, 185
clay 79, 185
clean 83, 185
cleaned 256
cleaner 246
clear 113
cleft 185, 192
clemency 244
clement 267
clench 185, 195
clerk 102
cliché 162
click 185
cliff 149, 185
climax 170
climb 143
cling 148
clinical 264
clink 185
clip 69, 185
clipping 225
clique 138
Clive 151
cloak 92
clock 137, 185
clog 72
cloister 110
clone 91
close 91, 185
closet 158
closure 163
clot 72
cloth 185
clothe 153
clout 109
clove 91
cloy 109
club 74, 185
cluck 137
clue 97
clueless 273
clump 192
clumsiness 250
clumsy 83, 274
clung 148
clutch 166
coach 92
coal 92, 172

coarse 105, 154, 193
coast 92
coat 92
coax 92
cobble 174
cobra 112
cock 137
cod 134, 135
code 91
coelacanth 86
coffee 149
coffin 149
cog 135
coherence 245
coherent 267
coil 110, 172
coin 110
coke 91
cold 193
colicky 229
collaborate 282
collage 282
collapse 195
collar 111, 244
collate 282
collateral 282
colleague 140, 282
collection 160, 252
college 282
collide 282
collision 163
collocate 282
colloquial 282
collusion 163, 282
Cologne 145
colonel 108, 203, 207
colour 112, 251
column 143
columnar 266
coma 112
comb 143
combine 282
come 75
comely 231
comfortable 264
comfortably 277
comic 136, 271
comical 265
comically 278
coming 230
comma 112
command 282

commando 239
commandoes 239
commandos 239
commemorate 282
commend 260
commentary 244
commentate 260
commiserate 282
commitment 249
committed 227
commotion 160, 252
communicate 282
communication 160
communism 247
communist 248
community 282
compact 192
companion 282
comparative 273
compare 282
compartment 282
compassion 161, 251, 282
compatibility 248
compatible 271, 282
compatriot 282
compendia 241
compendium 241, 248, 282
compete 85, 282
competence 245
competency 244
competent 267
competition 160, 252
complained 256
complement 206
complete 85
completeness 250
completion 160, 252
compliment 206, 249
composition 160, 252
compound 282
comprehensible 270
comprehension 162, 251
compromise 261, 282
con 135
concede 85
conceit 84

conceive 84
concert 155, 283
concertos 240
conclave 283
conclusion 163
concoct 283
concord 283
concrete 85
concur 283
condemn 143
condolence 283
cone 91
confectionery 246
confederacy 283
conference 283
confide 283
confidence 245
confident 267
confidential 160
confluence 283
conform 283
confraternity 283
confusion 163
congestion 167
conglomerate 283
congregate 283
congress 283
congruence 283
conical 264
conjoin 283
conjugal 265, 283
conjugate 283
conjure 167
conjuror 76, 250
conker 207
connection 252
connection 160, 252
conquer 139, 207
conquest 141
conscience 163
conscious 163, 272
consign 145
consonant 283
constabulary 244
consultative 273
contagious 272
contemporaneous
    268
contempt 194
contentious 272
continua 241
continuum 241
contour 117

contraband 282
contraceptive 282
contractor 250
contradict 282
contradistinction
    282
contraindicate 282
contraltos 240
contraposition 282
contraption 282
contrary 282
contravene 282
contravention 282
controlled 229
convalescence 156
convene 85
convenience 245
convenient 180, 267
convey 80
convoy 109
cook 99, 136
cool 96, 172
coop 96
coordinate 262, 267
cop 72, 135
cope 91
copies 239
copious 272
copper 130
copying 234
coral 177
cord 102
core 103
corn 102
corner 103
corporate 266
corporation 160,
    252
corpse 195
corpulence 245
corpulent 267
correlate 262, 267,
    283
correspond 283
correspondence 245
corridor 177
corroborate 283
corrupt 193
corruptible 270
cosmetics 158
cost 72, 190
cot 72, 135
cottage 168

cotton   146
couch 109
crouch 109
cougar 244
cough 74, 150
could 100
council 176
councillor 208
counsellor 208
countenance 243
country 76
couple 76, 175
coupon 98
courage 76, 168,
    243
courageous 232, 273
course 105, 154, 203
court 105, 203
courteous 268
cousin 76, 158
cove 91
cover 75
coverage 243
covered 256
cow 108
cowardice 247
cower 119
cowl 172
coy 109
crab 66, 184
crack 137
craft 101, 184, 192
craftsmanship 251
crag 66, 184
cram 66, 184
cramp 184
crane 77, 184
crank 184, 191
crash 159, 184
crashes 237
crass 154, 184
crate 77
crave 78
crawl 104
craze 78, 157
crazily 276
crazy 274
creak 83
cream 83
creamed 256
create 260
creature 166, 252
crèche   162

credibility 248
credible271
creed 82
creep 82
creepy 274
crept 257
crescent 156
crest 184
crevice 247
crew 97, 184
crib 69, 184
crick 137
cringe 195
cripple 174
crises 240
crisis 240
crisp 184, 190
crisply 275
criteria 240
criterion 240
critical 175
critique 138
crochet 81, 162
crock 184
crockery 246
crook 99
croon 96
crop 72, 184
croquet 81, 139
cross 154, 184
crosses 237
crouch 109
crow 92
crowd 108, 184
crown 108, 184
crucial 161
crude 99
cruise 98
crumple 175
crush 159, 184
cry 87, 184
crypt 70
crystal 70
cub 74, 131, 135
Cuba 95
cube 94
cubic 271
cubicle 95
cucumber 95
cud 74
cuddle 174
cuddly 274
cue 202

cuff 149
cull 173
culture 166, 252
cup 74, 130, 135
cupid 95
curb 107, 207
cure 120
curfew 94
curios 240
curiosity 248
curious 272
curl 172
currant 206
current 206
curricula 241
curriculum 241
curry 177
curse 107, 154
curtain 107, 147
curve 107
cusp 190
custard 111
cut 74,132, 135
cute 94
cyanide 156
cyberspace 156
cyclamen 156
cycle 88, 156
cyclone 88, 156
cygnet 70, 156, 208, 249
cylinder 156
cymbal 156
cynic 156
cyst 156
dab 131, 134
dabble 174
Dad 66, 134
daffodil 149
daft 101, 192
dairies 239
dairy 115
daisies 239
daisy 78
damage 143, 168, 243
dame 77
damn 143
damp 66, 192
dampen 260
Dan 66, 134, 144
dance 101, 155
dandle 175

Dane 77
dangle 148, 174
dank 66
dapple 174
dare 116
dark 100
darken 260
darkness 250
darling 249
darn 100
dash 66, 159
data 241
date 77
datum 241
daughter 105
daunt 105
dawdle 104
dawn 104
day 79
daze 78, 157
dazzle 174
dead 68
deaden 260
deaf 68
deafen 260
deal 83, 172
dealt 257
dean 83
dear 113, 204
death 68
debar 288
debarred 227
debase 288
debilitate 288
debrief 288
debt 211
debut 214
decadence 245
decadent 267
decalcify 288
decapitate 288
deceit 84
deceive 84, 288
December 155
decide 155
decimal 155
decipher 150
decision 163
deck 137
declare 288
decline 288
decode 288
decompose 288

decompress 288
decorate 260
decoration 160, 252
deduct 288
deed 82
deem 82
deep 82
deer 113, 204
defame 288
default 288
defend 260, 288
defiance 243
defiant 265
deficient 267
deflate 260, 288
deform 288
deft 192
degrade 288
dehydrate 288
deify 261
deign 80, 145
deject 288
delayed 234, 256
delegate 262, 267
deliberate 262, 267
delicate 266
delicious 161, 272
delight 88
delighted 255
delirium 248
delphinium 248
delude 99
deluge 164
delusion 163
demagogue 140
demolish 262
demonstrate 260
demoralise 288
demur 107
demure 120
den 67, 134, 144
denounce 288
dense 154
dent 67, 191
dental 265
denture 166, 252
depart 288
departure 252
depend 288
dependence 245
dependency 244
dependent 267
depletion 160, 252

deploy 288
deport 288
deportee 245
depot 214
depth 196
deride 87, 288
derive 87
descend 156, 260, 288
descent 156
describe 288
desert 158
desiccated 138
design 145
desk 67
desperate 266
despondency 244
despondent 267
dessert 158
destroy 109
destroyed 234, 256
deuce 95
develop 174
development 249
deviate 288
device 87, 155
devious 272
devise 158
devotee 245
devotion 160, 252
devour 119
dew 94, 169
diabetic 271
dialogue 140
diaphragm 150, 212
diarrhoea 114, 113, 118. 178
diary 118
dice 86, 155
Dick 137
dictionary 160, 244, 252
did 69, 124
die 89, 201
differ 149
difference 245
different 267
dig 69, 134, 139
digestion 167
digital 265
digitally 276
dignify 261
dignitary 244

dilemma 112
dim 69, 134, 142
dime 87
diminish 145, 262
dimple 175
dimply 274
din 69, 134, 144
dine 86
dinghy 141
dinner 144
dinosaur 105
dint 70, 191
dip 69, 130, 134
diploma 112
dipper 130
dipping 225
dire 117
direction 160
director 250
dirt 106
disability 281
disaccord 281
disadvantage 281
disaffect 281
disagree 281
disallow 281
disappear 281
disappoint 281
disapprove 281
disarray 281
disbelieve 281
disc 191
discard 281
discern 156
disciple 156
disclaim 281
disclose 19
discolour 281
discomfort 281
disconnect 281
disconsolate 281
discontent 281
discontinue 281
discord 281
discount 281
discourage 281
discover 281
discovery 246
discredit 281
discreet 200
discrepant 281
discrete 200
discussion 161, 251

disease 158, 281
disenchant 281
disenfranchise 281
disengage 281
disentangle 281
disfavour 281
disfigure 281
disgorge 281
disgrace 281
disgruntle 281
disgust 281
dish 70, 159
disharmony 281
dishes 237
dishonest 281
disillusion 281
disingenuous 281
disintegrate 281
disinterest 281
disk 191
dislike 281
dislocate 281
disloyal 281
dismal 175
dismantle 281
dismember 281
dismiss 281
dismount 281
disobedient 281
disorder 281
disown 281
dispel 281
dispensary 244
displace 281
displease 281
disquiet 281
dissidence 281
dissimilar 281
dissipate 281
dissolve 158, 281
dissuade 281
distinct 194
distracted 255
distraction 281
distraught 105
distress 281
distrust 281
disturb 107, 281
disused 281
ditch 166
ditches 237
dive 86
diversion 162, 251

divine 87
divisible 270
divorcee 245
dizzy 157
do 96
dock 137
doctor 111, 250
document 249
dodge 168
doe 93, 202
does 76
dog 72, 134, 139
dole 172
doll 173
dolphin 150
dome 91
domestic 136, 271
domestically 278
dominion 180
dominoes 239
done 75
donkey 84
doom 96
door 104
dope 91
dormitory 250
dosage 243
dose 91, 154
dot 72, 133, 134
dote 91
double 76
doubt 211
dough 93, 202
dour 117
douse 109, 154
dove 75, 151
dower 119
down 108
doze 91
dozen 75
drab 183
drag 183
dragon 140, 146
drain 79, 183
drake 77
dram 183
drama 112
dramatic 271
dramatise 261
drank 191
drank 136, 191
drape 77, 183
draught 102, 150

draw 104, 183
dread 183
dreaded 226
dream 83
dreamed 257
dreamt 68, 257
dreary 113
dredge 168
drench 183, 195
dress 154, 183
dresses 237
drew 97
drey 80
drift 183, 192
drill 173, 183
drink 137, 183, 191
drip 69, 183
dripping 225
drive 87, 183
driven 259
driving 230
drizzle 174
drizzly 274
droll 173
dromedary 244
drone 91
drool 96
droop 96
drop 72, 183
dropped 225
dropping 225
drove 91
drown 108
drug 183
drum 74, 183
drunk 191
dry 87, 183
dual 169, 206
dub 134
dubious 169, 272
duck 137
duckling 249
dud 74, 134
due 94, 169
duel 169, 176, 206
duet 169
dug 74, 134, 139
dukedom 245
dull 173
dumb 143
dump 75, 192
dune 94
dung 75, 147

dunk 75, 191
duplicate 262, 267
duration 120
duress 120
during 169
dusk 75, 191
Dutch 166
duties 239
duty 169
dwarf 104, 188
dwell 173, 188
dwindle 175, 188
dye 89, 201
dying 232
dyke 87
dynamic 88
dynamite 88
dynamo 88
dynamos 240
each 83
eagle 175
ear 113
earl 107
earldom 245
early 83, 107
earn 107, 203
earnest 107
earth 107
easel 176
easily 276
eastern 147, 270
easy 83, 274
eat 83
eaten 146, 259
ebb 132
eccentric 171
echo 138
echoes 239
economic 136
edge 168
edible 271
edifice 247
edify 261
edition 160
educability 248
educable 264
educate 260
education 160, 252
eel 82
eerie 113, 204
effect 149, 210
effete 85
effort 149

egg 140
Egypt 70, 168
eight 80, 200
eighth 152
either 90
eke 85
elaborate 262, 267
elastic 136
elation 160
elbow 92
election 160
elector 250
electric 136, 271
electrically 278
electrify 261
elegance 243
elegant 265
elegantly 275
elephant 150
eleventh 152
elf 67, 194
elopement 249
eloquence 245
eloquent 267
elves 238
embalm 101
embellish 174, 262
embroidery 246
eminence 245
eminent 267
emperor 111, 250
emphases 240
emphasis 150, 240
employ 109
employee 245
employment 249
enactment 249
enclosure 163
encouragement 249
end 67, 191
ended 255
endure 120, 169
energetic 271
energetically 278
energy 168
enforceable 264
engagement 249
engineer 245
England 70
enhance 155
enigma 112
enjoy 109
enjoyable 264

enjoyment 249
enormity 248
enough 76, 150
enquire 141
ensign 145
entered 227
entrepreneur 247
environment 249
epilogue 140
epistle 156
equal 265
equally 276
equate 260
equipped 227
era 112, 114
ergonomic 136
erosion 163
erotic 271
erroneous 268
esoteric 136
especially 161
espionage 164
essential 160
establish 262
Esther 134
estimate 262, 267
etch 166
eternity 248
etiquette 246
eucalyptus 95
Eucharist 95
eugenic 95
eulogy 95
euphonium 95
euphoria 95
euphoric 271
euro 120
Europe 120
euthanasia 95
eve 85
ever 110, 151
evidence 245
evil 176
ewe 95, 202
exact 171
exaggerate 169, 171
exam 171
examination 160,
  252
examinee 245
example 171
exasperate 171, 288
exceed 171

excel 171
excellence 245
Excellency 244
excellent 171, 267
except 171, 209
exception 171
excerpt 171
excess 171
exchange 170
exchequer 139
excise 171
excite 155, 171
excitement 249
exclaim 170
exclude 170, 288
exclusion 163
excruciate 288
excuse 94, 170, 288
exemplary 266
exempt 194
exercise 170, 288
exhale 164
exhaust 170, 171,
  213
exhibit 170, 213
exhilarate 213
exhume 288
exile 171, 288
exist 171
exit 170, 288
exodus 288
exonerate 288
exotic 271, 288
expand 170
expatriate 88, 262,
  267
expect 170, 192
expel 288
expense 170
experience 114
expert 106
expire 288
explain 170
explicable 264
explode 288
explore 103
explosion 163
export 170
express 170, 288
expression 161, 251
extension 162, 251
extensive 273
extensively 275

extent 170
external 288
extinct 170
extol 288
extra 170
extraction 288
extracurricular 288
extramarital 288
extraneous 268, 288
extraordinary 288
extrapolate 288
extrasensory 288
extraterrestrial 288
extravagance 243
extravagant 170,
    265, 288
extreme 85
exude 288
eye 89, 201
eyelet 249
eyrie 114, 204
fab 131
fable 175
face 78
fact 192
faction 160
factor 250
factory 250
factual 166
fade 78
faded 255
fading 230
fag 149
fail 78, 172
failed 256
faint 78, 200
fair 115, 204
fairies 239
fairly 275
fake 77, 136
fall 103, 173
fallen 259
falsehood 247
falsify 261
fame 77
familiar 180
family 83
famish 143, 262
famous 230
fan 66, 144, 149
fanatical 265
fancy 83
fang 66

fantastic 136, 271
fantastically 278
far 100
farce 155
fare 116, 204
farm 101
fart 100
fascia 163
fascinate 156
fascism 163, 247
fascist 163, 248
fast 101, 190
fasten 101, 260
fastened 227
fastidious 272
fat 132, 149
fatal 265
fatality 248
fatally 276
fate 77
fateful 231, 270
father 101, 110, 246
fatigue 140
fatten 224
fatter 224
fattest 224
fattish 272
fatty 224
fatuous 274
fault 105
faulty 274
favour 112, 251
fawn 104
faze 78, 206
fear 113
feared 256
feat 83, 200
feather 68
feature 166, 252
febrile 87
February 214, 244
fed 67, 134, 149
fee 82
feebly 277
feed 82
feeding 226
feel 82, 172
feet 82, 200
feign 80, 145
feint 80, 200
fell 173
felt 257
femur 112

fence 155
fend 67, 191
fennel1 144
fern 106
ferry 177
fervent 267
fervour 251
fester 110
festive 273
festively 275
festivity 248
fetch 166
fetid 133, 272
fetter 133
fettle 174
feud 95
few 94
fey 80
fib 69, 131
fibre111
fickle 174
fiddle 174
fiddly 274
fidget 168
fiefdom 245
field 84
fierce 114, 155
fiery 118
fifth 152
fig 69, 139, 149
fight 88
figure 140
fill 173
filled 256
fin 69, 149
final 265
finality 248
finally 276
find 89
fine 86
finely 276
finesse 246
finger 148
finish 145, 207, 262
Finnish 207
fir 106
fire 117
firm 106
firmament 249
first 106
fish 70, 159
fishmonger 76
fist 70

fit 69, 132, 149
fitness 250
five 86, 151
fix 170
fixture 166, 252
fizz 157
flab 66, 186
flaccid 272
flag 186
flagon 140
flail 79
flair 115
flake 77, 186
flamboyant 265
flame 77, 186
flan 186
flank 136, 186, 191
flap 66, 186
flare 116
flash 159, 186
flask 101, 186, 191
flat 66, 186
flatulence 245
flaunt 105
flavour 112, 251
flaw 104
flax 170
flaxen 267
flay 79
flea 83, 200
fleck 137, 186
fled 67
flee 82, 200
fleeing 232
fleet 82
flesh 186
flew 97
flex 170
flick 186
flight 88
flinch 186, 195
fling 148, 186
flint 191
flip 69, 186
flirt 106
flit 69, 186
float 92
floated 226
flock 137, 186
floe 93
flog 72, 186
flood 76
floor 104

flop 72, 186
florescence 156
florid 272
florist 177
floss 154, 186
flour 119, 205
flourish 76, 262
flout 109
flow 92, 186
flower 119, 205
flue 97
fluency 244
fluent 267
fluently 275
fluff 149
flume 99
flummox 170
flung 148
flurry 177
flush 159, 186
flute 99
flux 170
fly 87, 186
flying 234
foal 92, 172
foam 92
fob 72
focus 153
fodder 135
foe 93
foetus 86
fog 72, 139, 149
foil 110, 172
fold 90, 193
folk 93
follow 173
fond 72, 191
fondle 175
font 191
food 96
fool 96, 172
foot 99
for 102, 203
forbear 289
forbid 289
forbidden 227, 259
force 103, 155
forceful 270
forcefully 276
fore 103, 203
forearm 286
foreboding 286
forecast 286

forefather 286
forego 286
foreground 286
forehead 286
foreign 145
forelock 286
foreman 286
foremost 286
forename 286
foreshorten 286
foresight 286
forest 177
forestall 286
foretaste 286
forethought 286
forewarn 286
foreword 286
forfeit 81, 289
forgery 246
forget 289
forgetful 270
forgive 289
forgiven 259
forgotten 259
fork 102
forlorn 289
form 102
formalise 229
formality 229
formatting 228
formed 256
formula 112
forswear 289
fort 102, 203
forth 102, 203
fortunate 266
forty 103
fought 106, 203
foul 109, 172, 204
found 109
fountain 147
four 105, 203
fourth 152, 203
fowl 108, 172, 204
fox 72, 149, 170
foxes 237
fraction 160, 252
fragile 168
fragment 249
fragrance 243
fragrant 265
frail 79, 172
frailty 252

frame 77, 184
France 101, 155
frank 184
frantic 136, 271
frantically 278
fratricide 244
fraud 105
fraudulence 245
fraudulent 267
fraught 105
frazzle 174
freak 83
freckly 274
Fred 184
free 82, 184
freedom 245
freeing 232
freeze 200
freight 80
French 184
frenetic 271
fresh 184
fret 67
friar 118
fridge 168
friend 68
friendliness 250
friendship 251
frieze 200
frigate 140
frigid 272
frill 173, 184
fringe 195
fringeing 232
frisk 184
frizz 157
frizzle 174
frog 72
frolicked 229
from 72, 184
front 75
frost 190
frown 108
frowning 225
frozen 259
frugal 265
fruit 98
frump 184, 192
frustration 160
fry 87, 184
fudge 168
fuel 176
fugitive 273

fugue 140
fulfil 289
full 100, 173
fulsome 289
fumble 175
fun 74, 144, 149
function 160, 252
fund 191
funeral 95
fungal 265
fungicide 244
fungus 153
funnel 144, 176
funny 83, 144, 274
furl 172
furnish 107, 262
furniture 166, 252
further 107
fuse 94
fusion 163
fuss 154
future 166, 252
fuzz 157
gadget 168
gaelic 81
gag 139
gaggle 174
gain 78
gait 78, 200
gale 77
gall 103, 173
gallery 173
galley 84
galloped 227
gamble 207
gambol 207
game 77
gap 66, 130, 139
gape 77
garage 177, 243
garb 101
garbage 243
gardener 246
garnish 262
gas 139, 153
gaseous 268
gases 237
gash 66, 159
gashes 237
gasp 190
gate 77, 200
gauge 168, 215
gave 78

gay 79
gaze 78, 157
gear 113, 139
gel 168
gelding 249
gem 67, 168
gene 85
general 168
generate 260
generosity 248
genius 168
genocide 244
gentle 168
gently 277
geography 150, 168
geology 168, 250
George 168
Georgian 265
geranium 248
germ 168
German 168, 265
gesture 166, 252
get 77, 133, 139
ghastly 141
ghost 141
ghoul 98, 141
giant 168
gibbon 132
gift 70, 139, 192
gig 139
giggle 174
giggly 274
gild 206
gill 139
gilt 206
gimlet 249
gin 69, 168
ginger 168
giraffe 149, 168
gird 106
girl 106, 139, 172
gist 168
give 139, 151
given 146, 259
giving 230
glad 185
glade 78, 185
glamour 112, 143, 151
glance 155
gland 185, 191
glare 116, 185
glass 185

glasses 237
glaze 78
gleam 83, 185
glean 83, 185
glee 82
glen 185
glib 185
glide 87
glided 255
glimpse 195
glint 185, 191
glisten 156
gloat 92
globe 91, 185
gloom 96, 185
glorify 261
glory 185
gloss 154
glottal 265
glove 75, 151
glow 92, 185
glower 119
glue 97, 185
glug 74
glum 75, 185
gnarl 145
gnash 145
gnat 145
gnaw 104, 145
gnome 145
go 90, 139
goal 92, 172
goat 92
gobble 174
goblet 249
god 134, 139
goggle 174
going 90
gold 90, 193
golden 146, 267
golf 194
gone 73, 139
gong 147
good 99
goodbye 89
goose 97, 154
gore 103
gorgeous 268, 274
gormless 273
gorse 102, 154
gosh 159
gosling 249
got 72, 133, 139

gourmet 81
gout 109
govern 75, 147
government 249
grab 184
grace 78, 155
graceful 231, 270
gracefully 276
gracious 161
graduate 262, 267
graft 184
grail 79
grain 79, 184
gram 184
grammar 111, 244
Gran 184
granary 244
grand 191
grange 195
Granny 144
grant 184
grape 77
graph 150
grapheme 150
graphics 150
graphite 150
grapple 174
grasp 190
grass 154, 184
grate 77, 200
grated 255
grateful 270
gratify 261
grave 151
graze 78, 157
great 79, 200
greed 82, 184
greedily 276
greedy 83, 284
Greek 82
green 82, 184
greet 82
Greg 184
Gregorian 265
grenadier 114
grew 97
grey 80
grid 69, 184
grief 84
grieve 84
griffin 149
grill 173, 184
grim 184

grime 87
grin 184
grind 184, 191
grip 69, 184
gripe 87
gripping 225
gristle 156
grit 184
grizzle 174
groan 92, 184, 202
groaning 226
grocery 246
groin 206
groom 96
grope 91
gross 154
grotesque 138
ground 109
group 98
grouse 109, 154
grout 109
grove 91, 151
grow 92, 184
growl 108
grown 202
groyne 206
grub 74, 184
grudge 168
gruesome 274
gruff 149, 184
grumble 175
grunt 184
guarantee 140
guard 140
guardianship 251
Guernsey 140
guerrilla 140
guess 140
guest 140
guide 140
guild 71, 140, 206
guile 140
guillotine 140
guilt 71, 140, 206
guilty 140
guinea-pig 140
guitar 140
gulf 194
gulfs 238
gull 173
gulp 75
gum 74, 139
gun 74, 139

gurgle 107
gush 75, 159
gust 75
gut 74, 132, 139
guy 87, 140
gymkhana 168
gymnasia 241
gymnasium 168,
   241, 248
gymnastics 168
gypsum 168
gypsy 70, 168
gyrate 118, 168
habit 132
hack 137
had 66, 134, 164
haemoglobin 86
hag 66, 139, 164
haggle 174
hail 78, 172
hair 115, 204
hake 77
hale 77
half 101
hall 103, 173, 203
halt 103
halves 238
ham 66, 142, 164
hamlet 249
hammer 142
hampered 228
hand 66, 164, 191
handed 255
handkerchief 212
handkerchiefs 238
handle 175
handsome 274
handsomely 275
hang 147
hangar 244
hapless 273
happen 146
happened 228
happily 276
happiness 250
happy 83, 130, 274
harangue 148
harbour 112, 251
hard 100
harden 260
hardship 251
hare 116, 204
hark 100

harmlessness 250
harmonious 272
harp 101
harsh 101
has 158, 164
hash 159
hassle 174
haste 78
hasten 156
hastened 228
hat 66, 132, 164
hatch 166
hatched 256
hate 77
hated 255
haughty 105
haul 105, 203
haunch 105
haunt 105
have 151, 164
hay 79
hazard 158
haze 78
hazy 274
he 81
head 68, 164
heal 83, 172, 200
health 68, 195
heap 83
hear 113, 204
heard 107, 203
hearth 102
hearse 107, 154
heart 102
heartily 276
hearty 274
heat 83
heather 68
heaven 68
heavy 68
heckle 174
hedge 168
heed 82
heel 82, 172, 200
heifer 69
height 88
heinous 274
heir 115, 204
held 67, 164, 193
helium 248
hell 164, 173
hellish 272
help 67, 164, 193

helped 256
hem 67
hen 67, 144
hence 155
her 164
herb 106
herbaceous 162, 268
herd 203
here 114, 204
hermit 106
hero 90
heroes 239
heroic 18, 136
heroin 207
heroine 207
heron 177
hers 158
Hertford 102
heterodox 289
heterogeneous 268,
   289
heterosexual 289
hiccup 138
hid 69, 134, 164
hidden 146, 259
hide 86
hideous 268
high 88
hike 87, 136
hiked 257
hilarious 272
hill 164, 173
him 69, 142, 164,
   199
hind 89, 191
hindered 228
hindrance 243
hint 70, 164, 191
hip 69, 130, 164
hippo 130
hippy 130
hire 117
hireling 249
his 158, 164
hiss 154
historic 136
historically 278
histories 271
history 250
hit 78, 132, 164
hitch 166
hive 86, 151
hoarse 105, 154

hob 92, 164
hobble 174
hobby 132
hock 137
hockey 84
hoe 93
hog 72, 139, 164
hold 90, 193
holder 225
hole 91, 207
hollow 173
holy 83
homage 143, 243
home 91
homeless 273
homicide 244
homogeneous 268,
   289
homograph 289
homonym 70, 289
homophone 150,
   289
homosexual 289
hone 91
honest 145, 213
honey 75, 84, 145
honk 164
honorary 266
honour 112, 251,
   213
hood 99
hoof 96, 164
hook 99, 136
hoop 96
hoot 96
hop 72, 91, 130
hope 91
hoped 230, 257
hopeful 231, 270
hopeless 231, 273
hopped 224
hopper 224
hopping 224
horn 102
horrible 271
horribly 277
horrid 177, 272
horrific 271
horrifically 278
horrify 261
horse 102, 154
hose 91, 158
hostel 176

hot 72, 133, 164
hound 109
hounded 255
hour 119, 205, 213
house 109, 154
how 108
howl 108, 172
hub 74
huddle 174
huff 149, 164
hug 74, 139, 164
hugged 225
hugging 225
hulk 164, 193
hull 173
hum 74, 142, 164
human 146, 265
humanise 261
humble 175
humbly 277
humming 225
humorous 273
humour 112, 251
hump 75, 164
hunch 164
hung 75, 147
hunger 148
hungry 274
hunk 75, 164, 191
hunt 164, 191
hunted 255
hurl 107, 172
hurried 233
hurrying 234
hurt 107
hush 75, 159
husk 75
hustle 156
hut 74, 132, 164
hutch 166
hydrant 88
hygiene 88
hymn 70, 143, 199
hyperbole 82
hyphen 150
hypnosis 70
hypocrite 70
hypotheses 240
hypothesis 240
hysterics 70
I 88, 201
ice 155
icy 156

idea 114
identify 261
idiom 247
idiotic 271
idle 175, 207
idol 207
if 149
igneous 268
ignorance 243
ignorant 265
ill 173
illegal 280
illegible 280
illiberal 280
illicit 280
illimitable 280
illiterate 280
illogical 280
illusion 163
image 143, 243
imbalance 279
immaterial 279
immature 279
immense 154
imminence 245
imminent 267
immobile 279
immoral 279
immortal 279
immune 279
immutable 279
imp 192
impair 115
impartial 279
impassable 279
impatient 279
impeccable 138, 264, 279
impecunious 279
impede 85
impenitent 279
impermeable 279
impersonal 279
impervious 279
impetuous 274
impious 279
implement 249
impolite 279
impolitic 279
imponderable 279
impossible 279
impotent 279
impractical 279

impregnable 279
impression 161, 251
improper 279
improvise 261
impudence 245
impudent 267
impugn 145
impunity 248
impure 279
in 69, 144
inaccessible 278
inaccurate 278
inactive 278
inadequate 279
inappropriate 279
inarticulate 279
incapable 279
incarnate 266
inch 105
include 199
inclusion 163
incomprehensible 279
inconsistent 279
incorrect 279
increment 249
independence 245
independent 279
index 240
indices 240
indict 212
indifferent 279
indirect 278
indiscrete 278
indispensable 278
individual 265
indolence 245
indomitable 279
inducement 249
inedible 279
ineffable 279
ineligible 279
inept 279
inertia 160
inestimable 279
inevitable 264
inexpensive 279
inexplicable 279
inextricable 279
infallible 278
infirmity 248
inflate 260
influential 160

influx 170
informant 265
information 160, 252
infringement 249
ingenious 272
ingratiate 260
inhale 164
inherit 164
iniquity 248
initial 160
initiate 260
ink 136, 191
inkling 249
innocuous 278
innuendo 239
innuendoes 239
innuendos 239
innumerable 278
inoperable 279
inordinate 279
inorganic 279
insane 279
inscription 160
inscrutability 248
inscrutable 264
insecure 279
insidious 272
insincere 279
insolence 245
insolent 267
insomnia 279
inspection 160
instance 243
instant 265
instantaneous 268
instantly 275
instead 68
institution 160, 252
instructor 250
insulate 260
insupportable 279
insure 160
intelligence 245
intelligent 173, 267
intelligently 275
intelligibility 248
intelligible 271
intend 260
intention 160
interact 289
interbreed 289
intercede 289

intercept 289
interchange 289
intercom 289
interconnect 289
interface 289
interfere 114, 289
interlace 289
intermediate 289
intermittent 267,
   289
internal 289
international 289
internee 245
interpret 289
interred 227
interrogate 289
interrupt 289
intersection 289
intervene 289
interview 289
interviewee 245
intimate 262, 267
intrepid 272
intricate 266
intrude 99
intrusion 163
invasion 163
inveigh 80
inveigle 84
invention 160
investiture 252
investment 249
invincible 271
invisible 279
iodine 119
iridescence 156
iridescent 267
irksome 274
irrational 279
irreconcilable 279
irrecoverable 279
irredeemable 279
irreducible 279
irrefutable 279
irregular 279
irrelevant 279
irreparable 279
irreplaceable 279
irrepressible 279
irreproachable 279
irresistible 279
irresolute 279
irrespective 279

irresponsible 279
irretrievable 279
irreverent 279
irreversible 279
irrevocable 279
is 158
island 215
isle 201
it 69, 132
itch 166
itinerary 244
jab 66, 131
Jack 137
jail 78
Jake 77
jam 66, 142, 167
jammed 224
jamming 224
jammy 224
Jane 77
January 244
Japan 167
Japanese 246
jar 100, 167
jaundice 247
jaunt 105
jaw 167
jay 79, 167
jazz 157, 167
jealous 68, 273
jealously 275
Jean 83
jeep 82
jeer 113
jellies 239
jelly 83
jeopardy 69
jersey 84
jet 67, 167
Jew 97, 167
jewel 176
jewellery 246
jig 69, 139, 167
Jim 167
jingle 148
jive 86, 151, 167
job 72, 84, 131
jockey 84
jodhpurs 112
Joe 93
jog 72, 139, 167
John 167
join 110, 167

joinery 246
joint 110
joke 91, 136, 167
jolly 167
jostle 156
jot 82, 167
journal 108
journalese 246
journey 84, 108
jowl 172
joy 109
joyful 234, 270
Judaism 247
judge 167, 168
judgeship 251
judo 167
jug 74, 139, 167
juice 98
juicy 156
July 87, 167
jump 75, 167, 192
junction 160, 252
June 99, 167
jungle 148
junior 167
junk 137, 167, 191
just 167, 190
justice 247
jut 132
jute 99
juvenile 99
karate 82
keel 82, 172
keen 136
keep 82
Ken 136
kennel 144, 176
kept 257
kerb 106, 207
kernel 106, 203, 207
ketch 166
kettle 174
key 84, 201
khaki 213
kick 137
kid 69, 136
kidnapped 228
kidney 84
kill 136, 173
kin 136
kind 89, 136, 191
kindly 275
kindness 250

king 70, 136, 147
kingdom 245
kink 70, 136, 191
kip 69
kipper 130
kiss 136, 154
kissed 256
kisses 237
kit 69, 136
kite 86
knack 137
knapsack 145
knave 145, 207
knead 83, 145, 201
knee 145
kneel 82, 145, 172
knelt 145, 257
knew 94, 145, 202
knickers 145
knife 87, 145
knight 88, 145
knighthood 247
knit 145
knives 238
knob 145
knock 137, 145
knoll 145, 173
knot 145, 207
know 92, 145, 202,
   207
knowledge 145
knowledgeable 232
knuckle 145
lab 131, 172
labelled 229
laboratory 250
laborious 272
labour 112, 251
lace 78, 155, 172
lack 137, 172
lacquer 139
lacy 156
lad 66, 134, 172
ladies 239
ladle 175
lady 83
lag 66, 139, 172
laid 78
lain 78, 200
lair 115
lake 77, 136, 172
lamb 143
lame 77, 172

lamp 66, 172, 192
lance 155
land 66, 172, 191
landed 255
lane 77, 200
language 169
languid 272
lank 66
lap 66, 130, 172
lapse 195
larch 101
lard 100
largesse 246
lark 100
lash 66, 159, 172
lass 154
last 101, 172, 190
latch 166
latches 237
late 77, 172
lately 231, 276
latency 244
latent 267
lather 101, 110
laud 105, 203
laugh 102, 150
laughed 256
launch 105
launderette 246
lavish 262
law 104
lawn 104
lawyer 180
lax 170
lay 79
layer 116
laze 78
lazily 276
laziness 250
lazy 274
lead 68, 83, 199
leaden 267
leaf 83, 172
leaflet 249
league 140
leak 83, 201
leaking 226
lean 83
leaned 257
leant 257
leap 83, 172
leaped 257
leapt 257

learn 107
lease 154
least 190
leather 68, 110
leaves 238
leaving 230
lecture 166, 252
led 67, 134, 172, 199
ledge 168
lee 82
leech 82
leek 82, 201
leer 113
left 172, 192
leg 67, 139, 172
legal 265
legalese 246
legalise 229
legality 229
legend 169
legibility 248
legible 271
legislature 166, 252
leisure 69, 163
lemming 142
lemon 143, 146
lend 172, 191
lengthen 260
leniency 244
lenient 267
lent 67, 191
leopard 69
lessee 245
lessen 260
lest 67
let 133, 172
lethal 265
letter 246
lettuce 71
leukaemia 86, 99
lewd 97
liaise 78
liaison 78
liar 118, 205, 266
library 214, 244
lice 86, 155
licence 155, 210
license 154, 210
licensee 245
lick 137, 172
lid 69, 134, 172
lie 89
life 87, 172

lift 70, 192
light 88
lighten 260
lightly 275
like 87, 136
liked 257
likelihood 247
lily 174
limb 143
lime 87
limitation 228
limp 70, 172, 192
limped 226
line 86, 172
linger 110, 148
link 70, 136, 172, 191
linoleum 246
lint 70, 191
lip 69, 130, 172
liquefy 260
liquor 139
liquorice 247
lisp 70, 190
list 70, 190
listen 156
lit 69, 132, 172
literature 166, 252
litigious 272
litre 111
little 174
live 86, 151, 172
liven 260
lives 238
livid 272
lizard 158
load 92
loaf 92
loam 92
loan 92, 202
loath 152
loathe 153
loaves 238
lob 72, 131, 172
lobe 91, 172
local 265
locus 153
lock 137, 172
lodge 168
loft 72, 172, 192
log 72, 139, 172
logic 168
logical 265

lollipop 173
London 75
lone 202
lonesome 274
long 147, 172
look 99, 136
loom 96
loop 96
loose 97, 154
loot 96, 202
lop 72
lope 91, 172
lord 102, 203
lordship 251
lore 103
lose 96
loss 154
lost 172, 190
lot 72, 133, 172
lotion 160, 252
lotus 153
loudly 275
loudness 250
louse 154
lout 109
lovable 264
love 75, 151, 172
loved 230
loveless 273
loveliness 250
lovely 231
low 92, 172
lowered 256
loyal 109, 265
loyalty 252
luck 137, 172
luckily 276
luckless 273
lucky 83, 274
Lucy 156
lug 139, 172
luggage 140, 168, 243
Luke 99
lull 173
lumbar 210, 266
lumber 210
luminary 244
luminescence 156
lump 75, 192
lunar 266
lunch 195
lung 75, 147

lunge 195
lure 120
lurid 272
lurk 107
luscious 163
lush 75,159
lustre 111
lute 99, 202
luxury 163
lying 232
lynx 70, 170
lyre 118, 205
mace 78
machete 82, 162
machine 162
machinery 246
mackerel 176
mad 66, 134, 142
madden 260
made 78, 200
maestro 90
maggot 140
magic 136, 168
magical 264
magnetic 136, 271
magnificence 245
magnificent 267
magnify 261
magnitude 94
maid 78, 200
mail 78, 172, 200
maim 78
main 78, 200
maintenance 243
maize 78, 200
majesty 167
major 167
majority 167
make 77, 136
making 230
male 77, 200
malice 247
malign 145
mall 103
malt 103
mammal 175
mammalian 265
man 66, 142, 144
manage 145, 169
manageable 232
management 249
mane 77, 200
mange 195

mangle 148, 174
manhood 225, 247
manic 271
manoeuvre 111
manor 145
mansion 162, 251
mantle 175
manual 265
manufacture 166,
   252
manure 120
many 68, 83
map 66, 130, 142
maple 175
march 101
mare 116, 204
marital 265
mark 100
marketed 228
marquee 139
married 233
marrow 177
marry 177
marrying 234
marsh 101
martyrdom 245
marvellous 273
mash 66, 159
mask 101, 191
masquerade 139
mass 154
massacre 111
massage 164
masseur 247
massive 273
mast 101, 190
master 101
masterful 270
mat 66, 142, 209
match 166
matched 226
matches 237
matching 226
mate 77
matrices 240
matricide 244
matrix 240
matt 133, 209
matted 225
matting 225
mattress 133
mature 120
mausoleum 246

maxim 170
maximum 170
may 79
mayor 116, 204
maze 78, 157, 200
me 81, 142
mead 83
meadow 68
meagre 111
meal 83, 172
mean 83, 201
meanness 250
meant 68, 257
measure 68, 163
meat 83, 200
mechanic 138
medal 135, 175
meddle 174
media 241
mediocre 111
mediocrity 248
medium 241, 248
medley 84
meek 82
meet 82, 200
Meg 139, 142
megaphone 150
men 67, 142, 144
mend 67, 191
mended 255
mental 265
mentally 276
mention 160, 252
mere 114
meringue 148
merrily 276
merry 177, 274
mesh 159
mess 154
messiah 113
met 67, 133, 142
metal 133, 175
metamorphoses 240
meticulous 274
meticulously 275
metre 86, 111, 155
mice 155
Mick 137
microphone 150
middle 174
midge 168
mien 84, 211
might 88, 111

Mike 87,136
mild 89, 193
mildly 275
mile 87
military 266
milk 193
mill 173
million 180
mime 87
mimicked 229
mind 88, 191
mine 86
mingle 148, 174
miniature 213
minstrel 176
mint 70, 191
minus 153
minute 71
minutiae 90
minx 170
mire 117
mirror 111, 250
misadventure 281
misadvise 281
misalign 281
misapply 281
misbelieve 281
miscarry 281
miscellaneous 268
mischief 281
misconception 281
miscreant 281
miscue 281
misdeed 281
misdemeanour 281
miser 158
misery 158
misfire 281
misfit 281
misfortune 281
misgiving 281
mishap 281
misinform 281
misjudge 281
mislay 281
mislead 281
mismatch 281
misnomer 281
mispronounce 281
misread 281
miss 154
missed 256
misshapen 281

mission 161, 251
misspell 281
misspend 281
mist 70, 190
mistake 281
mistletoe 156
mistrust 281
misunderstand 281
misuse 281
mite 86, 201
mitre 111
mix 170
mixing 227
mixture 166, 252
mnemonic 214
moan 92
moat 92
mob 131, 142
mock 137
modal 264
modality 248
model 135
moderate 262, 267
modern 135, 147, 270
modify 261
moisten 260
mole 91
mollify 173, 261
monastery 246
Monday 75
money 75, 84, 145
mongrel l76
monitor 111, 250
monk 75, 191
monkey 75
month 75, 152, 196
monthly 275
monument 249
mood 96
moon 96
moor 117, 203
moose 97
moot 96
mop 72, 130, 142
mope 91
moral 177
morbid 272
morbidity 248, 275
more 103, 203
morning 103
mortgage 214
mosque 138

mosquito 139
mosquitoes 239
moss 154
moth 152
mother 75, 110, 246
motherese 246
motherhood 247
motion 160, 252
motor 111, 250
motto 239
mottoes 239
mottos 239
mould 93
moult 93
mound 109
mountain 147
mountaineer 245
mourn 105
mournful 270
mouse 109, 154
moustache 162
mouth 109, 152
mouthful 270
movable 230
move 96, 151
movement 249
mow 92
Mozambique 138
much 75, 165
muck 137
mud 74, 134, 142
muddle 174
muffin 149
muffle 174
mug 74, 139, 142
mule 94
mull 173
mum 74
mumble 175
Mummy 142
munch 195
municipal 265
murder 107
murmur 107, 112
muscle 156, 208
muse 94
museum 246
mush 75
music 95
musical 264
musicality 248
musician 161
musk 75

mussel 176, 208
must 75, 190
mutant 265
mute 94
mutineer 245
mutton 146
muzzle 174
my 87, 142
myopic 271
mysterious 272
mystery 70
mystique 138
myth 70
nag 66, 139, 144
nail 78, 172
name 77
Nan 144
nap 66, 130, 144
narrative 177
nasty 101
natal 265
nation 160, 252
naturalise 261
nature 166, 252
naughty 105
nauseous 268
nautical 105
nave 207
navel 176
near 113
neaten 260
neatness 250
necessarily 276
necessary 266
necessity 248
neck 137
Ned 144
need 82, 201
needed 226, 255
needing 226
needle 175
negative 273
negativity 248
negligence 245
negligent 267
negotiate 260
neigh 80
neighbour 80, 112, 251
neither 90
nephew 94, 150
nestle 156
net 67, 133, 144

netted 225
netting 225
nettle 174
neuron 120
neurotic 271
neuter 95
neutral 95
neutron 95
never 110, 151
new 94, 202
next 193
nib 69, 131, 144
nibble 174
nice 86, 155
nicely 231, 276
niche 162
niece 84, 155
niggle 174
night 88
nihilism 247
nimble 175
nimbly 277
ninth 152
nip 69, 130, 144
nipple 174
nit 144
no 90, 144, 202, 207
noble 175, 277
nod 134, 144
nodding 225
node 91
noise 110
noiseless 273
noisily 276
noisy 274
nominee 245
nonchalant 162
none 75, 199
nonsense 154
nook 99, 136
noon 96
noose 97, 154
nor 102
norm 102
Norman 265
Norse 102
north 102, 152
northern 147, 270
nose 91
not 72, 133, 144, 207
notch 166
note 91

notelet 231, 249
nothing 75
notice 247
noticeable 231, 264
notify 261
notion 160, 252
notoriety 252
nought   106
nourish 76, 262
novice 247
now 108
nozzle 174
nude 94
nudge 168
nugget 140
nuisance 98
numb 143
numbered 228
nun 74, 144, 199
nurse 107, 154
nursery 246
nut 74, 132, 144
nuzzle 174
nylon 88
nymph 150
oaf 92
oafs 238
oak 92
oar 105, 203
oases 240
oasis 240
oats 92
obdurate 266
obedience 245
obedient 267
obediently 275
obey 80
obeyed 234
oblique 138
obscure 120
observation 160
observatory 250
obsolete 85
obvious 272
occasion 138,163
occident 171
occult 138
occupy 138
occur 138
ocean 162
odd 135
oddly 275
odour 112,251

of 72
off 72, 149
offend 149, 260
offered 228
office 149, 247
official 161
ogle 175
ogre 111
oil 110
old 90
omniscience 156
on 72, 144
once 179
one 179, 199
onion 180
only 83
onslaught 105
ooze 97
opaque 138
operatic 271
operation 160
opinion 180
opium 248
opportunity 111,
   248
oppression 161, 251
opprobrium 248
optic 271
optimism 247
optimist 248
opulence 245
opulent 267
or 102, 203
orange 177, 195
orbited 228
orchestra 138
ordinary 266
ore 103, 203
organ 146
organic 271
organise 261
oriental 264
ornament 249
orphan 146, 150
orphanage 243
orthography 150
orthopaedic 86
osprey 80
ostrich 165
other 75
ouch 109
ought 106
our 119, 205

oust 109
out 108
outbidden 227
outrageous 232,
   268, 273
outwitted 227
ovary 244
oven 75
over 110
overwhelm 179
own 92
ox 170
Oxford 170
oxygen 70, 170
oyster 109
pace 78, 155
paced 257
pacify 261
pack 137
package 243
pact 192
pad 66, 130
paddle 174
paediatric 86
pagan 265
page 78, 168
pageant 169
paid 78
pail 78, 172, 200
pain 78, 200
painlessly 275
paint 78
pair 115, 205
palace 174
pale 77, 200
pall 103, 173
pallid 173, 272
palm 101
Pam 66, 120, 142
pamphlet 150
pan 66, 130, 144
panacea 114
panache 162
pane 77, 200
panel 176
pang 66, 147
panic 136
panicked 229
panicky 229
pant 66
papal 265
par 100
parachute 162

paradigm 212
paragraph 150
parallel 173
parcel 155
parch 101
pare 116, 205
pariah 113
park 100
parliament 213, 249
parlour 112, 251
parlous 274
parochial 138
parsimonious 272
parsley 84
part 100
partial 160
particular 266
parties 239
party 83
pass 154
passion 161, 251
passive 273
passively 275
passivity 248
past 101, 190
paste 78
pat 66, 120, 132
patch 166
path 101, 152
pathetic 271
pathology 250
patient 160
patricide 244
patriotic 271
patrolled 229
patted 225
pattern 147
patting 225
Paul 105
pause 158
pave 78, 151
pavement 231
paw 104, 203
pawn 104
pay 79
payee 245
pea 83
peace 155, 200
peaceful 270
peacefully 276
peach 83
peak 83, 200
peal 83, 172, 200

pear 116, 205
pearl 107, 172, 203
peasant 68
peat 83
pebble 174
peck 137
pedal 135, 207
pedalled 229
pedalling 229
peddle 174, 207
peek 82, 200
peel 82, 172, 200
peep 82
peeped 256
peer 113, 204
peerage 243
peerless 273
peg 67, 130, 139
pen 67, 130, 144
penal 265
pence 155
pencil 155, 176
pendulum 169
pension 162, 251
people 85, 175
perceive 84
perfection 160
perhaps 164
peril 176, 177
perilous 273
perilously 275
period 114
perish 262
perjury 167
permissible 270
permission 161, 251
permitted 227
perplex 170
persistence 245
persistency 244
persistent 267
personal 106
persuade 179
Perth 106
pessimism 247
pessimist 248
pest 67
pesticide 244
pestle 156
pet 67, 130, 133
petal 133
petroleum 246
petulance 243

petulant 265
pew 94
pewter 94
phantom 150
pharmacy150
phase 78, 150, 158,
  206
pneasant 150
phenomenon 150
phial 118, 150
philately 150
Philip 150
phlegm 150, 212
phoenix 86
phone 150
phoneme 150
phoney 150
phonic 150
phosphate 150
photo 150
phrase 78, 150, 158
physical 150
physics 70, 150
physique 138
pi 201
pianos 240
pick 137
picnic 136
picnicking 229
picture 166, 252
picturesque 138
pie 89, 201
piece 84, 155, 200
pier 114, 204
pierce 114, 155
piety 252
pig 69, 130, 139
pigeon 169
pike 87, 136
pilgrimage 243
pill 173
pillar 111, 173, 244
pin 69, 130, 144
pinch 195
pine 86
ping 147
pink 70, 136, 191
pint 89
pioneer 245
pip 69, 130
pipe 87
pipette 246
pique 138

pirouette 246
pit 69, 130, 132
pitch 166
piteous 268
pity 133
pivotal 228
pixie 84, 170
place 78, 155, 185,
  200
placid 272
placidly 275
plague 140
plaice 200
plaid 67
plain 79
plait 67
plan 185
plane 77
planet 185
plank 136, 185, 191
plant 185, 191
plaster 101
plastic 136
plate 77
plateau 93
platelet 249
platitude 94
play 79, 185
played 234
pleaded 255
please 158
pleasure 68, 163
pledge 168
pliers 118
plight 88
plonk 191
plop 72, 185
plot 72, 185
plough 109
ploy 109
pluck 137
plug 74, 185
plum 75, 185
plumage 243
plumb 143
plumber 246
plump 185, 192
plunge 195
plural 265
plus 153, 185
plush 185
pneumatic 95, 214
pneumonia 95, 214

poach 92
pocketed 228
pod 130, 134
podium 248
point 110
poise 110
poison 110
poke 91, 136
poked 257
poker 230
polar 266
pole 91, 202
police 155
polish 174, 262
polite 87
politician 161
poll 90, 173, 202
pollution 160
pond 72, 191
pong 147
poodle 175
pool 96, 172
poor 117, 203
poorly 275
pop 72, 130
pope 91
popping 225
poppy 130
popular 111, 244,
  266
popularly 275
population 160
populous 274
porcelain 147
porch 103
pore 103, 203
pork 102
port 102
portend 260
portion 160
portmanteau 93
Portuguese 246
pose 91
posh 159
position 160
positive 273
positively 275
posse 82
possess 158
possession 161, 251
possibility 248
possible 271
possibly 277

post 190
posterior 290
postgraduate 290
posthumous 290
post-mortem 290
postpone 290
postscript 290
posture 252
pot 72, 130, 133
potassium 248
potato 90
potatoes 239
potential 265
potion 160
pouch 109
pound 109
pour 105, 203
pout 109
powder 108
power 119
powerfully 276
practical 265
practice 155, 210, 247
practise 154, 210
praise 78
pram 183
prance 155
prawn 104
pray 79, 200
prayed 234
prayer 116
preamble 286
prearrange 286
precarious 272
precaution 286
precede 286
precinct 194
precious 161
precision 163
preclude 286
precognition 286
preconception 286
precursor 286
predate 286
predecease 286
predicate 262, 267
predilection 286
predisposition 286
predominant 286
pre-eminent 286
pre-empt 286
preen 82

preface 286
prefect 286
preference 286
preferred 227
prefix 170, 286
prejudge 286
prejudice 167, 247, 286
premature 286
premise 286
premium 248
premonition 286
preoccupation 286
prepare 286
preposition 160, 286
prerogative 286
presage 286
prescience 286
presence 245
present 158, 183, 267
presently 275
press 154, 183
prestige 164
presumptuous 274
presuppose 286
pretend 260
pretentious 272
pretty 70, 83, 274
prevent 286
previous 272, 286
prey 80, 183, 200
price 87, 155
prick 137, 183
prickly 274
priest 84
prig 69
prim 69, 183
principal 210, 265
principle 210
prior 119
prism 194
prison 158
privilege 169
prize 157
probably 277
probe 91
proceed 290
process 290
procession 290
procreate 290
prodding 225
produce 290

product 290
profession 161, 251
professor 250
profit 206
profited 228
profiteer 245
progress 290
prologue 140
prominence 245
prominent 267
promise 143
promote 290
prong 148
pronounceable 231
pronouncement 249
proof 96
prop 72, 183
prophet 206
propitious 272
propriety 252
prosperity 248
protection 160
protein 84
proudly 275
prove 96
provide 290
provision 163
prudery 246
pry 87
psalm 101, 157
pseudonym 157
psoriasis 157
psyche 157
psychedelic 157
psychiatry 157
psychic 157
psychology 157, 250
psychometric 157
psychotic 157
ptarmigan 214
pterodactyl 214
pub 131
public 136
publicity 248, 278
publish 262
puddle 174
puff 149
puffin 149
pull 100, 173
pulley 84
pump 75, 192
pun 74, 144
punch 195

punctuality 248
puncture 166, 252
punish 145, 262
punt 191
puny 95
pup 74, 130
puppy 130
purchase 107
purdah 113
pure 120
purely 231, 277
purify 261
purl 203
purple 107
purpose 107
purr 107
purse 107, 154
pursuit 98
pus 74, 153
put 100
putrefy 260
putrid 272
putt 133
puzzle 174
pygmy 70
pylon 88
pyramid 70
pyre 118
quack 137, 141
quad 73, 141
quail 79
quaint 78, 141
quake 141
qualify 73, 261
quality 73, 248
qualm 101
quandary 244
quantify 261
quantity 73, 248
quarrelled 229
quarry 177
quart 104
quarter 104
quay 85, 139, 201
queen 82, 141
queer 113, 141
quest 141
question 141, 167
queue 95, 139, 202
quibble 174
quiche 139, 162
quick 137, 141
quickly 275

quid 141
quiet 141
quietly 275
quill 141
quilt 141
quip 141
quite 141
quiver 141
quiz 158
quota 112, 141
quote 141
rabbit 132
rabble 174
rabid 132, 272
raccoon 138
race 78, 155
raced 257
rack 137, 176
racket 207
racquet 139, 207
racy 156
radiator 250
radios 240
radish 135
radium 147, 248
raffle 174
raft 101, 192
rag 66, 139, 176
rage 168
raid 78
raided 255
rail 78, 172
rain 78, 200
raise 78, 158, 200
raisin 158
rake 77
raked 257
ram 66, 176
ramble 175
ramify 261
ramp 66, 192
ran 66, 144, 176
ranch 195
rang 66, 147
range 195
rank 66, 136, 191
rankle 175
rant 66, 191
rap 66, 176, 208
rapid 131, 272
rapidity 248
rapidly 275
rapist 248

rapport 214
rapt 193
rare 116
rarefy 260
rascal 101
rash 66, 159, 176
rashes 237
rasp 190
rat 66, 132, 176
ratchet 166
rate 77
rather 101, 110
ratify 261
rattle 174
rave 78, 151
ravish 262
raw 104, 203
ray 79
raze 78, 200
razor 157
reach 83
read 68, 83, 176, 200
readily 276
readiness 250
reading 226
readjust 290
ready 68, 83, 274
realise 261
ream 83
reap 83
reapply 290
rear 113
rearrange 290
reason 158
rebel 132, 176
rebelled 229
rebuild 290
recall 290
recede 85
receipt 84, 214
receive 84, 290
receivership 251
recipe 82
recluse 99
recognition 160
recommence 290
recompose 290
recruit 98
recruitment 249
rectify 261
recur 290
recurred 227
red 77, 176

reddish 272
redress 290
reduce 290
redundant 265
reed 82, 200
reek 208
reel 82, 172
refectory 250
referee 245
referenda 241
referendum 241
referral 227
refine 87
refinery 246
reflection 160
refuse 94
regain 290
regal 265
regatta 112
reggae 81
regime 164
regress 290
regretted 227
regular 266
regularity 248, 275
rehearse 107, 164
reign 80, 145, 200
rein 80, 200
reindeer 80
relapse 195
relax 170, 290
release 154
reliability 248
reliable 264
relief 84
relieve 84
religious 272
relish 174, 262
reluctance 243
reluctant 265
renal 265
rend 67
rent 67, 91
reopen 290
repeat 290
repelled 229
repetition 160
replenish 145, 262
replete 85
replica 112
reply 87
reptilian 265
republic 136

request 141
require 141
rescue 94
residue 94
resign 145
resin 158
respect 192
respite 87
responsibility 248
responsible 271
responsive 273
rest 67, 176
restaurateur 247
retirement 249
retrieve 290
reverence 245
reverent 267
revise 158, 290
revision 163
revive 290
reward 104
rewind 290
rhapsody 178
rhea 178
rhesus 178
rhetoric 178
rheumatic 99, 271
rheumatism 178
rhinoceros 178
rhizome 178
Rhodes 178
rhodium178
rhododendron 178
rhubarb 178
rhyme 88, 178
rhythm 178, 196
rib 69, 131, 166
ribbon 132
rice 86, 155
rich 70, 165, 176
riches 237
rick 137
ricochet 81, 162
rid 69, 134
ridden 259
riddle 174
ride 86
ridge 168
ridicule 94
ridiculous 273
ridiculously 275
rife 87
rifle 175

rift 70, 192
rig 69, 176
right 88, 201, 208
righteous 268
rigid 168, 272
rigidity 248
rigidly 275
rigour 140
rile 87
rim 69, 142, 176
rimless 225
rind 89, 191
ring 70, 147, 208
rink 70, 136, 191
rinse 154
riot 119
rip 69, 130, 176
ripe 87, 176
ripping 225
ripple 174
rise 87, 158
risen 259
risk 70, 191
rite 201
road 92, 176, 202
roam 92, 202
roar 105, 203
roast 92, 190
rob 72, 131, 176
robber 246
robbing 225
robin 132
rock 137, 176
rod 176
rode 91, 202
roe 93, 202
rogue 140
roll 90, 173, 176
Roman 265
Rome 91, 202
romp 72
roof 96
rook 99, 136
room 96
root 96, 202
rope 91, 176
rose 91
rosette 246
rot 72, 133, 176
rote 91, 202, 208
rotten 146
rough 76, 150
roulette 246

round 109
rout 109
route 98, 202
rove 91
row 92, 108, 202
rowing 227
Roy 109
royal 109, 265
royalty 252
rub 74, 131, 176
rubbish 132
rude 99
rudely 277
rudeness 231
rue 97
ruffle 174
rug 74, 139, 176
rum 74
rumble 175
rumour 112, 251
rump 75, 192
run 74, 144, 176
rung 75, 147, 208
runner 225
running 225
runny 144, 225
runt 191
ruse 99
rush 75, 159, 176
rushed 256
rusk 75
Russia 161
rust 75
rustle 156
rut 74, 132
Ruth 98
ruthless 273
ruthlessly 275
rye 89, 208
Sabbath 132
sable 175
saboteur 247
sabre 111
sachet 81, 162
sack 137
sacrilegious 272
sad 66, 134, 153
sadden 260
saddle 174
sadistic 271
sadly 225, 275
sadness 250
safe 78

safely 231, 277
safety 231
sage 78
said 68
sail 79, 172, 200
saint 78
sainthood 247
sake 77
salad 174
salary 244
sale 200
salmon 213
salt 103
Sam 66, 142, 153
same 77
sample 175
sanctify 261
sanctimonious 272
sanctity 248
sanctuary 266
sand 66, 191
sandwich 165
sane 77
sanely 277
sang 66, 147
sank 66, 36, 191
sap 66, 153
sapling 249
sapphire 214
Sarah 113
sarcasm 194
sash 66
sat 66, 132, 153
satchel 166, 176
satiate 260
satin 133
Saturday 112
saucer 105
saunter 105
sausage 74, 169, 243
savage 169
save 78, 151
saved 230
saviour 112, 251
saw 104, 203
say 79
saying 227
scab 187
scaffold 149
scald 103, 193
scale 77
scalp 187, 193
scalpel 176

scam 187
scamp 187, 192
scan 187
scant 191
scar 100, 187
scare 116
scarf 187
scarily 276
scarves 238
scary 274
scene 85, 156, 200,
    208
scenery 156
scent 156, 208
sceptre 156
schedule 138
scheme 85, 138
schizophrenia 138
scholarship 251
school 96, 138
sciatica 156
science 156
scientific 136, 271
scintillate156
scion 156
scissors 156, 158
scold 187, 193
scone 73
scoop 96
scoot 96, 187
scorch 103
score 103
scorn 103
Scot 72, 187
scotch 166
scour 119
scout 109
scrap 189
scrape 189
scratch 166, 189
scream 189
screech 189
screed 82
screen 189
screw 97, 189
script 189
scroll 173
scrub 189
scrum 189
scull 187, 207
scum 74, 187
scurrilous 274
scythe 156

sea 83, 200
seal 83
sealing 200, 208
seam 83, 200
sear 113
search 107
seat 83
secretary 244
sectarian 265
section 160
secure 120
sedate 260
see 82, 200
seed 82
seeing 232
seek 82
seem 82, 200
seen 82, 200, 208
seep 82
seize 84, 157
seizure 164
selection 160
self 67, 194
sell 173, 208
seller 208
selves 238
seminary 244
send 67, 191
senile 87
senior 180
sense 154
sensibly 277
sensitive 273
sensitivity 248
sent 67, 191, 208
sententious 272
separate 262, 267
sepulchre 111
serene 85
serf 203
sergeant 102, 169
serial 114, 208
series 114
serious 272
serve 106
service 155, 247
serviceable 231
serviette 246
session 161, 251
set 67, 133 153, 209
settle 174
seventh 152
severe 114

severely 231, 277
sew 92, 202
sex 170
shabbily 276
shabby 132
shack 137, 159
shackle 174
shade 78, 159
shaded 255
shadow 135
shaft 101, 159
shake 77
shaken 146, 259
shale 77
shall 159, 173
sham 159
shamble 175
shame 77, 159
shameful 231
shampoo 159
shape 77, 159
shard 100
share 116, 159
shark 100, 159
sharp 101
shave 78, 151, 159
shawl 104
she 81, 159
sheaf 159
shear 159, 204
sheaves 238
shed 159
sheen 82, 159
sheep 82, 159
sheer 204
sheet 82, 159
shelf 194
shell 159
shelves 238
sherry 159
shield 84
shift 192
shin 69, 159
shine 87, 159
shingle 174
ship 159
shirt 106, 159
shoal 92, 159
shock 137, 159
shoe 98, 159, 202
shone 73, 159
shoo 202
shook 99, 159

shoot 96, 9
shop 159
shopper 246
shore 103, 159, 203
shorn 103, 159
short 103
shorten 260
shot 72, 159
should 100
shoulder 93
shout 109
shove 75, 151, 159
show 92, 159
shower 119
shrank 189
shred 189
shrew 97, 189
shrewd 97
shriek 84, 189
shrill 173, 189
shrimp 189
shrine 189
shrink 136, 189, 191
shroud 189
shrub 189
shrug 189
shudder 135
shuffle 174
shun 159
shunt 159
shut 159
shuttle 174
shy 87, 159
sibling 249
sick 137
sickle 174
side 86
sidle 175
siege 84
sieve 71
sift 70, 192
sigh 88
sight 88, 201
sign 145
signal 175
signalled 229
signet 208
significance 243
significant 265
silence 245
silent 267
silently 275
silhouette 213, 246

silk 193
silliness 250
silly 83, 173, 274
silver 110, 246
similar 266
simile 82
simple 175
simply 277
simulate 260
simultaneous 268
sin 69, 144, 153
sing 70, 147
singe 195
singeing 232
single 148, 174
singly 277
singular 244, 266
sink 70,136, 191
sip 69, 130, 153
sire 117
sister 110, 246
sisterhood 247
sit 69, 132, 153
site 86, 201
six 170
sixth 152
sizzle 174
skate 77
skeletal 265
sketch 166, 187
sketches 237
skew 94
ski 187
skid 187
skiing 232
skill 173, 187
skim 187
skimp 192
skin 69, 187
skip 69, 187
skipped 225
skipper 225
skipping 225
skirt 106, 187
skive 87
skull 173, 187, 207
sky 87, 187
slab 186
slack 186
slacken 260
slain 79
slam 186
slant 191

slap 186
slash 159, 186
slat 186
slate 77
slaughter 105
slave 78, 151
slay 79, 186, 200
sled 67, 186
sledge 168
sleek 82
sleep 82
sleepless 273
sleet 82
sleigh 80, 200
sleight 88, 201
slept 257
sleuth 99
slice 155
slick 186
slid 69, 186
slide 87
slight 191
slim 69, 186
sling 148
slink 137, 191
slip 69, 186
slipping 225
slit 69, 186
slob 186
sloe 93
slog 72
sloop 96
slope 91
sloppiness 250
slosh 186
slot 72
slow 92
sludge 168
slug 74
sluggish 272
sluice 98
slum 74
slump 192
slush 159, 186
sly 87
smack 137, 187
small 103, 173, 187
smash 159, 187
smear 113
smell 187
smelled 257
smelly 274
smelt 257

smile 87, 187
smite 87
smog 72, 187
smoke 136, 187
smother 75
smudge 168
smug 74
smut 187
snack 137, 187
snag 66, 187
snail 79, 172
snake 77
snap 66, 187
snapping 225
snare 116
snatch 166
sneak 83
sneer 113
sniff 149
sniffed 256
sniffle 174
snip 69, 187
snipe 87
snob 187
snobbish 272
snoop 96
snooze 97
snore 103
snort 103
snout 109
snow 92, 187
snub 74,187
snuff 149
snuffle 174
snuggle 174
so 90, 202
soak 92
soap 92
soar 105, 203
sob 72, 131, 153
sobbing 225
sobriety 252
social 161
sociology 250
sock 137
soft 72, 192
soften 260
softness 250
soil 110, 172
solar 266
sold 90, 193
soldier 169
sole 91, 202

solely 277
solemn   143
solicitor 250
solid 174, 272
solidity 248
solitary 266
solo 90
solos 240
solstice 247
solution 160
solvency 244
solvent 267
sombre   111
some 75, 199
somersault 75
son 75, 199
song 147
soon 96
sop 72
sopranos 240
sordid 272
sordidness 250
sore 103, 203
sorely 277
sort 102, 203
soubriquet 81
sought 106, 203
soul 93, 202
sound 109
soup 98
sour 119
south 109
southern 76, 147,
   270
sovereign 145
sovereignty 252
sow 92, 108, 202
space 78, 186
spacious 272
spade 78, 186
spaghetti 141
Spain 79, 186
spam 66, 186
span 66
spank 191
spar 100
spare 116
spark 186
spasm 194
spat 66, 186
spatter 188
spawn 104
spay 79

speak 83
speaker 226
speaking 226
spear 113
special 161
specialty 252
species 161
specify 261
specious 274
speck 137, 186
spectre 111
sped 67
speech 82
speed 82
spell 173
spelled 257
spelt 257
spend 191
spent 191
sphere 114, 150
sphincter 150
sphinx 150, 170
spice 87, 155
spiced 257
spicy 156
spike 87, 136
spill 173
spillage 243
spilled 257
spilt 257
spin 69, 186
spine 87
spineless 231, 273
spinelessly 275
spinning 225
spit 69, 186
spitting 225
splash 159, 188
splashes 237
splay 188
spleen 188
splendid 188
splice 87, 155, 188
splint 188
splinter 188
split 188
splodge 188
splutter 188
spoil 110, 172
spoke 91
spoken 259
sponge 75
sponsor 111

spontaneous 268
spooky 274
spool 96, 172
spoon 96, 186
spore 103
sport 103
sportsmanship 251
spot 72
spouse 109, 154
sprain 79, 189
sprang 189
sprat 189
sprawl 189
spray 79, 189
spread 68, 189
spree 82, 189
sprig 189
spring 148, 189
spruce 189
sprung 189
spry 189
spud 74
spun 74
spur 107
spurious 120, 272
spurn 107
spy 87
squabble 73
squad 73
squadron 73
squalid 141, 174
squalor 73
squander 73
square 141
squash 73, 141
squat 73, 141
squeak 141
squeal 141
squire 141
squirm 141
stab 66, 186
stable 175
stack 186
stadium 248
staff 101, 149
stag 66, 186
stage 78
staid 79
stain 79
stair 115, 205
stake 77, 200
stale 77
stalk 104

stall 103, 173
stamp 192
stamped 226
stampede 85
stance 101, 155
stand 186, 191
standardise 261
stank 156, 191
staple 175
star 100, 186
starch 101
stare 116, 205
stark 100
starlet 249
starling 249
start 100
stash 159, 186
state 77
stated 255
stateless 273
statement 249
static 271
station 160
stationary 210, 266
stationery 210, 246
statuesque 138
statuette 246
stature 166, 252
status 153
stave 78
stay 79
stayed 234
steadily 276
steadiness 250
steady 68, 274
steak 79, 200
steal 83, 172, 200
stealth 68, 195
steam 83
steel 82, 200
steep 82
steeple 175
steer 113
stem 67,186
stench 195
stencil 176
step 186
stern 106
stew 94
stick 137, 186
stiff 149, 186
stile 87
still 173, 186

sting 147
stink 137, 186, 191
stint 191
stir 106
stitch 166
stitches 237
stoat 92
stock 186
stoke 91
stole 91
stolen 146
stolid 174, 272
stomach 138
stomp 72, 192
stone 91
stood 99
stool 96, 172
stoop 96
stop 72, 186
stopped 225
stopper 225
stopping 225
store 103
storey 200
stork 103
storm 103
story 84, 200
stove 91, 151
stow 92
straggle 174
straggly 274
straight 80, 200
strain 79, 189
strait 200
strand 189, 191
strange 189, 195
strangeness 250
strangle 148
strap 189
strategic 271
straw 104, 189
stray 189
streak 189
stream 189
street 82, 189
strengthen 260
stress 154, 189
stretch 166, 189
strict 189
stricture 252
strident 267
strife 87, 189
strike 189

string 148, 189
strip 189
stripe 87, 189
strive 189
striven 259
strobe 91
stroke 189
stroll 173, 189
strong 147, 189
strove 91
structure 166, 252
struggle 174
strum 189
stub 74, 186
stuck 137, 186
stud 74
study 135
studying 234
stuff 149, 186
stultify 261
stumble 175
stump 192
stun 74, 186
stung 148
stunt 186, 191
stupefy 260
stupid 272
stupidity 248
stupidly 275
style 87
stylish 230, 272
sub-aquatic 290
subconscious 290
subcontinent 290
subcontract 290
subdivide 290
subdue 94, 290
subeditor 290
subject 290
subjective 290
subjugate 290
sublime 87, 290
submarine 290
submerge 290
submit 290
subordinate 262,
    267, 290
subscribe 290
subservient 290
subsidence 290
subsidy 290
subsist 290
subsoil 290

substance 290
substantiate 260
substitute 290
subsume 290
subterranean 290
subterraneous 268
sub-terrestrial 290
subtle 211
subtract 290
suburb 107, 290
subversive 290
subway 290
success 171
succession 161, 251
successor 250
succinct 194
succour 138
succulent 138
succumb 138, 143
such 75, 165
suck 137
suckle 174
sudden 135
Sue 97
suede 179
suffer 149
sufficient 161, 267
suffix 149, 170
suffragette 246
sugar 140, 160
sugary 274
suggest 169
suggestion 167
suicide 244
suit 98
suitably 277
suite 200
sulphur 112
sultan 146
sum 74, 142, 199
summary 244
summer 142
summit 142
sun 74, 144, 153, 199
sundae 200
Sunday 200
sung 75, 147
sunk 75, 191
superb 291
superficial 291
superhuman 291
superintendent 291

superlative 291
supermarket 291
supernatural 291
supernova 291
superpower 291
superstition 291
supervise 261, 291
supple 174
supplement 249
suppression 161, 251
sure 117, 160, 203
surely 277
surf 203
surface 107
surfeit 71
surgeon 178
surname 107
surplus 107
surprise 107, 158
survey 80
survive 107
suspicion 161
swab 188
swallow 73, 173
swam 188
swamp 192
swan 73, 188
swap 73, 188
swarm 104
swathe 153
sway 79
swayed 234
swear 116
sweat 68
sweater 68
swede 85
sweep 82
sweet 82, 200
sweetly 275
swell 173
swept 257
swift 192
swig 188
swill 173
swim 69, 188
swimming 225
swine 87
swing 148
swipe 87
swiped 257
swirl 106
Swiss 154

switch 166
swizz 157
swoon 96
swoop 96
sword 103, 215
swore 103
sworn 103
swum 74
sycamore 70
syllable 70
symbiosis 291
symbol 70, 291
symmetry 70, 291
sympathetic 271, 291
sympathy 70
symphonic 291
symphony 150, 291
symposium 291
symptom 70, 291
synagogue 140
synapse 291
synchromesh 291
synchronise 291
syndicate 262, 267, 291
syndrome 291
synecdoche 82
synergy 168
synod 291
synonym 70, 291
synonymous 291
synopses 240
synopsis 240, 291
syntheses 240
synthesis 240
synthetic 271, 291
syringe 70
syrup 70
system 70
tab 66, 131, 132
table 175
tableau 93
tack 137
tackle 174
tact 192
tag 66, 132, 139
tail 79, 172, 200
take 77, 136
taken 146, 259
taking 230
tale 77, 200
talent 174

talk 104
tall 103, 173
tame 77
tan 66, 132, 144
tang 66, 147
tangle 148, 174
tank 66, 136, 191
tannin 144
tap 66, 130, 132,
tape 77
tar 100
tart 100
task 101, 191
taste 78
tasteless 231
tattoo 133
taught 105
taut 105
tautology 250
tavern 147
tax 170
taxes 237
taxidermy 170
taxiing 232
taxonomy 170
tea 83, 201
teach 83
teacher 246
teak 83
teal 83
team 83
tear 113, 116 204
teat 83
technical 138
technique 138
Ted 132
tedious 272
tedium 248
tee 82, 201
teem 82
teen 82
telegraph 150
telescopic 271
television 163
tell 173
temperate 266
temple 175
temporarily 276
temporary 266
tempt 194
ten 67, 132, 144
tend 67, 191
tendency 244

tendentious 272
tenor 145
tense 154
tension 162, 251
tent 67, 191
tenth 152, 196
tepid 272
tequila 139
term 106
terrapin 177
terrible 271
terribly 277
terrific 136, 271
terrifically 278
terrify 261
territory 250
Tess 154
test 67
tether 110
Teutonic 95
text 193
Thailand 134
Thames 134
than 153
thank 136, 152, 191
thanked 256
that 153
thatch 166
thaw 104
the 111,153
theatre 111
their 115, 205
them 153
then 153
theorem 114
theory 114
therapist 248
there 115, 205
thesaurus 105
these 85
theses 240
thesis 240
they 80, 153
thick 137, 152
thicken 260
thief 84
thieves 238
thigh 88
thimble 175
thin 69, 144, 152
thing 148
think 136, 152, 191
thinly 225

thinned 225
thinner 225
thinnest 225
thinning 225
third 106
thirteen 106, 152
thirteenth 152
thirty 106, 152
this 153
thistle 156
Thomas 134
thong 167
thorn 152
thorough 112
thoroughly 112
those 153
though 93
thought 106
thrash 159, 190
thread 68, 190
threat 68, 190
three 82, 152, 190
threw 97, 190, 202
thrift 190
thrill 173
throat 92, 190
throb 190
throes 93
throne 91, 190, 202
throng 190
through 98, 190, 202
throw 92, 190
thrown 202
thrush 159, 190
thrushes 237
thrust 190
thumb 143
thump 75, 192
Thursday 107
thwack 190
thwart 190
thyme 88, 134, 201
tick 137
tickle 174
tickly 274
tidal 264
tidally 276
tide 86
tie 89
tier 114, 204
tighten 260
tightly 275
tile 87

till 173
Tim 69, 132, 142
time 87, 201
timeless 273
timely 231
times 68
timid 143, 272
timidity 248, 275
tin 69, 132, 144
tincture 252
tingle 148, 174
tint 70, 191
tip 69, 130, 132
tipple 174
tire 205
tireless 231
title 175
titular 266
to 96, 202
toad 92
toast 92
today 79
toddle 174
toe 93, 202
toffee 149
toggle 174
toil 110, 172
toilet 110
told 90, 193
toll 173
Tom 72, 132, 142
tomato 90
tomatoes 239
tomb 143
tome 91
ton 75
tonal 264
tonality 248
tone 91
toneless 231
tongue 76, 148
tonic 136
tonight 88
too 202
took 99, 136
tool 96, 172
tooth 96
top 72, 130, 132
topic 131, 136
topical 265
topple 174
tore 103, 203
torn 103

tornado 239
tornadoes 239
tornados 239
torpedoes 239
torrential 160
torrid 272
toss 154
tot 72
touch 76, 165
tough 76, 150
toughen 260
tour 117, 203
tourniquet 81, 139
tow 92, 202
toward 104
towel 119
tower 119
town 108
toy 109
trace 78, 155
traceable 231
track 137, 183
tract 183
tractor 111, 250
trade 78
traded 255
traffic 136
trafficking 229
tragedy 169
tragic 136, 168
trail 79, 172
train 79
trainee 245
trait 79
tram 66, 183
tramp 183, 192
trample 175
trance 101, 155
transaction 291
transatlantic 291
transcend 260
transcendental 291
transcribe 291
transfer 291
transform 291
transgress 291
transient 291
transit 291
translate 291
transmission 161,
251
transmit 291
transparent 291

transplant 291
transport 291
transverse 291
trap 66, 183
trash 159, 183
travel 176
travelled 229
traveller 229
trawl 104
tray 79
tread 183
treasure 68, 163
treat 83
tree 82
tremendous 273
tremor 143
trench 183
trend 191
trestle 156
trial 118
triangle 287
tribal 265
tribally 276
tribunal 287
tributary 244
trice 287
trick 183
tricolour 287
tricycle 287
trident 287
triennial 287
trifle 175
trifoliate 287
trigonometry 287
trilateral 287
trill 183
trilogy 287
trim 69, 183
trimester 287
trinity 287
trinomial 287
trip 69, 183
tripe 87
triple 287
triplet 287
triplicate 287
tripod 287
tripping 225
triptych 287
trireme 287
trite 87
triumph 150
trodden 259

troll 173
trolley 84
troop 96
trophy 150
tropic 131
tropical 265
trot 72
trotting 225
trouble 76
trough 74, 150
trousseau 93
trout 109
trove 91
truck 137
trudge 168
true 97
truffle 174
trump 192
trunk 137, 191
trust 190
trusted 226
trustee 245
truth 98, 152
try 87
trying 234
tub 74, 131, 132
tuba 166
tube 94, 166
tuck 137
Tudor 166
Tuesday 166
tuft 192
tug 74, 132, 139
tuition 166
tulip 166
tumble 175
tummy 142
tuna 166
tune 166
tuneless 273
tunic 95, 166
tunnel 176
turbine 107
turbulence 245
turbulent 267
turkey 84, 107
turnip 107
turtle 107
tusk 75
tussle 174
tweak 83
twelfth 152, 196,
    212

twelve 188
twenty 188
twice 155, 188
twig 69, 188
twin 188
twine 87
twirl 106
twist 188
twit 188
two 97, 202
tying 232
type 87
typhoid 88
typical 70
tyrant 118
tyre 118, 205
ugliness 250
ugly 274
ukulele 82
umpire 117
unaccountable 280
unaffected 280
unassailable 280
unattached 280
unavailing 280
unaware 280
unbidden 280
uncommon 280
uncompromising
    280
unconscionable 280
unconscious 280
uncouth 98
uncover 280
under 110
undo 280
undoubted 280
uneasy 280
unemployed 280
unexceptional 280
unfortunate 280
unfounded 280
unfriendly 280
unguarded 280
unhappy 280
unhinge 280
unimpeachable 280
union 180
unique 138
unitary 266
universal 265
university 248
unjust 280

unkempt 280
unkind 280
unmitigated 280
unnatural 280
unnecessary 280
unpack 280
unpick 280
unpopular 280
unravel 280
unreliable 280
unruly 280
unsavoury 280
unsightly 280
unspeakable 280
unsteady 280
unsung 280
untie 280
untrue 280
unwell 280
unwieldy 280
unwilling 280
unwitting 280
up 74
urban 265
urchin 107
urge 107
urgent 107, 267
urgently 275
urine 120
urn 107, 203
us 74, 153
use 94, 154
usherette 246
usual 163, 265
usually 276
utilitarian 265
uxorious 170
vacant 265
vacantly 275
vaccinate 171
vacuous 273
vagrant 265
vague 140
vagueness 250
vain 151, 200
valance 174
vale 77, 200
valet 81
valley 84
valour 251
vamp 66, 151
van 66, 151
vane 77, 200

vanish 145, 262
vanquish 262
vapid 272
vapour 112, 251
variety 252
various 272
vast 101, 151
vat 66, 151
vault 105
vaunt 105
veal 151, 172
veer 113
vegan 265
vehement 213
vehicle 213
veil 80, 200
vein 80, 200
velar 266
venal 265
vendetta 112
vent 151, 191
venture 166, 252
veranda 112
verb 106, 151
verify 261
verse 106
version 162, 251
very 151, 177
vessel 176
vest 67, 151
vet 67, 151
vex 170
vibe 151
vibrant 265
vibrantly 275
vicar 244
vice 151, 155, 86
vicious 161
Victorian 265
victorious 272
view 94
vigilante 82
vigour 112, 140, 251
vile 87, 151
vilify 261
village 169, 243
villain 147
vim 151
vindictive 273
vine 86, 151
vinegar 111, 244
violate 119
violence 245

violent 119, 267
violently 275
violet 119
virulence 245
virulent 267
visibility 248
visible 271
visitor 250
visual 163
vital 265
vivacious 161
vocal 265
vogue 140
voice 110, 155
void 110
volcano 239
volcanoes 239
volcanos 239
vole 91
volley 84
volt 151
voluntarily 276
voluntary 266
vote 91, 151
vouch 109
voucher 109
vow 108, 151
vowel 119
voyage 109
voyeur 247
vying 232
wade 78
waded 255
wading 230
waffle 174
waft 192
wag 66, 139, 178
wage 78, 168
wagged 225
waggle 174
wagon 140
waif 78
waifs 238
wail 79, 172
waist 200
wait 78, 200
waited 255
waive 78, 200
wake 77, 136
walk 104
walked 256
wall 103, 173
wallet 73

wallow 73, 173
wan 73
wand 73, 191
wander 73
wandered 256
wangle 174
want 73, 191
wanted 255
wanting 226
wanton 73
war 104, 203
ward 104
ware 116
warm 104
warmth 196
warn 104
warp 104
wart 104
was 73, 158, 178
wash 73, 159, 178
washes 258
wasp 73
waste 78, 190
watch 73, 166
watches 237
watt 73, 133, 209
wattle 73, 174
wave 78, 200
wax 170, 178
way 79, 178, 200
we 81, 178, 201
weak 83, 201
weaken 260
weal 83
wealth 68, 195
wean 83
weapon 68
wear 116
wearily 276
weariness 250
weary 274
weather 68, 110, 199
web 131, 178
wed 67, 134, 178
wedge 168
Wednesday 212
wee 82, 201
weed 82
week 82, 201
weep 82, 178
weevil 176
weigh 80, 200
weight 80, 191

weir 114
weird 114
weld 193
well 173, 178
wend 67, 191
went 178, 191
wept 257
were 108
west 67, 178
western 147, 270
wet 67, 133, 178
wetter 225
wettest 225
wetting 225
whack 137, 179
whale 179
wham 179
wharf 179
what 179, 209
wheat 83, 179
wheedle 179
wheel 179
wheeze 179
whelk 179
whelp 179, 193
when 179
where 115, 179
whet 179
whether 110, 179, 209
whey 80, 179, 200
which 165, 179, 209
whiff 179
while 87, 179
whilst 179
whim 179
whimper 179
whine 87, 179, 209
whinge 179
whingeing 232
whinny 179
whip 179
whippet 179
whirl 106, 172, 179
whisk 179, 191
whisker 179
whisky 179
whisper 179
whist 179
whistle 156, 179
white 87, 179
whiting 179
whittle 179

whiz 158, 179
who 96, 165
whoever 165
whole 165, 207
wholly 165
whom 165
whoop 96
whooping 165
whose 96
why 87, 179
wick 137
wide 86, 178
widely 277
widen 260
widow 135
widowhood 247
width 196
wield 84
wife 87
wig 69, 139, 178
wigwam 178
wild 89, 193
will 173, 178
wimp 192
wimple 175
win 69, 144, 178
wince 155
winch 195
wind 70, 89, 191
wine 86, 178, 209
wing 70, 147
wink 70, 136, 191
winkle 175
winsome 274
winsomely 275
wipe 87
wire 117
wisdom 245
wise 87, 158

wisely 277
wish 70, 159, 178
wished 256
wishes 237
wisp 190
wit 69, 132, 178
witch 166, 209
witches 237
wives 238
wizard 111, 158
wobble 174
wobbly 274
woe 93
woke 91
woken 259
wolf 194
wolves 238
woman 143, 146
womanhood 247
womb 143
women 71, 143
won 75, 178, 199
wonder 75
wonderful 270
wood 99, 178, 205
wooden 146, 267
wool 172, 178
woollen 146
word 107, 178
wore 103, 203
work 107, 178
worker 246
workmanship 251
world 107
worm 107
worn 103
worry 75, 177
worrying 234
worse 107, 154

worship 107
worshipped 228
worth 107
would 100, 205
wound 98, 109
wove 91
woven 259
wow 108
wrangle 174, 177
wrap 177, 208
wrath 177
wreak 208
wreath 177
wreathe 153
wreck 137, 177
wreckage 243
wren 177
wrench 177
wrestle 156, 177
wretch 177
wriggle 174, 177
wring 148, 177, 208
wrinkle 175, 177
wrist 177
writ 177
write 177, 201, 208
writhe 153, 177
written 146, 259
wrote 177, 202, 208
wrought 106, 177
wrung 208
wry 177, 208
xenophobia 159
xylophone 88, 159
yam 180
yap 66, 130, 180
yard 100, 180
yarn 100, 180
yawn 180

year 180
yell 173, 180
yellow 180
yelp 180, 193
yeoman 93
yes 153, 180
yet 133, 180
yew 180
Yiddish 135
yield 84
yodel 180
yoghurt 213
yoke 180, 202
yolk 93, 180, 202
yore 103
York 180
you 95, 98, 180, 202
young 76, 180
your 180
youth 180
yo-yo 180
zany 157
zap 66
zeal 157
zealous 273
zealously 273
zebra 157
Zen 157
zero 114, 157
zigzag   157
zinc 157
zip 69, 157
zither 157
zodiac 157
zone 157
zoo 157
zoology 250
zoom 157
Zulu 157